HIGH BEGINNING
Workbook

OXFORD
PICTURE
DICTIONARY

SECOND EDITION

OPD

Marjorie Fuchs

OXFORD
UNIVERSITY PRESS

198 Madison Avenue
New York, NY 10016 USA

Great Clarendon Street, Oxford OX2 6DP UK

Oxford University Press is a department of the University of Oxford.
It furthers the University's objective of excellence in research, scholarship,
and education by publishing worldwide in

Oxford New York

Auckland Cape Town Dar es Salaam Hong Kong Karachi
Kuala Lumpur Madrid Melbourne Mexico City Nairobi
New Delhi Shanghai Taipei Toronto

With offices in

Argentina Austria Brazil Chile Czech Republic France Greece
Guatemala Hungary Italy Japan Poland Portugal Singapore
South Korea Switzerland Thailand Turkey Ukraine Vietnam

OXFORD and OXFORD ENGLISH are registered trademarks of
Oxford University Press.

© Oxford University Press 2009

Database right Oxford University Press (maker)

Executive Publishing Manager: Stephanie Karras
Managing Editor: Sharon Sargent
Development Editor: Katie La Storia
Design Director: Susan Sanguily
Design Manager: Maj-Britt Hagsted
Designer: Jaclyn Smith
Project Manager: Allison Harm
Project Coordinator: Sarah Dentry
Cover Design: Stacy Merlin
Image Editor: Robin Fadool
Manufacturing Manager: Shanta Persaud
Manufacturing Controller: Eve Wong

ISBN: 978 0 19 474044-9 OPD High Beginning Workbook with Audio CDs (Pack)
ISBN: 978 0 19 474007-4 OPD High Beginning Workbook
ISBN: 978 0 19 474045-6 Audio CDs (4)

Printed in China

10 9 8 7 6 5

Chapter icons designed by Von Glitschka/Scott Hull Associates

Art

Vilma Ortiz-Dillon: 2 (top); 250 (female sewing and male working in flower shop);
277; Andrea Champlin: 6 (desk with school supplies); 55; 121; 182; Mike Gardner: 7;
10; 35; 137; 142; 315; Janos Jantner/Beehive Illustration: 11; 111; 266; 250 (waitress
and customer); Ben Shannon/Magnet Reps: 12; 26; 64; 96; 105; 148; 161; 174; 179;
Gary Antonetti/Ortelius Design: 13; 200; 210; Barb Bastian: 14; 40 (chart); 50; 54; 57;
67; 74; 92; 95; 98; 114; 144; 184; 209; 217 (chart); 220; 221; 250 (swimming pool);
262; Jody Emery: 17 (books); 24; 47; 48; 78; 83; 84; 127; 142 (TV Guide): 152; 176; 236;
291; 295 (map); 317; Argosy: 18; 46; 80; 91; 94;102; 104; 105; 108; 113; 119; 151; 157;
194; 250 (respirator); 294; 308; Karen Minot: 21; 32; 82 (Guest Check); 97; 133; Zina
Saunders: 22; 33; 40; 59; 60; 81; 82; 86; 99; 100 (skirts); 107 (top); 125; 178 (adhesive);
206; Ken Batelman: 23; 38; 53; 66 (bottom); 70 (meat and poultry); 100 (sewing box);
110; 136; 215; 224; 227; 240 (bottom); Glenn Gustafson: 27 (top); 75; 76; 79; 101; 117;
128; 155; 271; Mike Renwick/Creative Eye: 28; 56; 62; 66 (top); 73; 85; 89; 126; 138;
141; 146; Simon Williams/Illustration Ltd.: 38 (top right); 39; 44; 45; Bob Kaganich/
Deborah Wolfe: 41; Kev Hopgood: 42; Nina Wallace: 63; 268; Annie Bissett: 65; 77
(h. turn on oven); 90 (catalog and text); 129; 134; 150; 158; 167; Ken Joudrey/Munro
Campagna: 68; 69; 177; 218; 239; 272; 286; Scott MacNeill: 51; 61; 112; 208; 225; 238;
313; Mary Chandler: 71; 213; 246; 250; Stacey Schuett: 72; Jim Delapine: 77; 109; 214;
235; Ralph Voltz/Deborah Wolfe: 90; 154; 162; 258; 295 (signs); Garth Glazier: 107;
Tony Randazzo: 156; 232; Mark Reidy/Scott Hull Associates: 163 (stamp); Kevin Brown:
242; 243; 253; 263; 289; Rob Schuster: 166; 168; 183; 195; 214; 226; 228; 234; 264;
290; Mohammad Masoor: 178; 180; Eileen Bergman: 202; Shelley Himmelstein: 204;
Dennis Godfrey/Mike Wepplo: 204 (island); Sally Bansusen: 211; 310; Barbara Harmon:
212; 243; Alan Male: 210; 212; Paul Mirocha: 216; 217; Jeff Sanson: 240; Pamela Johnson:
244; 252; Chris Pavely: 245; Uldis Klavins/Hankins & Tegenborg, Ltd.: 247; Anna
Veltfort: 248; 249; Jeff Lindberg: 250 (nurse and patient); Adrian Mateescu/The Studio:
250 (female painting).

Cover Art: CUBE/Illustration Ltd. (hummingbird), 9 Surf Studios (lettering).

Pronk&Associates: 4; 5; 6 (Back to School and Spelling Test); 8; 9; 15: 16; 17 (pie chart);
19; 20; 25; 27 (Be a Smart Shopper); 29; 30; 33; 35 (note at bottom); 36; 37 (crossword);
38 (To Do List); 43; 47 (Home Preference Checklist); 49; 52; 60 (To Do List); 61 (To Buy);
63; 66 (shopping list); 68 (web browser); 68 (chart); 69 (chart); 70 (chart); 73 (Grocery
List); 81 (Food Order Form); 86 (Clothing Rules); 88; 89 (Hotel Stationary); 91 (receipt);
97; receipt); 100 (form); 102 (price stickers); 103; 105 (Patient Form); 108 (list); 109
(To Buy list); 110 (Patient Form); 111 (forms); 117 (check list); 118; 121 (Supply List);
123; 130 (Mall Directory); 131; 132; 138 (chart); 139; 140 (forms); 145 (newspaper
headlines); 146 (Emergency Plan and Disaster Checklist); 148 (Oak Street Association);
149; 152; 156 (chart); 158 (list); 163 (postcard); 165; 170; 172 (form); 173; 174 (forms);
175; 176 (checklist); 177 (chart); 179 (checklist); 181 (chart); 183 (clipboard); 187; 189;
190; 192; 196; 197; 198; 203; 207; 210 (chart); 214 (chart); 218 (newspaper headlines);
221 (postcard); 223; 229; 230; 231 (chart); 237; 241; 243 (crossword); 244 (word search);
251; 252 (crossword puzzle); 254 (forms); 260; 261; 269; 273; 274; 276; 279; 283; 285;
287; 292; 293; 296; 298; 299; 300; 301; 302; 305; 309; 316.

Photos

Shutterstock: 2 (bottom right); Photodisc/Age Fotostock: 3; United States coin
image from the United States Mint: 26 (coins); Dennis Kitchen: 26 (dollar bills);
Jack Hollingsworth/Photodisc/Inmagine: 31 (African American male student); Asia
Pix/Age Fotostock: 31 (Asian middle-aged male); Siri Stafford/Taxi/Getty Images:
31 (elderly Hispanic female); Philip Brittan/Alamy: 31 (10 year-old Caucasian girl);
Shutterstock: (two year-old Hispanic boy); Alexander Crispin/Johner Images/Getty
Image: 31 (2-month-old Caucasian baby); Image Source/Inmagine: 32 (Asian young
female); Photodisc/Inmagine: 32 (Caucasian male, 30's); Brand X/Jupiter Unlimited: 32
(African American female); Goodshoot/Jupiter Unlimited: 32 (young Caucasian male
in wheelchair); Corbis/Age Fotostock: elderly Caucasian female); Dennis Kitchen: 37;
istock.com: 38 (PDA); istockphoto.com: (Hispanic male); istockphoto.com: 58; Mixa/
Inmagine: 66 (Asian female shopper); istockphoto.com: 71 (sandwich); Photodisc/Age
Fotostock: 113 (medicine cabinet); Digital Vision/Punch Stock: 120; istockphoto: 130
(eyeglasses); Shutterstock: 130 (work boots); Keith Leighton/Alamy: 130 (children's
blocks); Shutterstock: 130 (MP3 Player); Ingram Publishing/Age Fotostock: 130 (dog
bone); Shutterstock: 130 (earrings); Time & Life Pictures/Getty Images: Urbano
Delvalle, 130 (Franz Liszt CD); Digitalvision/Inmagine: 130 (flowers); istockphoto.com:
130; Graeme Teague: 135; Shutterstock: 136; Reuters: Gregg Newton, 140 (peaceful
assembly); Comstock/Jupiter Unlimited: 140 (courtroom scene); bigstockphoto: Rahul
Sengupta 140 (freedom of speech); istockphoto.com: 140 (mosque); Reuters: Sam
Mircovic, 140 (freedom of press); Superstock: Dean Fox, 141 (U.S. Supreme Court);
Age Fotostock: Jack English, 145 (tidal wave); Getty Images: Sandy Huffake, 145
(firefighters); Alamy: Frances M. Roberts, 145 (street explosion); Associated Press: Jack
Smith, 145 (volcano); Associated Press: 145 (rescue flood); Associated Press: 145 (child
and parent); AFP/Getty Images: Yuri Cortez, 147; Dennis Kitchen: 151 (ten dollar bill);
Imagesource/Inmagine: 172; Istockphotos.com: 179 (warning symbols); Istockphotos.
com: 180 (can of yellow paint); Dennis Kitchen: 180 (screws, nuts, bolts, washers,
and hooks); Istockphotos.com: 181; Istockphotos.com: 193; Istockphotos.com: 197
(bike); Hulton Archive/Stringer/Getty Images: 199 (WWII); The Image Works: 199 (The
Wright Brothers); Newell Convers Wyeth/The Bridgeman Art Library/Getty Images:
199 (Lewis & Clark); Time & Life Pictures/Getty Images: Robert W. Kelley, 199 (equal
rights march); Hulton Archive/Getty Images: 199 (Ellis Island); GhostWorx Images/
Alamy: William Baker, 100 (musical score); Jon Arnold Images Ltd/Alamy: 199 (The
Acropolis); dbimages/Alamy: Marcia Chambers, 199 (Singapore); V&A Images/Alamy:
199 (young Queen Elizabeth); Istockphotos.com: 201; Istockphotos.com: 211 (ground);
; Istockphotos.com: 231; Istockphotos.com: 244 (pan, pot, and fence); Istockphotos.
com: 246 (tie, ring); Istockphotos.com: 247 (nurse); Istockphotos.com: 250 (pipe and
rake); Istockphoto.com: 254 (cell phone); Somos Images LLC/Alamy: 258 (Hispanic
female); istockphoto.com: 262; Istockphotos.com: 217; Courtesy of the MTA: 294; Age
Fotostock: 310 (honeybee); istockphoto.com: 314.

This book is printed on paper from certified and well-managed sources.

Acknowledgments

The publisher and author would like to acknowledge the following individuals for their invaluable feedback during the development of this workbook:

Patricia S. Bell, Lake Technical County ESOL, Eustis, FL

Patricia Castro, Harvest English Institute, Newark, NJ

Druci Diaz, CARIBE Program and TBT, Tampa, FL

Jill Gluck, Hollywood Community Adult School, Los Angeles, CA.

Frances Hardenbergh, Southside Programs for Adult and Continuing Ed, Prince George, VA

Mercedes Hern, Tampa, FL

(Katie) Mary C. Hurter, North Harris College, Language and Communication, Houston, TX

Karen Kipke, Antioch Freshman Academy, Antioch, TN

Ivanna Mann-Thrower, Charlotte Mecklenburg Schools, Charlotte, NC

Holley Mayville, Charlotte Mecklenburg Schools, Charlotte, NC

Jonetta Myles, Salem High School, Conyers, GA

Kathleen Reynolds, Albany Park Community Center, Chicago, IL

Jan Salerno, Kennedy-San Fernando CAS, Grenada Hills, CA

Jenni Santamaria, ABC Adult School,Cerritos, CA

Geraldyne Scott, Truman College/ Lakeview Learning Center, Chicago, IL

Sharada Sekar, Antioch Freshman Academy, Antioch, TN

Terry Shearer, Region IV ESC, Houston, TX

Melissa Singler, Cape Fear Community College, Wilmington, NC

Cynthia Wiseman, Wiseman Language Consultants, New York, NY

Special thanks to:

Stephanie Karras and Sharon Sargent for their dedication and hard work in managing a very complex project; Jaclyn Smith, Robin Fadool, and Maj-Britt Hagsted for ensuring that the many graphic elements illustrated and enhanced the text; and Pronk&Associates for their commitment and skill.

Bruce Myint, who contributed to the early stages of the *Workbook* and made excellent suggestions for bringing this new edition into a new century;

Katie La Storia, who applied her sharp mind and eyes to the manuscript, always offering excellent advice. With her steadfast energy, enthusiasm, and encouragement, she was a pleasure to work with;

Vanessa Caceres, who worked hard and fast on the manuscript. The *Workbook* has benefited greatly from her classroom experience;

Alexis Vega-Singer, who carefully checked text, art, photos, and facts. Her suggestions were always thoughtful and intelligent, even at 3:00 in the morning;

Ellen Northcutt, who made insightful comments and queries.

Sarah Dentry, who made things flow smoothly, assuring that I always had what I needed wherever I was;

Jayme Adelson-Goldstein, who provided support and who, along with Norma Shapiro, created a rich trove of materials on which to base the exercises in the *Workbook*;

Rick Smith, as always, for his unswerving support and for his insightful comments on all aspects of the project. Once again, he proved himself to be equally at home in the world of numbers and the world of words.

The publisher would like to thank the following for their permission to reproduce copyrighted material:

pp. 134, 135, 289: U.S. Postal Service Corporate Logo, Express Mail Logo, Certified Mail, Letter Carrier Uniform, Postal Clerk Uniform, Round Top Collection Mailbox, Priority Mail Logo, Media Mail, and Certified Mail are trademarks of the United States Postal Service and are used with permission.

pp. 151, 294: Metrocard is an MTA trademark and is used with permission.

To the Teacher

The *Low Beginning*, *High Beginning*, and *Low Intermediate Workbooks* that accompany *The Oxford Picture Dictionary* have been designed to provide meaningful and enjoyable practice of the vocabulary that students are learning. These workbooks supply high-interest contexts and real information for enrichment and self-expression.

Writing a second edition has given us the wonderful opportunity not only to update material, but also to respond to the requests of our first-edition users. As a result, this new edition of the *High Beginning Workbook* contains more graphs and charts, more writing and speaking activities, more occasions for critical thinking, opportunities to use the Internet, and a brand-new listening component. It still, of course, has the features that made the first edition so popular.

The *Workbooks* conveniently correspond page-for-page to the 163 topics of the *Picture Dictionary*. For example, if you are working on page 50 in the *Dictionary*, the activities for this topic, Apartments, will be found on page 50 in all three *Picture Dictionary Workbooks*.

All topics in the *High Beginning Workbook* follow the same easy-to-use format. Exercise 1 is always a "look in your dictionary" activity where students are asked to complete a task while looking in their *Picture Dictionary*. The tasks include answering questions about the pictures, judging statements true or false, counting the number of illustrated occurrences of a vocabulary item, completing a time line, or speculating about who said what.

Following this activity are one or more content-rich contextualized exercises, including true or false, matching, categorizing, odd-one-out, and completion of forms. These exercises often feature graphs and charts with real data for students to work with as they practice the new vocabulary. Many topics include a personalization exercise that asks "What about you?" where students can use the new vocabulary to give information about their own lives or to express their opinions.

The final exercise for each topic is a Challenge which can be assigned to students for additional work in class or as homework. Challenge activities provide higher-level speaking and writing practice, and for some topics will require students to interview classmates, conduct surveys, or find information outside of class by looking in the newspaper, for example, or online.

Each topic also has a listening activity recorded on CDs which come with the *Workbook*. The CDs give students the opportunity to hear the language of each topic in natural, real-life contexts including short conversations, classroom instructions, news and weather reports, radio ads, and store and airport announcements. The listening exercises are in the back of the *Workbook* beginning on page 258. In some cases, the target language is in the listening itself and students need to recognize it. In other cases, the target language is in the exercise text and students need to interpret the listening to choose the correct answer.

Each of the 12 units ends with Another Look, a review which allows students to practice vocabulary from all the topics of a unit in a game or puzzle-like activity, such as picture crosswords, word searches, and C-searches, where students search in a picture for items which begin with the letter c. These activities are at the back of the High-Beginning Workbook on pages 242–253.

Throughout the *Workbook*, vocabulary is carefully controlled and recycled. Students should, however, be encouraged to use their *Picture Dictionaries* to look up words they do not recall, or, if they are doing topics out of sequence, may not yet have learned.

The Oxford Picture Dictionary Workbooks can be used in the classroom or at home for self-study.

I hope you and your students enjoy using this *Workbook* as much as I have enjoyed writing it.

Marjorie Fuchs

Marjorie Fuchs

To the Student

The Oxford Picture Dictionary has over 4,000 words. This workbook will help you use them in your everyday life.

It's easy to use! The *Workbook* pages match the pages in your *Picture Dictionary*. For example, to practice the words on page 23 in your *Picture Dictionary*, go to page 23 in your *Workbook*.

It has exercises you will enjoy. Some exercises show real information. A bar graph of people's favorite colors is on page 24 and a chart showing popular sports in the United States is on page 229. Another exercise, which asks "What about you?" gives you a chance to use your own information. You will find stories, puzzles, and conversations, too.

At the end of each topic there is a Challenge, a chance to use your new vocabulary more independently. There are also listening exercises where you hear conversations, TV and radio ads, and store announcements. And finally, every unit has a game or puzzle activity called Another Look. This can be found at the back of the book.

Learning new words is both challenging and fun. I had a lot of fun writing this workbook. I hope you enjoy using it!

Marjorie Fuchs

Marjorie Fuchs

Table of Contents

1. Everyday Language

2. People

3. Housing

4. Food

5. Clothing

6. Health

Contents

10. Areas of Study

11. Plants and Animals

12. Recreation

1. Look in your dictionary. Label the pictures.

a. _____Shake hands._____

b. _____

c. _____

d. _____

e. _____

f. _____

2. Circle the answer.

a. **Say, "Hello."**

Good evening.   (Hi.)   Fine, thanks.

b. **Introduce a friend.**

Ana, this is Meng.   Hi, I'm Ana.   Nice to meet you, Ana.

c. **Greet people.**

Luis, this is Mia.   Hello, everyone.   Fine, thanks.

d. **Say, "Goodbye."**

Good evening.   Hello.   Good night.

3. What about you? Imagine Jessica is your friend. You see her in school. Check (✓) the things you do.

☐ Say, "Hello."   ☐ Ask, "How are you?"

☐ Introduce yourself.   ☐ Smile.

☐ Wave.   ☐ Hug.

☐ Kiss.   ☐ Bow.

☐ Shake hands.   ☐ Say, "Goodbye."

Jessica

4. Look in your dictionary. *True* or *False*?

a. Picture A: He introduces himself.   *false*

b. Picture C: She introduces a friend.   _____

c. Picture D: He waves.   _____

d. Picture E: They hug.   _____

e. Picture F: She smiles.   _____

f. Picture H: They bow.   _____

g. Picture I: She introduces a friend.   _____

h. Picture J: They shake hands.   _____

5. What about you? Complete the conversations. Use the instructions in parentheses ( ).

Miguel

a. You: *Hello, I'm* _____

      (Introduce yourself to Miguel.)

Miguel: Hi. I'm Miguel.

b. You: _____

      (Say, "Hello," to a friend.)

Friend: Hi.

c. You: _____

      (Ask your friend, "How are you?")

Friend: Fine, thanks.

d. You: _____

      (Introduce your friend to Miguel.)

Miguel: Nice to meet you.

Friend: Nice to meet you, Miguel.

e. You: _____

      (Say, "Goodbye.")

Miguel and Friend: Goodbye!

Challenge Introduce yourself to two classmates. Then, introduce the two classmates to each other.

See page 258 for listening practice.

1. Look in your dictionary. What is Carlos Soto's . . . ?

  a. ZIP code   <u>33607–3614</u>   c. apartment number   _____

  b. area code   _____   d. Social Security number   _____

2. Match.

<u> 9 </u> a. middle initial   1. female

____ b. signature   2. California

____ c. city   3. (310)

____ d. sex   4. 548-00-0000

____ e. area code   5. Los Angeles

____ f. Social Security number   6. Miriam S. Shakter

____ g. name   7. 90049-1000

____ h. ZIP code   8. *Miriam S. Shakter*

____ i. state   9. S.

3. What about you? Fill out the form. Use your own information.

L.A. Adult Center

REGISTRATION FORM
(Please print.)

Last name _____ First name _____ Middle initial _____

Sex: ☐ Male ☐ Female

Place of birth _____ Date of birth _____

Address _____ Apartment number _____

_____ _____
(City)   (State)   (ZIP code)

Phone _____ Cell phone _____

_____
Signature

Challenge Interview a classmate. Find out his or her last name, first name, middle initial, address, and place of birth.

     See page 258 for listening practice.

1. Look in your dictionary. Put the words in the correct columns.

People	Places	
principal	quad	

2. Look at the floor plan. Match the rooms on the directory with the letters.

Directory

	Room(s)
Auditorium	C
Cafeteria	
Classrooms	
Gym	
Library	
Lockers	
Restrooms	
Men's	
Women's	

3. What about you? Check (✓) the places your school has.

☐ auditorium   ☐ library   ☐ track   ☐ computer lab   ☐ cafeteria

Challenge Draw a floor plan or write a directory for your school.

See page 258 for listening practice.

1. Look at the top picture in your dictionary. How many . . . are in the classroom?

a. teachers ___1___   c. students ____   e. bookcases ____

b. computers ____   d. desks ____   f. chairs ____

2. Look at the list of school supplies. Check (✓) the items you see in the picture.

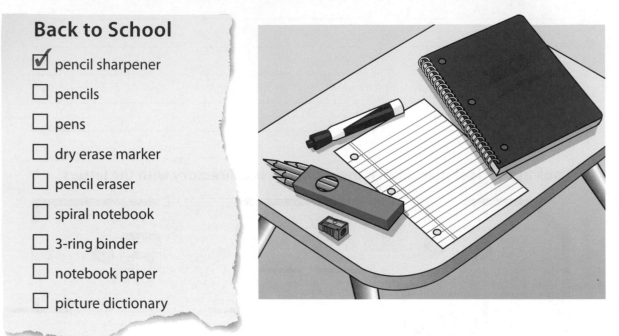

Back to School

- ☑ pencil sharpener
- ☐ pencils
- ☐ pens
- ☐ dry erase marker
- ☐ pencil eraser
- ☐ spiral notebook
- ☐ 3-ring binder
- ☐ notebook paper
- ☐ picture dictionary

3. Complete the spelling test.

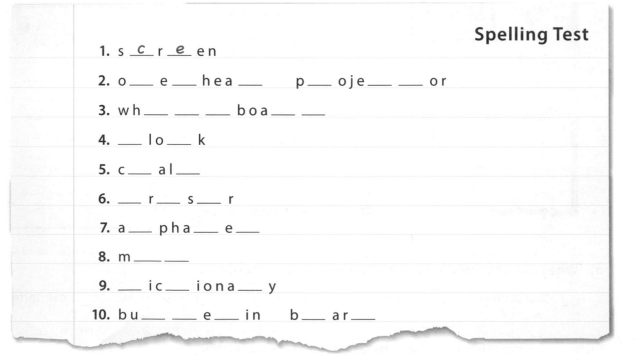

Spelling Test

1. s _c_ r _e_ e n

2. o ___ e ___ h e a ___   p ___ o j e ___ ___ o r

3. w h ___ ___ ___ b o a ___ ___

4. ___ l o ___ k

5. c ___ a l ___

6. ___ r ___ s ___ r

7. a ___ p h a ___ e ___

8. m ___ ___ ___

9. ___ i c ___ i o n a ___ y

10. b u ___ ___ e ___ i n   b ___ a r ___

4. Label the pictures. Use the words in the box.

Listen to a CD.	~~Open your workbook.~~	Stand up.
Pick up your pencil.	Close your workbook.	Put down your pencil.
Take a seat.	Raise your hand.	Talk to the teacher.

a. <u>Open your workbook.</u>

b. _____

c. _____

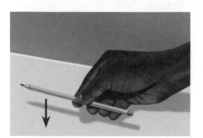

d. _____

e. _____

f. _____

g. _____

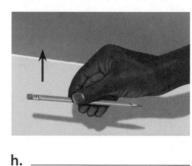

h. _____

i. _____

5. What about you? Check (✓) the items you use in your classroom.

☐ pencils   ☐ headphones   ☐ pens

☐ spiral notebook   ☐ markers   ☐ 3-ring binder

☐ pencil sharpener   ☐ notebook paper   ☐ LCD projector

☐ dictionary   ☐ picture dictionary   ☐ workbook

☐ textbook   ☐ computer   ☐ chalkboard

☐ Other: _____

Challenge Write about the items in Exercise 5. **Example:** *I have one dictionary. I have two pens. I don't have any pencils.*

See page 259 for listening practice.

1. Look in your dictionary. *True* or *False*?

a. **Picture A:** The student is copying a word.   _____false_____

b. **Picture C:** The student is translating the word.   _____

c. **Picture J:** The students are sharing a book.   _____

d. **Picture K:** The woman is asking a question.   _____

e. **Picture M:** The students are putting away their books.   _____

f. **Picture N:** The man is dictating a sentence.   _____

2. Match.

__3__ **a.** Ask a question.

1. pencil/ˈpensl/

2.
pencil

pencil

_____ **b.** Answer the question.

3. What's a pencil?

_____ **c.** Look up the word.

4.

_____ **d.** Translate the word.

5.
pence /pens/ *n.* (*pl.*) pennies.
pencil/ˈpensl/ *n.* instrument for writing
and drawing, made of a thin piece of wood
with lead inside it.
penetrate /ˈpenɪtreɪt/ *v.* go into or through
something: *A nail penetrated the car tire.*

_____ **e.** Check the pronunciation.

6. A pencil is something
    you write with.

_____ **f.** Copy the word.

7. This is a pen / pencil.

_____ **g.** Draw a picture of the word.

8.
pencil = えんぴつ

_____ **h.** Circle the answer.

3. Complete this test.

Name: _____   Class: _____

1. Fill in the blanks. Use the words in the box.

away	~~in~~	out

a. I'm filling ___*in*___ the blanks.

b. The students are taking _____ their picture dictionaries.

c. The teacher is putting _____ the books.

2. Cross out the word that doesn't belong.

a. help   share   ~~match~~   brainstorm

b. ask   underline   circle   fill in

c. brainstorm   copy   dictate   discuss

3. Underline the words that begin with *c*.
Circle the words that begin with *d*.

read   <u>copy</u>   (draw)   share   help

dictate   circle   check   discuss   choose

4. Match.

_3_ a. Look up   1. a picture.

___ b. Draw   2. a question.

___ c. Ask   3. a word.

5. Unscramble the words.

a. tedicta ___*dictate*___   c. scudiss _____

b. wrad _____   d. lastetran _____

4. What about you? Look in your dictionary. Which classroom activities do you like to do? Which activities don't you like to do? Make two lists.

Challenge   Look up the word *thimble* in your dictionary.
a. Translate the word.
b. Draw a picture of a thimble.
c. Label the picture.

See page 259 for listening practice.

1. Look in your dictionary. *True* or *False*?

    a. Picture A: Sergio is taking notes.   *false*

    b. Picture B: He is participating in class.   _____

    c. Picture D: He is studying at home.   _____

    d. Picture G: He is not making progress.   _____

    e. Picture H: He is getting good grades.   _____

    f. Picture J: He is asking for help.   _____

    g. Picture K: He is taking a test.   _____

    h. Picture L: He is not checking his work.   _____

    i. Picture N: He is correcting the mistake.   _____

2. Sergio is taking a test. Number the activities in the correct order. (1 = the first thing Sergio does)

    ____ **a.** He checks his work.

    ____ **b.** He bubbles in the answer on the answer sheet.

    ____ **c.** He hands in his test.

    _1_ **d.** He clears off his desk.

    ____ **e.** He corrects the mistake.

    ____ **f.** He passes the test.

    ____ **g.** He erases the mistake.

3. What about you? Check (✓) the things you do.

    ☐ set goals   ☐ bubble in answers

    ☐ participate in class   ☐ check my work

    ☐ take notes   ☐ ask my teacher for help

    ☐ study at home   ☐ ask my classmates for help

Challenge   Write three study goals. **Example:** *Learn five words a day.*

    a. _____

    b. _____

    c. _____

1. **Look in your dictionary. Circle the words to complete the sentences.**

    a. Five students (enter the room) / leave the room.

    b. The teacher <u>runs to class / turns on the light</u>.

    c. One student is carrying <u>books / trash</u>.

    d. He's delivering them to room <u>102 / 202</u>.

    e. Two teachers <u>have a conversation / buy a snack</u> during the break.

    f. After the break, they <u>leave / go back to</u> class.

2. **Look at the pictures. Match.**

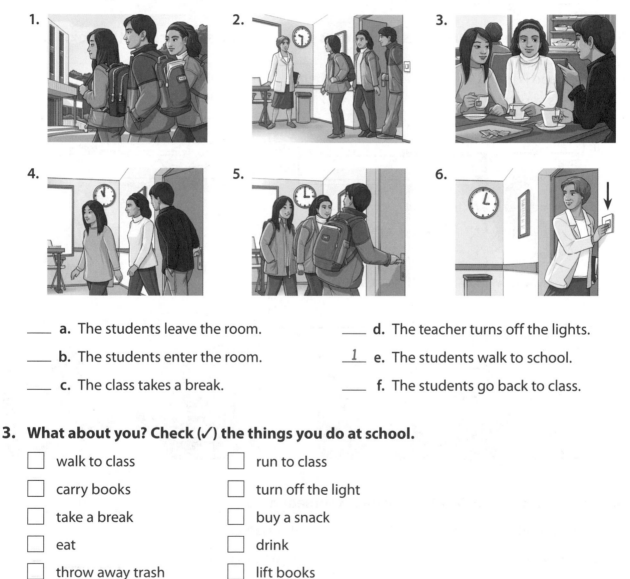

    _____ **a.** The students leave the room.

    _____ **b.** The students enter the room.

    _____ **c.** The class takes a break.

    _____ **d.** The teacher turns off the lights.

    _1_ **e.** The students walk to school.

    _____ **f.** The students go back to class.

3. **What about you? Check (✓) the things you do at school.**

    ☐ walk to class   ☐ run to class

    ☐ carry books   ☐ turn off the light

    ☐ take a break   ☐ buy a snack

    ☐ eat   ☐ drink

    ☐ throw away trash   ☐ lift books

    Challenge Look in your dictionary. Write sentences about pictures H–L. What are people eating?
    What are they drinking? What are the teachers having a conversation about?

See page 260 for listening practice.   11

1. Look in your dictionary. Circle the correct words.

a. | Hi. I'm Danny. | make small talk / (start a conversation)

b. | Is that *Donny*? | check your understanding / explain something

c. | Nice day, isn't it? | compliment someone / make small talk

d. | That's a nice jacket. | agree / compliment someone

e. | I'm having a party tonight. Please come. | accept an invitation / invite someone

2. Complete the conversations from Amy's party. Use the sentences in the box.

| This food is great! | ~~Coats go in there.~~ | Oh! Sorry! | There? |
| No. It's very bad! | Here's a napkin. | Thanks! | That's OK. |

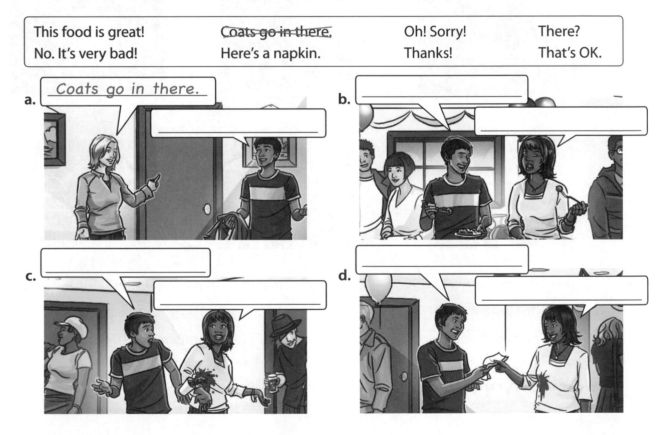

a. *Coats go in there.*

3. Look at Exercise 2. In which picture is someone . . . ?

1. accepting an apology   _c_
2. apologizing   ___
3. checking understanding   ___
4. disagreeing   ___
5. offering something   ___
6. thanking someone   ___

Challenge What are good topics for small talk? What are bad topics? Make a list.

1. Look in your dictionary. Describe the temperatures.

    a. Fahrenheit: 95°   _hot_   35°   _____   60°   _____

    b. Celsius: 25°   _____   −10°   _____   40°   _____

2. Look at the weather map. Circle the words to complete the sentences.

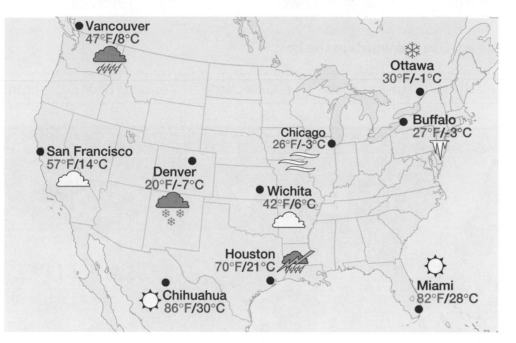

  a. It's foggy / (windy) in Chicago.

  b. There's a heat wave / snowstorm in Denver.

  c. Houston is having a dust storm / thunderstorm.

  d. It's clear / cloudy in Chihuahua.

  e. The temperature is cold / freezing in Ottawa.

  f. It's raining / snowing in Vancouver.

  g. It's icy / smoggy in Buffalo.

  h. It's cloudy / raining in San Francisco.

  i. It's hot / warm and sunny in Miami.

  j. It's cloudy and cool / cold in Wichita.

3. What about you? What kinds of weather do you like? Check (✓) the columns.

	I like it.	It's OK.	I don't like it.
humid			
cool and foggy			
raining and lightning			
warm and sunny			
hailstorm			

Challenge Write a weather report for your city. **Example:** *Monday, January 25. Today it's sunny and warm in San Antonio. The temperature is . . . .*

See page 260 for listening practice.

The Telephone

1. Look in your dictionary. Check (✓) the things with numbers.

a. ✓ phone bill   e. ☐ cord   i. ☐ key pad

b. ☐ phone jack   f. ☐ star key   j. ☐ pound key

c. ☐ charger   g. ☐ calling card k. ☐ pay phone

d. ☐ country code   h. ☐ receiver   l. ☐ antenna

2. Complete the ad. Use the words in the box.

> answering machine   smart phone   ~~cellular phone~~   cordless phone   headset

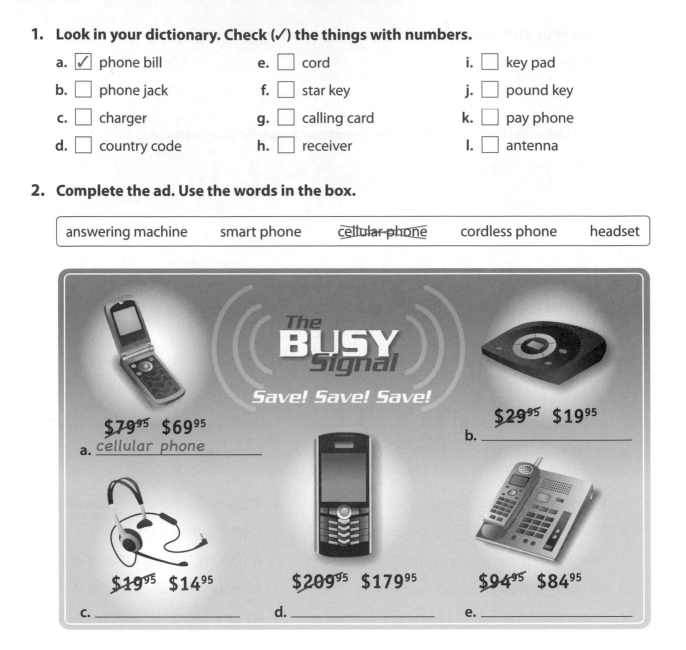

The
BUSY
Signal

Save! Save! Save!

$79⁹⁵ $69⁹⁵

a. cellular phone

$29⁹⁵ $19⁹⁵

b. _____

$19⁹⁵ $14⁹⁵

c. _____

$209⁹⁵ $179⁹⁵

d. _____

$94⁹⁵ $84⁹⁵

e. _____

3. Circle the words to complete the sentences.

> Hi. It's me.
> I'll be home late.

a. This is a text / (voice) message.

> This call requires a coin deposit.
> Please hang up and dial again.

c. This is a smart / pay phone.

> Can you hear me now?
> Can you hear me now?

b. The cellular phone has a weak / strong
signal.

> Please press 1 for
> customer service.

d. This is an automated phone system /
Internet phone call.

4. Look in your dictionary. Match.

<u>2</u> **a.** (505)

___ **b.** 411

___ **c.** 0

___ **d.** 56-2-555-1394

___ **e.** 911

1. emergency call

2. area code

3. operator

4. directory assistance

5. international call

5. Circle the words to complete the instructions.

Follow these instructions for an (emergency) / international call:
　　　　　　　　　　　　　　　　　　　　　a.

First, dial <u>411 / 911</u>. Give your <u>calling card / name</u> to the operator. Then <u>state / spell</u> the
　　　　　　　b.　　　　　　　　　　　**c.**　　　　　　　　　　　　**d.**

emergency. Is there a fire? Do you need a doctor? Tell the operator. Stay on the line.

<u>Hang up / Don't hang up</u>! The operator will ask you other questions.
　　　　e.

6. What about you? Complete the chart.

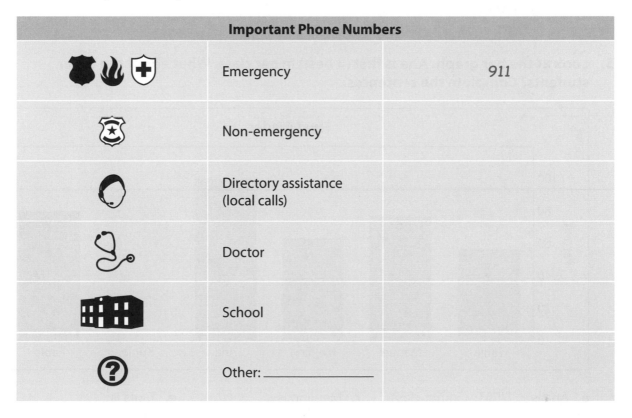

Important Phone Numbers		
🛡🔥✚	Emergency	911
⭐	Non-emergency	
👤	Directory assistance (local calls)	
🩺	Doctor	
🏢	School	
⍰	Other: _____	

Challenge Find out the area codes for five cities. Look in a phone book, on the Internet, or ask your classmates. **Example:** *Houston—713*

See page 261 for listening practice.

1. Look in your dictionary. Write the types of numbers. What comes next?

   a. ___Ordinal numbers___ : tenth, twentieth, thirtieth, ___fortieth___

   b. _____ : VI, VII, VIII, _____

   c. _____ : 70, 80, 90, _____

2. Complete the chart.

Word	Number	Roman Numeral
ten	10	X
		III
	15	
		L
	20	
one hundred		
		D
one thousand		

3. Look at the bar graph. Ana is first (= best) in her class. What about the other students? Complete the sentences.

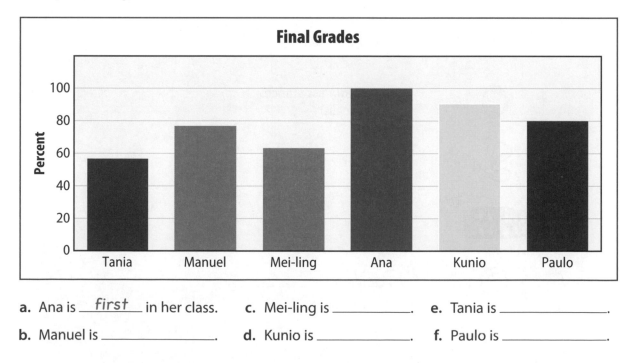

Final Grades

a. Ana is ___first___ in her class.　　c. Mei-ling is _____.　　e. Tania is _____.

b. Manuel is _____.　　d. Kunio is _____.　　f. Paulo is _____.

Challenge Work with a partner. Where can you see cardinal numbers? Ordinal numbers? Roman numerals? Write sentences. Compare your answers with a classmate's.
Example: *Telephone numbers have cardinal numbers.*

1. **Look in your dictionary. What kind of numbers are these?**

a. 1/5 _____fraction_____   **b.** 20% _____   **c.** .20 _____

2. **Look at the chart. Complete the sentences.**

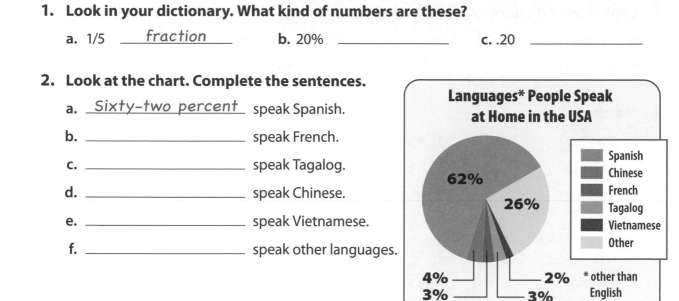

a. __Sixty-two percent__ speak Spanish.

b. _____ speak French.

c. _____ speak Tagalog.

d. _____ speak Chinese.

e. _____ speak Vietnamese.

f. _____ speak other languages.

Languages* People Speak at Home in the USA

Spanish
Chinese
French
Tagalog
Vietnamese
Other

62%   26%   4%   3%   2%   3%

* other than English

Based on information from: *US Census Bureau, American Community Survey, 2005.* Table C16001

3. **Look at the books. Complete the sentences.**

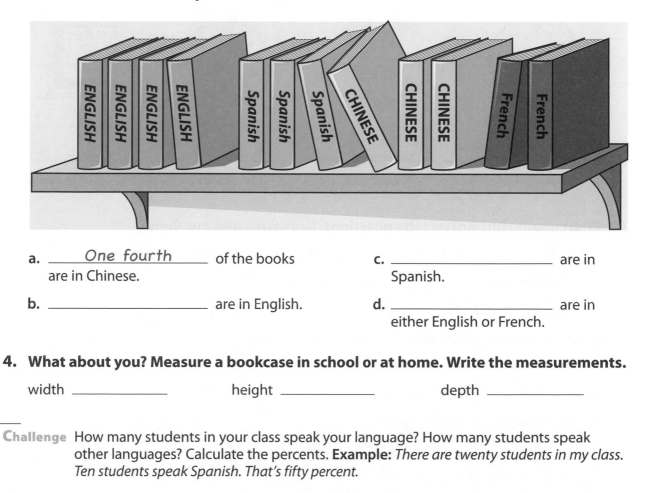

a. _____One fourth_____ of the books are in Chinese.

b. _____ are in English.

c. _____ are in Spanish.

d. _____ are in either English or French.

4. **What about you? Measure a bookcase in school or at home. Write the measurements.**

width _____   height _____   depth _____

Challenge How many students in your class speak your language? How many students speak other languages? Calculate the percents. **Example:** *There are twenty students in my class. Ten students speak Spanish. That's fifty percent.*

See page 262 for listening practice.

1. Look in your dictionary. What's another way to say . . . ?

a. ten-thirty   _half past ten_

b. two-forty-five   _____

c. a quarter after three   _____

d. twenty after six   _____

2. Match.

_3_ a. 3:00

___ b. 5:25

___ c. 2:30

___ d. 6:45

___ e. 8:50

___ f. 6:15

___ g. 9:10

___ h. 5:45

1. It's ten to nine.

2. It's a quarter to seven.

3. It's three o'clock.

4. It's a quarter after six.

5. It's a quarter to six.

6. It's two-thirty.

7. It's five-twenty-five.

8. It's ten after nine.

3. Complete the clocks.

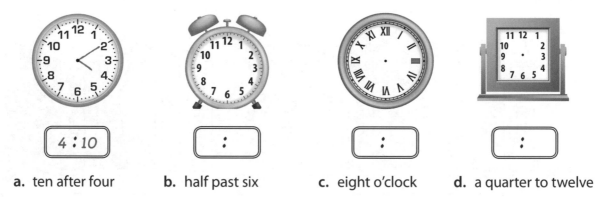

4:10

:

:

:

a. ten after four   b. half past six   c. eight o'clock   d. a quarter to twelve

4. What about you? Answer the questions. Use words and numbers.

Example: What time is it? It's _____ _four-fifteen p.m. (4:15 p.m.)_ _____.

a. What time is it? It's _____.

b. What time is your class? It's from _____ to _____.

c. Do you come to class early, on time, or late? _____.

   If you come early or late, at what time? At _____.

d. What time do you leave class? At _____.

e. What time do you get home? At _____.

5. **Look at the map in your dictionary. In which time zone is . . . ?**

a. Caracas   _____Atlantic_____   c. Denver   _____

b. Chicago   _____   d. Vancouver   _____

6. **Look at the chart. It's 12:00 noon in New York City. What time is it in . . . ?**
Use numbers and the words in the box.

At 12:00 noon, Eastern Standard Time, the time in . . . is . . .			
Athens	7 P.M.	Mexico City	11 A.M.
Baghdad	8 P.M.	Montreal	12 noon
Bangkok	12 midnight*	New York City	12 noon
Barcelona	6 P.M.	Panama	12 noon
Buenos Aires	3 P.M.	Paris	6 P.M.
Frankfurt	6 P.M.	Rio de Janeiro	3 P.M.
Halifax	1 P.M.	Riyadh	8 P.M.
Hanoi	12 midnight*	Rome	6 P.M.
Havana	12 noon	St. Petersburg	8. P.M.
Hong Kong	1 A.M.*	San Juan	1 P.M.
Houston	11 A.M.	Seoul	2 A.M.*
Kolkata	10:30 P.M.	Sydney	4 A.M.*
London	5 P.M.	Tel Aviv	7 P.M.
Los Angeles	9 A.M.	Tokyo	2 A.M.*
Mecca	8 P.M.	Zurich	6 P.M.
* = the next day			

| in the morning | in the afternoon | in the evening | at night | noon | midnight |

a. Athens   _7:00 in the evening_   g. St. Petersburg   _____

b. London   _____   h. Bangkok   _____

c. Kolkata   _____   i. Mexico City   _____

d. Panama   _____   j. Frankfurt   _____

e. Halifax   _____   k. Los Angeles   _____

f. Tokyo   _____   l. Hanoi   _____

7. **What about you? Does your native country have . . . ? Write *Yes* or *No*.**

a. different time zones?   _____   b. daylight saving time?   _____

Challenge Find out the time for sunrise and sunset in your area. Look in a newspaper or online.

1. Look in your dictionary. In May, how many . . . are there?

a. days   _31_

b. Mondays ___

c. Thursdays ___

d. weekdays ___

e. two-day weekends ___

f. seven-day weeks ___

2. Unscramble the months. Then number them in order. (1 = the first month)

a. r a J n y u a   _January_   _1_

b. y a M   _____ ___

c. m e D b r e c e   _____ ___

d. n u J e   _____ ___

e. c h a r M   _____ ___

f. b r e t o c O   _____ ___

g. l i p r A   _____ ___

h. l y J u   _____ ___

i. p r e S e t m e b   _____ ___

j. b r u F y e a r   _____ ___

k. s A t u g u   _____ ___

l. v e N o m b e r   _____ ___

3. Write the seasons.

Seasons in the United States			
December 21 – March 20	March 21 – June 20	June 21 – September 20	September 21 – December 20

a. _winter_   b. _____   c. _____   d. _____

4. Look at the dates. Write the seasons. Use the information from Exercise 3.

a. January 5   _winter_

b. November 28   _____

c. March 22   _____

d. May 6   _____

e. December 19   _____

f. June 25   _____

5. Look at Antonio's calendar. *True* or *False*?

	SUN.	MON.	TUES.	WED.	THURS.	FRI.	SAT.
		1 Science Lab English	**2** Computer Lab Math	**3** English	**4** Gym Math	**5** Language Lab English	**6** To Los Angeles!
	7 Daylight Saving Time	**8**	**9**	**10** NO CLASSES	**11**	**12** To N.Y.	**13** Ana 7:00 p.m.
	14	**15** Science Lab English	**16** Auditorium 2:00 Math	**17** English	**18** Gym Math	**19** Language Lab English	**20** Track & Field
	21 Mary 6:00 p.m.	**22** Science Lab English	**23** Counselor's Office 3:15 Math	**24** English	**25** Gym Math	**26** Language Lab English	**27** Library with Frank
	28	**29** Science Lab English	**30**	**31**			

TODAY'S DATE

a. Antonio has class every day this month. _____false_____

b. He has Math twice a week. _____

c. He has Math on Wednesday and Friday. _____

d. He has English three times a week. _____

e. He has Gym once a week. _____

f. He was in Los Angeles last weekend. _____

g. Tomorrow he has Track & Field. _____

h. Yesterday was Tuesday. _____

i. He sees Mary Saturday night. _____

j. He sees Mary every weekend. _____

k. There were no classes last week. _____

l. Daylight saving time begins this week. _____

m. Next week Antonio sees the school counselor. _____

Challenge Make a calendar of your monthly activities. Write ten sentences about your calendar.

**1. Look in your dictionary. Number the legal holidays in order.
(1 = the first holiday in the year)**

___ **a.** Labor Day   ___ **e.** Memorial Day

___ **b.** Christmas   ___ **f.** Presidents' Day

___ **c.** Fourth of July   ___ **g.** Thanksgiving

_1_ **d.** New Year's Day   ___ **h.** Martin Luther King Jr. Day

2. Look at the pictures. Match.

_2_ **a.** Luisa's first doctor's appointment   ___ **d.** Our tenth anniversary

___ **b.** Our wedding   ___ **e.** Thanksgiving

___ **c.** Vacation, Summer 2007   ___ **f.** Luisa's eighth birthday

Challenge Bring some photos to class. Write captions on your own paper.

1. Look in your dictionary. Write the opposites.

a. big   _little_   d. cheap   _____

b. same   _____   e. ugly   _____

c. heavy   _____   f. slow   _____

2. Look at the classroom. *True* or *False*? Change the <u>underlined</u> word in the false sentences. Make the sentences true.

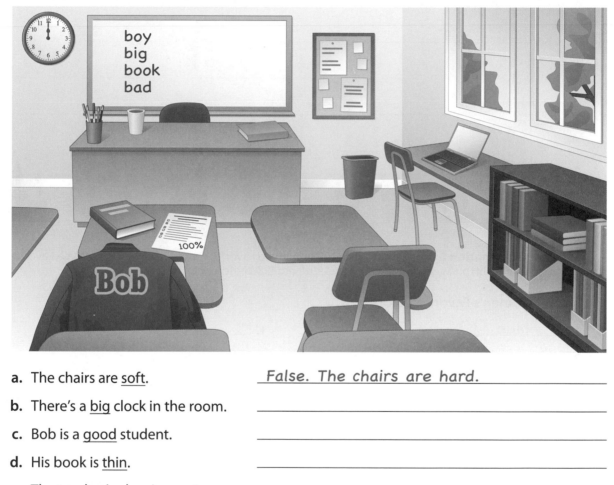

a. The chairs are <u>soft</u>.   _False. The chairs are hard._

b. There's a <u>big</u> clock in the room.   _____

c. Bob is a <u>good</u> student.   _____

d. His book is <u>thin</u>.   _____

e. The teacher's glass is <u>empty</u>.   _____

f. The words on the board are <u>easy</u>.   _____

g. The classroom is <u>noisy</u>.   _____

3. What about you? Check (✓) the words that describe your classroom.

☐ beautiful   ☐ big   ☐ quiet

☐ noisy   ☐ ugly   ☐ Other: _____

Challenge Describe your classroom. Write six sentences.

See page 263 for listening practice.

1. Look at page 156 in your dictionary. What color is the . . . ?

a. convertible ___red___

b. school bus _____

c. sedan _____

d. pickup truck _____

2. Look at the bar graph. Put the colors in order. (1 = favorite)

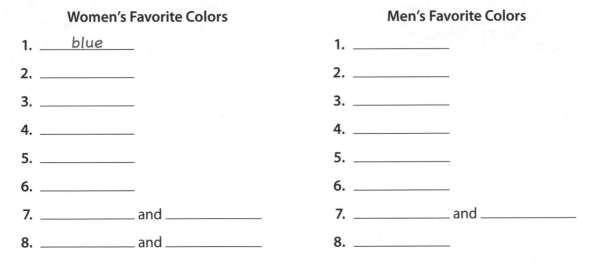

Based on information from: Hallock, Joe (2003) "Female Favorite Color Pie Chart" and "Male Favorite Color Pie Chart." http://www.joehallock.com/edu/com498/preferences.html

Women's Favorite Colors

1. ___blue___

2. _____

3. _____

4. _____

5. _____

6. _____

7. _____ and _____

8. _____ and _____

Men's Favorite Colors

1. _____

2. _____

3. _____

4. _____

5. _____

6. _____

7. _____ and _____

8. _____

3. What about you? Put the colors in order. (1 = your favorite)

___ red ___ turquoise ___ yellow ___ pink ___ violet

___ brown ___ light blue ___ dark blue ___ orange ___ beige

Challenge Make a list of the colors in Exercise 2. Ask five women and five men their favorite colors. Do their answers agree with the information in Exercise 2?

See page 264 for listening practice.

1. **Look at <u>page 24</u> in your dictionary. *True* or *False*?**

   a. The red sweaters are above the yellow sweaters.   <u>   true   </u>

   b. The purple sweaters are next to the orange sweaters.   <u>   </u>

   c. The white sweaters are between the black and gray sweaters. <u>   </u>

   d. The brown sweaters are on the left.   <u>   </u>

   e. The dark blue sweaters are below the turquoise sweaters. <u>   </u>

2. **Follow the instructions below.**

   a. Put the letter **W** in the pink box.

   b. Put a **Y** below it.

   c. Put an **E** in the yellow box.

   d. Put an **I** above the **E**.

   e. Put a **P** next to the **E**, on the left.

   f. Put a **U** in the green box.

   g. Put an **O** between the **Y** and the **U**.

   h. Put an **E** above the **U**.

   i. Put an **R** next to the **U**, on the right.

   j. Put an **H** between the **W** and the **E**.

   k. Put the letters **E, N, R,** and **S** in the correct boxes to complete the question.

3. **What about you? Look at Exercise 2. Answer the question.**

   _____

   |Challenge Draw a picture of your classroom. Write about the locations of the classroom items in
             your picture. **Example:** *The map is next to the board, on the right.*

1. Look in your dictionary. How much money is there in . . . ?

a. coins ___$1.91___   b. bills _____   c. coins and bills _____

2. Look at the money. How much is it? Use numbers.

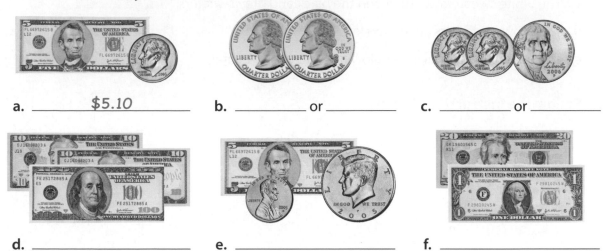

a. ___$5.10___   b. _____ or _____   c. _____ or _____

d. _____   e. _____   f. _____

3. Read the cartoon. Who . . . ? Check (✓) the correct column.

I need a quarter. Do you have change for $1.00?

No, sorry. But here's a quarter.

Here's your quarter.

Oh, thanks!

	The Man	The Woman
a. wants to gets change	✓	☐
b. lends money	☐	☐
c. borrows money	☐	☐
d. pays back money	☐	☐

Challenge How many different ways can you get change for a dollar? **Example:** *four quarters*

See page 264 for listening practice.

1. Look in your dictionary. Match.

1. 2. 3.

4. 5.

$12.50

Subtotal $25.00

Tax $2.06

TOTAL DUE $27.06

6.

___3___ **a.** SKU number   _____ **c.** use a debit card   _____ **e.** sales tax

_____ **b.** bar code   _____ **d.** use a gift card   _____ **f.** regular price

2. Complete the shopping tips. Use the words in the box.

~~cash register~~	credit	debit	exchange	pay	total
price	price tag	receipt	return	sales	

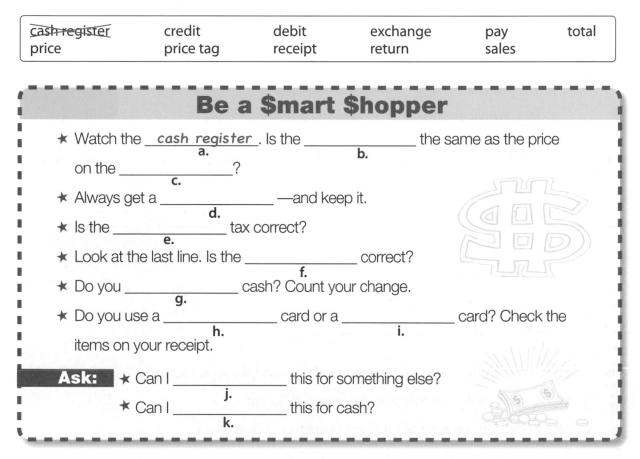

Be a $mart $hopper

★ Watch the __cash register__ . Is the _____ the same as the price
            a.   **b.**
  on the _____?
        c.
★ Always get a _____ —and keep it.
           d.
★ Is the _____ tax correct?
       e.
★ Look at the last line. Is the _____ correct?
                f.
★ Do you _____ cash? Count your change.
       g.
★ Do you use a _____ card or a _____ card? Check the
         h.   **i.**
  items on your receipt.

Ask: ★ Can I _____ this for something else?
            j.
★ Can I _____ this for cash?
         k.

3. What about you? What has sales tax in your state? How much is it?

Challenge Look at page 254 in this book. Complete the sales slip.

Go To Page 242 For Another Look (Unit 1). | See Page 265 For Listening Practice.

1. **Look in your dictionary. *True* or *False*?**

    a. Anya and Manda are twins.   _____true_____

    b. Mrs. Kumar is shopping for matching sweaters.   _____

    c. She buys two navy blue sweaters.   _____

    d. Manda is happy with her sweater.   _____

    e. Anya is happy with her sweater.   _____

    f. Mrs. Kumar looks disappointed.   _____

    g. Anya keeps her sweater.   _____

2. **Put the sentences in order. (1 = the first event) Use your dictionary for help.**

    ___ a. The twins look at the sweaters.

    _1_ b. Mrs. Kumar shops for Manda and Anya.

    ___ c. Anya exchanges her sweater.

    ___ d. Manda is happy with the sweater, but Anya is a little disappointed.

    ___ e. Mrs. Kumar pays for the sweaters.

    ___ f. The twins are happy with their sweaters.

    ___ g. Mrs. Kumar chooses matching green sweaters.

3. **What about you? Imagine a friend gives you this sweater. Answer the questions.**

    a. What color is the sweater? _____

    b. Are you happy or disappointed with it?

        _____ Why? _____

    c. Are you going to keep it? _____

    d. Are you going to exchange it? _____

        If *yes*, for what color? _____

4. **Look in your dictionary. Circle the words to complete the sentences.**

    a. Mrs. Kumar thinks her twins are (the same) / different.

    b. Mrs. Kumar buys the same / different sweaters for the twins.

    c. The regular / sale price of the sweater is $19.99.

    d. The total price / sales tax is $43.38.

    e. Mrs. Kumar pays cash / uses a credit card.

    f. Manda exchanges / keeps the sweater.

5. Look in your dictionary. Complete the receipt. Write the total and the change.

```
                A&G
        DATE: __10/20/09__
    ********************************
    ITEM
    1 GREEN SWEATER      $_____

    _____       $_____

    SUBTOTAL             $ 39.98

    SALES TAX            $  3.40

    TOTAL                $_____

    CASH                 $ 45.00

    CHANGE               $_____

    ********************************
        THANK YOU FOR SHOPPING WITH US.
```

6. Complete Manda's journal entry. Use the words in the box.

disappointed	happy	keep	matching
navy blue	~~shop~~	sweaters	twins

October 22

Mom really likes to ___shop___ for us! Yesterday, she gave us two beautiful
                        a.

_____ green _____. I'm very _____ with my sweater.
     b.   **c.**   **d.**

I love the color, and it's thick and warm. Anya was a little _____.
                                                                e.

She wants to be different. I'm going to _____ my sweater, but Anya
                                          f.

exchanged her sweater for a _____ sweater. Anya said to Mom,
                             g.

"Our sweaters are now different colors, but they are still the same sweaters."

And Mom said, "You're different people, but you're still _____!"
                                                          h.

7. What about you? Look in your dictionary. Which color sweater do you like?

Challenge Imagine you are Anya. Write a journal entry about the sweaters.

1. Look in your dictionary. How many . . . are there?

    a. men   _3_   **d.** infants   ____

    b. women   ____   **e.** teenagers ____

    c. senior citizens ____   **f.** girls   ____

2. Which words are for males? Which words are for females? Which words are for both? Put the words in the box in the correct spaces in the circles.

~~baby~~	infant	teen
boy	man	toddler
girl	senior citizen	woman

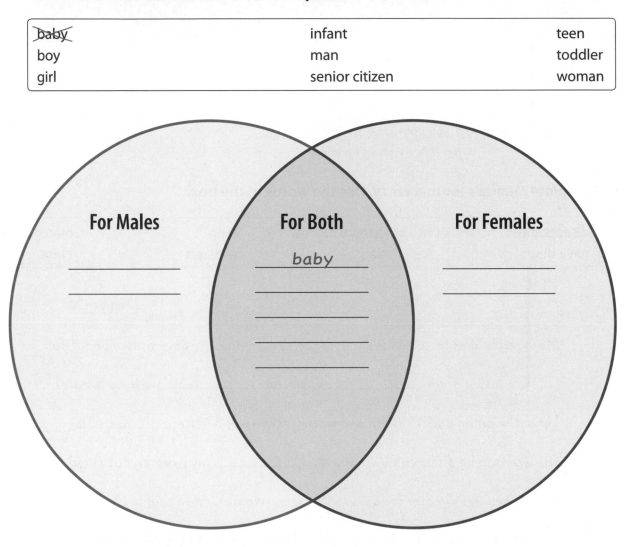

For Males

_____
_____

For Both

baby
_____
_____
_____
_____

For Females

_____
_____

3. What about you? How many . . . are in your class?

    men   ____

    women   ____

    senior citizens ____

    teenagers   ____

4. Look in your dictionary. *True* or *False*? Write a question mark (?) if you don't know.

a. The senior citizen is a woman. _____*true*_____

b. The toddler is a girl. _____

c. The infant is a boy. _____

d. The teenager is sitting next to a 10-year-old boy. _____

e. The baby is sitting next to a woman. _____

f. A man is holding the infant. _____

5. Match.

__2__ a. man

___ b. toddler

___ c. teen

___ d. girl

___ e. infant

___ f. senior citizen

1. 78 years old

2. 40 years old

3. 10 years old

4. 2 months old

5. 2 years old

6. 17 years old

6. Label the pictures. Use the words from Exercise 5.

a. _____*teen*_____

b. _____

c. _____

d. _____

e. _____

f. _____

Challenge Look in your dictionary. How old are the people? Discuss your answers with a classmate.
Example: *A: I think this man is 40. What about you? B: I think he's only 30.*

1. **Look in your dictionary. Write the opposites.**

a. young _____elderly_____

b. tall _____

c. thin _____ or _____

2. **Look at the ads. Circle the words that describe age and appearance.**
Match the ads with the photos.

CommunityPersonals.us 🔍 Search our Site | _____ **go**

1. 　 2. 　 3. 　 4. 　 5.

___3___ **a. Hi!:** I'm a (short), attractive middle-aged woman. You're smart, nice and funny. Appearance not important.
cutiepie@mid.us

_____ **b. Attractive:** Slender, elderly woman looking for relationship with honest man.
happyface@lcd.us

_____ **c. Young and Attractive:** Physically challenged man looking for someone to share the great things in life.
travelfun@eol.us

_____ **d. Short and Sweet:** Cute young woman of average weight seeks nice fun-loving man. No tattoos please!
sallyo@rcd.us

_____ **e. Friendly and Fun:** Great guy of average height and average weight. Looking for a happy woman who loves life.
ff@eol.us

3. **Look at the photos in Exercise 2. Do people have . . . ? Check (✓) the boxes.**
For the boxes with checks, write the number of the picture.

✓ pierced ears __1__ ☐ a mole _____ ☐ a tattoo _____

┊ **Challenge** Name a famous person who was or is . . . .
　　　　　　 a. physically challenged 　 **b.** sight impaired 　 **c.** hearing impaired.

1. **Look at the top picture in your dictionary. How many . . . do you see?**

   a. combs __5__
   b. rollers ___
   c. blow dryers ___
   d. brushes ___
   e. people with gray hair ___
   f. scissors ___

2. **Look at the pictures of Cindi. Check (✓) the things The Hair Salon did to Cindi's hair.**

   Before

   Now

   THE HAIR SALON

   ☑ cut
   ☐ set
   ☐ color
   ☐ perm

3. **Circle the words to complete the paragraph about Cindi.**

   Cindi is very happy with her new hairstyle. Before, she had short /(long) curly / straight,
                                                 a.   **b.**

   blond / brown hair with corn rows / bangs and a part / no part. Now she has very
        c.   **d.**   **e.**

   long / short, curly / straight, red / black hair. Cindi looks great!
      f.   **g.**   **h.**

4. **What about you? Draw a picture of a friend's hair. Check (✓) the correct boxes.**
   My friend has . . . .

   ☐ short hair   ☐ shoulder-length hair   ☐ long hair
   ☐ no hair (bald)   ☐ straight hair   ☐ wavy hair
   ☐ curly hair   ☐ a part   ☐ bangs
   ☐ corn rows   ☐ a mustache   ☐ a beard
   ☐ sideburns   ☐ _____ hair
                                   (list hair color)

Challenge   Find three pictures of hairstyles in your dictionary, a newspaper or magazine, or online. Write descriptions.

See page 266 for listening practice.

1. Look in your dictionary. Put the words in the box in the correct category.

~~aunt~~	brother-in-law	cousin	daughter	grandmother
husband	niece	parent	son	uncle

Male	Female	Male or Female
	aunt	

2. Look in your dictionary. *True* or *False*?

Tim Lee's family:

a. Tim has two sisters. _____*false*_____

b. Min is Lu's wife. _____

c. Dan is Min and Lu's nephew. _____

d. Tim and Emily have the same grandparents. _____

e. Rose is Emily's aunt. _____

Ana Garcia's family:

f. Ana is Carlos's sister-in-law. _____

g. Sara is Eva and Sam's granddaughter. _____

h. Felix is Alice's brother. _____

i. Marta is Eddie's mother-in-law. _____

j. Marta is Eva and Sam's daughter-in-law. _____

3. What about you? What is your . . . ? Answer the questions.

a. **name:** _____

b. **mother's name:** _____

c. **father's name:** _____

d. **marital status:** ☐ single ☐ married ☐ divorced

   If you are married, what is your husband's or wife's name? _____

e. **Do you have children?** ☐ yes ☐ no

   If *yes*, what are their names? _____

4. Look in your dictionary. Circle the answers.

a. Carol was Bruce's (wife) / sister.

b. Sue is Kim's stepmother / mother.

c. Rick is a single father / father.

d. David is Mary's brother / half brother.

e. Lisa is Bill's half sister / stepsister.

f. Bruce is Bill and Kim's father / stepfather.

5. Look at Megan's pictures. Put the sentences in order.

1. Megan and Chet—2004

2. Megan, Chet, and Nicole—2005

3. Megan   Chet

4. Megan and Nicole—2007

5. Megan, Brian, Nicole, and Jason—2009

6. Megan, Nicole, and Jason—2009

___ a. Megan is remarried.

___ b. Megan is a stepmother.

_1_ c. Megan is married.

___ d. Megan has a baby.

___ e. Megan is a single mother.

___ f. Megan is divorced.

6. Complete Nicole's story. Use the information in Exercise 5.

Name: Nicole Parker   October 10, 2012

My name is Nicole. My _____mother_____'s name is Megan.
                                   a.

My _____'s name is Chet. I have a _____.
            b.   c.

His name is Brian. Brian has a _____.
                                        d.

His name is Jason. Jason is my _____.
                                        e.

Challenge Draw your family tree. Use the family trees in your dictionary as a model.

See page 267 for listening practice.

1. Look in your dictionary. Who is . . . the child? Check (✓) the answers.

	Mother	Father	Grandmother
a. bathing	✓	☐	☐
b. reading to	☐	☐	☐
c. disciplining	☐	☐	☐
d. holding	☐	☐	☐
e. kissing	☐	☐	☐
f. undressing	☐	☐	☐
g. rocking	☐	☐	☐
h. buckling up	☐	☐	☐
i. feeding	☐	☐	☐
j. dressing	☐	☐	☐
k. praising	☐	☐	☐

2. Look at Sofia's *To Do* list. What is Sofia doing? Write sentences.

a. It's 10:00.   <u>She's bathing the baby.</u>

b. It's 12:00.   _____

c. It's 11:30.   _____

d. It's 10:30.   _____

e. It's 1:15.   _____

> **TO DO**
>
> 10:00 a.m. bathe Luisa
>
> 10:30 a.m. dress her
>
> 11:00–11:45 a.m. play with her
>
> 12:00 p.m. feed her
>
> 1:00–1:30 p.m. read to her

3. What about you? Check (✓) the things you can do.

	Yes	No
a. comfort a baby	☐	☐
b. read nursery rhymes to a child	☐	☐
c. feed baby food to a child	☐	☐
d. dress a child in training pants	☐	☐
e. change a cloth diaper	☐	☐
f. rock a baby to sleep	☐	☐

4. Cross out the word that doesn't belong.

a. Places to sit	high chair	~~diaper pail~~	potty seat
b. Things a baby wears	pacifier	bib	disposable diaper
c. Things a baby eats	formula	baby food	baby lotion
d. Things with wheels	rocking chair	carriage	stroller
e. Things to put in a baby's mouth	teething ring	baby bag	nipple
f. Things for changing diapers	baby powder	training pants	wipes
g. Things a baby plays with	night light	rattle	teddy bear
h. Things that hold a baby	safety pins	baby carrier	car safety seat

5. There are eight childcare and parenting words. They go across (→) and down (↓). Find and circle six more. Use the pictures as clues.

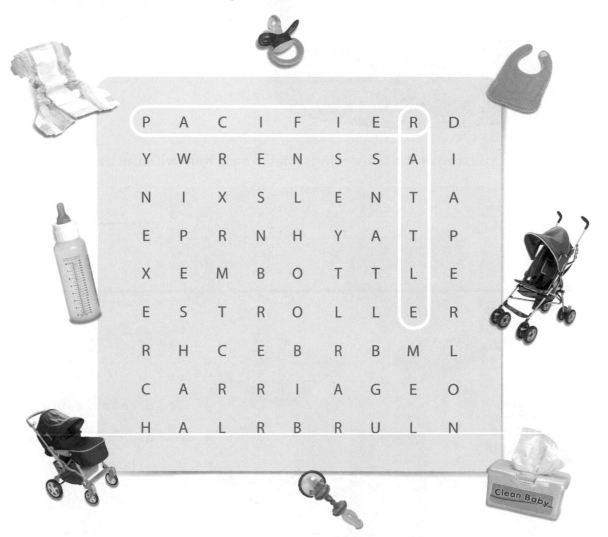

Challenge Make a list of things to put in a baby bag. What can you use them for?
Example: *bottle—to feed the baby*

See page 267 for listening practice.

1. Look in your dictionary. Complete Dan Lim's schedule.

6:00 A.M.	wake up
6:30 A.M.	get dressed
7:00 A.M.	
7:30 A.M.	
_____	drive to work
5:00 P.M.	
_____	exercise at the gym
_____	have dinner
8:00 P.M.	
8:30 P.M.	
_____	go to sleep

2. Look at the picture of the Lims' things. Match each item with the correct activity.

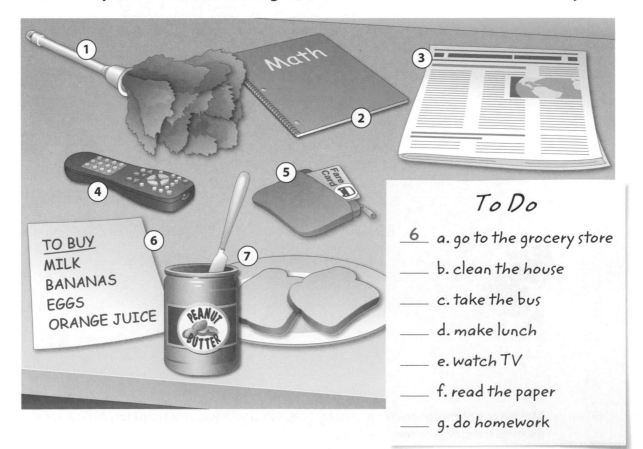

To Do

6 a. go to the grocery store
___ b. clean the house
___ c. take the bus
___ d. make lunch
___ e. watch TV
___ f. read the paper
___ g. do homework

3. Read about Nora Lim. Complete the story. Use the words in the boxes.

checks	eats	gets up	~~relaxes~~	takes

Nora Lim has a busy week. Sundays are busy, too,

but she ___*relaxes*___ a little more. She _____
         a.   **b.**

at 8:00 and _____ a long, hot shower. Then,
                 c.

she _____ email and _____ breakfast
       d.   **e.**

with her family.

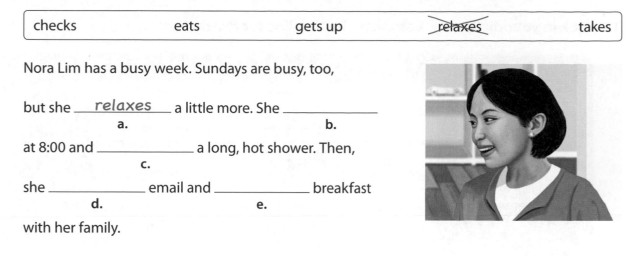

drives	goes	leaves	makes	picks up	works

After breakfast, she _____ her husband to the shoe store. (He _____ on
                 f.   **g.**

Sundays, too.) Then, she takes the children to visit their Aunt Ellen. Ellen _____ lunch
                                                        h.

for them. After lunch, Nora _____ Ellen's house and _____ to the library for
                              i.   **j.**

two hours. At 4:00, she _____ the children from Ellen's house.
                         k.

cooks	gets	goes	has	takes	watches

Nora _____ home at 5:00 and _____ dinner for her family. Her daughter,
       l.   **m.**

Sara, helps her. Dan _____ the bus home. The family _____ dinner at 6:00.
                     n.   **o.**

They talk about their day. After dinner, Nora _____ TV with her family. At 10:00,
                                           p.

Nora _____ to bed.
       q.

4. What about you? Complete your weekday or weekend schedule. Use the schedule in Exercise 1 as an example.

Challenge Interview someone you know (a friend, family member, or classmate). Write a schedule of his or her daily routine.

See page 267 for listening practice.

1. Look in your dictionary. Complete the timeline for Martin Perez.

YEARS	LIFE EVENTS
1935	*be born*
1940	start school
1950	
	graduate
1954	and become a citizen
	go to college
	get engaged
1959	
1961	
	buy a home
	become a grandparent
2000	
	travel
2008	

2. Complete the story about Rosa Lopez. Use the words in the box.

~~was~~	died	fell	got	graduated	had	got	learned

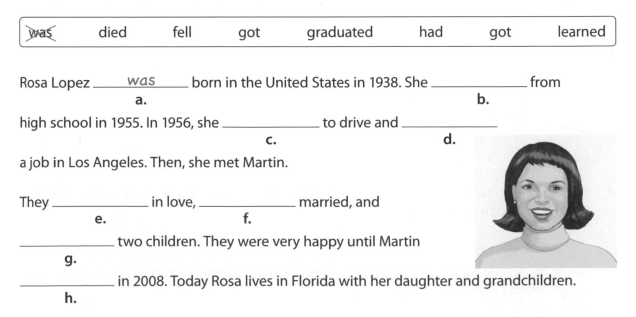

Rosa Lopez _____*was*_____ born in the United States in 1938. She _____ from
       a.   **b.**

high school in 1955. In 1956, she _____ to drive and _____
                                           c.   **d.**

a job in Los Angeles. Then, she met Martin.

They _____ in love, _____ married, and
           e.   **f.**

_____ two children. They were very happy until Martin
       g.

_____ in 2008. Today Rosa lives in Florida with her daughter and grandchildren.
     h.

3. Look at the documents. Answer the questions.

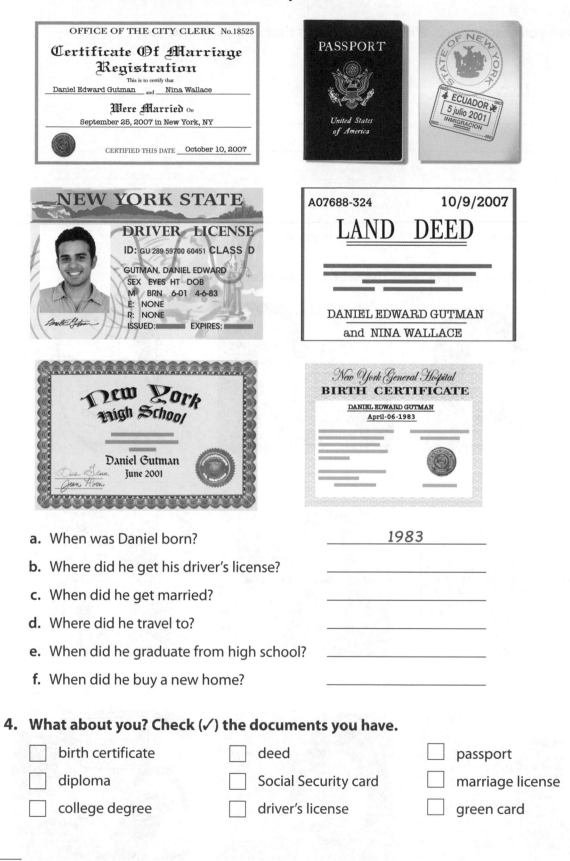

a. When was Daniel born? _____1983_____

b. Where did he get his driver's license? _____

c. When did he get married? _____

d. Where did he travel to? _____

e. When did he graduate from high school? _____

f. When did he buy a new home? _____

4. What about you? Check (✓) the documents you have.

☐ birth certificate   ☐ deed   ☐ passport

☐ diploma   ☐ Social Security card   ☐ marriage license

☐ college degree   ☐ driver's license   ☐ green card

Challenge Draw a timeline for important events in your life. Use the timeline in Exercise 1 for ideas.

See page 268 for listening practice.

1. Look in your dictionary. Write all the words that end in -y and -ed.

-y	-ed	
thirsty	satisfied	

2. How do these people feel? Use words from Exercise 1.

a. relieved

b. _____

c. _____

d. _____

e. _____

f. _____

g. _____

h. _____

i. _____

3. Put the words in the correct columns.

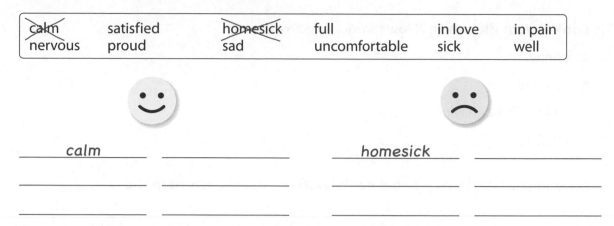

| calm | satisfied | homesick | full | | in love | in pain |
| nervous | proud | sad | uncomfortable | | sick | well |

(calm, homesick, sad crossed out)

😊   ☹️

_____calm_____   _____   _____homesick_____   _____

_____   _____   _____   _____

_____   _____   _____   _____

4. Complete the conversations. Use words from Exercise 3.

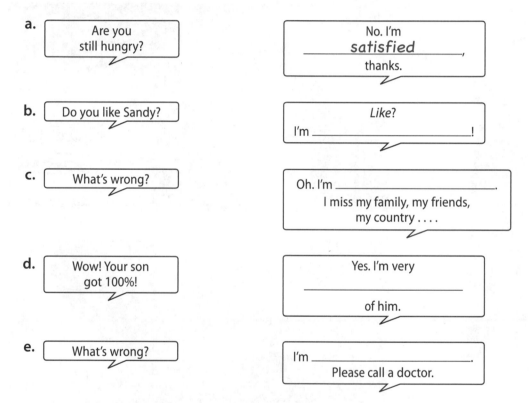

a.
Are you still hungry?

No. I'm
_____satisfied_____,
thanks.

b.
Do you like Sandy?

Like?
I'm _____!

c.
What's wrong?

Oh. I'm _____.
I miss my family, my friends, my country . . . .

d.
Wow! Your son got 100%!

Yes. I'm very
_____
of him.

e.
What's wrong?

I'm _____.
Please call a doctor.

5. What about you? How do you feel when you . . . ? Circle as many words as possible. Add new words, too.

a. **wake up**   sleepy   happy   calm   _____

b. **start a new class**   nervous   confused   excited   _____

c. **have problems in school** worried   upset   homesick   _____

d. **exercise**   happy   proud   uncomfortable _____

Challenge What do you do when you feel nervous? Bored? Homesick? Confused? Angry?
Discuss your answers with a classmate.

1. Look in your dictionary. How many . . . can you see?

a. banners   _1_

b. balloons   ___

c. children misbehaving   ___

d. relatives   ___

2. Look in your dictionary. Label Ben's relatives. Use the words in the box.

| ~~Ben~~ | aunt | grandfather | mother-in-law | son | cousin | wife |

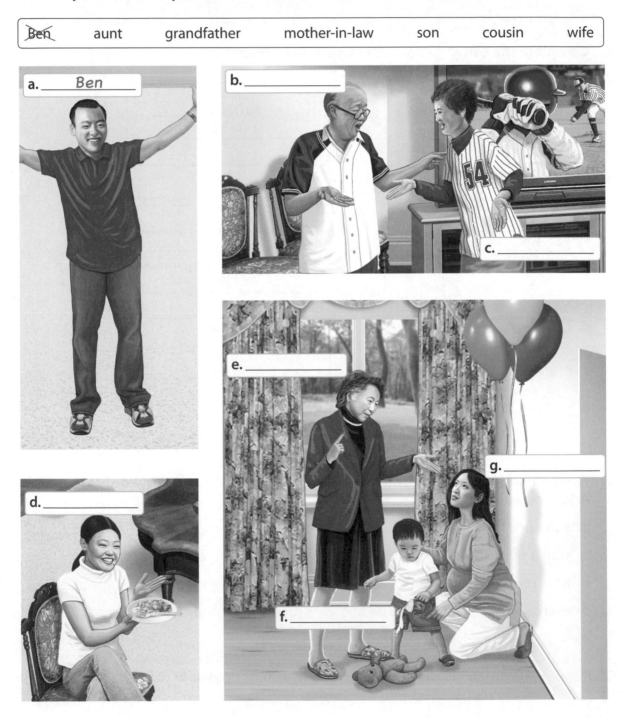

a. _____Ben_____

b. _____

c. _____

d. _____

e. _____

f. _____

g. _____

3. **Look in your dictionary. Who are Ben's other relatives? Guess. Complete the sentences. Then, discuss your answers with a classmate. Do you and your classmate agree?**

a. The woman to the right of Ben is his _cousin (or aunt or sister)_.

b. The physically-challenged man is his _____.

c. The little girl near the food table is his _____.

d. The boy watching TV is his _____.

4. **Look in your dictionary. What did people do at the reunion? Check (✓) the answers.**

☑ eat   ☐ misbehave

☐ clean   ☐ laugh

☐ go to sleep   ☐ exercise

☐ cook   ☐ check email

☐ talk   ☐ read

☐ watch TV   ☐ play baseball

☐ sing

5. **Look in your dictionary. Circle the words to complete the sentences.**

a. Ben Lu is single / (married).

b. He has a family reunion every year / month.

c. The reunion is at Ben's / his aunt's house.

d. Ben is talking to relatives / watching TV.

e. His grandfather and aunt have the same / different opinions about the baseball game.

f. His grandfather has a beard / gray hair.

g. His mother / son is misbehaving.

h. Ben is glad / sad his family is all there.

6. **What about you? Imagine you are at Ben's family reunion. Who do you want to talk to? Why?**

Example: *I want to talk to Ben's aunt and grandfather. I like baseball, too.*

Challenge Look in your dictionary. Choose three of Ben's relatives. Describe them to a partner. Your partner will point to the correct picture. **Example:** *She is elderly and has gray hair. She is near the food.*

See page 268 for listening practice.

1. Look in your dictionary. *True* or *False*?

a. This home has three bedrooms.   _____true_____

b. There's a door between the bedroom and the bathroom.   _____

c. The baby's room is next to the parents' bedroom.   _____

d. There's an attic under the roof.   _____

e. The kitchen is under the kids' bedroom.   _____

f. There's a window in the bathroom.   _____

g. There are books on the floor in the kids' bedroom.   _____

2. Look at the pictures. Which rooms do they go in? Match.

1.

2.

3.

4.

5.

6.

7.

8.

9.

____ a. living room   ____ d. garage   _1_ g. kitchen

____ b. bathroom   ____ e. baby's room   ____ h. kids' bedroom

____ c. dining area   ____ f. attic   ____ i. basement

3. What about you? Do you like the house in your dictionary? Why or why not? Talk about it with a partner.

4. Look in your dictionary. Complete the sentences.

   a. The mother is in the _____ *living room* _____.

   b. The father is in the _____.

   c. The teenage daughter is in the _____.

   d. The 10-year-old girl is in the _____.

   e. The baby is in the _____.

   f. The car is in the _____.

5. Look in your dictionary. Correct the mistakes in the ad.

FOR SALE

~~4~~ 3 bedroom house with 2 bathrooms

Large kitchen and dining area. Attic and basement,

2-car garage. Good for a family. Call 555-3434.

6. What about you? What's important to you in a home? Complete the chart.

Home Preference Checklist — J&R REALTORS

Number of bedrooms _____ Number of bathrooms _____

	very important	important	not important
Kitchen with a dining area?	☐	☐	☐
Window in the kitchen?	☐	☐	☐
Window in the bathroom?	☐	☐	☐
A basement?	☐	☐	☐
An attic?	☐	☐	☐
A garage?	☐	☐	☐

Challenge Write an ad for a home. It can be for your home, a home that you know, or for the home on <u>page 53</u> of this workbook. Use the ad in Exercise 5 as an example.

See page 269 for listening practice.

1. Look at pictures 1 and 2 in your dictionary. *True* **or** *False*?

Internet Listing

a. The Internet listing is for a house. _____*false*_____

b. It has one bedroom. _____

c. The rent is $900 a week. _____

Classified Ad

d. The classified ad is for a furnished apartment. _____

e. Utilities are included. _____

f. It has two bathrooms. _____

2. Check (✓) the things people do when they rent an apartment and / or buy a house.

	Rent an Apartment	Buy a House
a. make an offer	☐	✓
b. sign a rental agreement	✓	☐
c. get a loan	☐	☐
d. ask about the features	☐	☐
e. take ownership	☐	☐
f. move in	☐	☐
g. pay the rent	☐	☐
h. make a mortgage payment	☐	☐
i. unpack	☐	☐
j. arrange the furniture	☐	☐
k. meet with a realtor	☐	☐
l. put the utilities in their name	☐	☐
m. meet the neighbors	☐	☐
n. submit an application	☐	☐

3. What about you? Look at the Internet listing and the classified ad in your dictionary. Which apartment do you like better? Why? Tell a partner.

4. **Look in your dictionary. Circle the words to complete the sentences.**

   a. The woman in picture A wants to buy / (rent) an apartment.

   b. She talks to the manager / realtor.

   c. The rent is $850 / $1,700 a month.

   d. The man and woman in picture H are looking at a new apartment / house.

   e. The realtor makes / man and woman make an offer.

   f. The rent / mortgage is $2,000 a month.

5. **Look at the listings.** *True* or *False*?

   a. The Westside apartment is furnished.   _true_

   b. The Eastside apartment has a new kitchen.   _____

   c. The Eastside apartment has more bedrooms.   _____

   d. The Westside apartment has more bathrooms.   _____

   e. The Eastside apartment's rent is more.   _____

   f. Utilities are included for both apartments.   _____

   g. Both apartments have the same manager.   _____

   h. You can call the manager in the morning.   _____

6. **What about you? Check (✓) the things you and your family did the last time you moved.**

   ☐ rented an apartment   ☐ looked at houses

   ☐ submitted an application   ☐ signed a rental agreement

   ☐ paid rent   ☐ met with a realtor

   ☐ made an offer   ☐ got a loan

   ☐ made a mortgage payment   ☐ called a manager

   ☐ painted   ☐ met the neighbors

Challenge How did you find your home? Write a paragraph.

See page 269 for listening practice.

1. Look at page 50 in your dictionary. Circle the words to complete the sentences.

a. There's a fire escape on the first / (second) floor.

b. The building on the right has a playground / roof garden.

c. A tenant / The manager is hanging a vacancy sign.

d. A tenant / The manager is entering the building.

e. There's an intercom in the entrance / lobby.

f. The mailboxes are in the entrance / lobby.

g. A tenant is using the elevator / stairs.

h. There's a big-screen TV in the laundry room / recreation room.

i. There's a security camera in the garage / recreation room.

j. There's a pool table / washer in the recreation room.

2. Look at the sign. *True* or *False*?

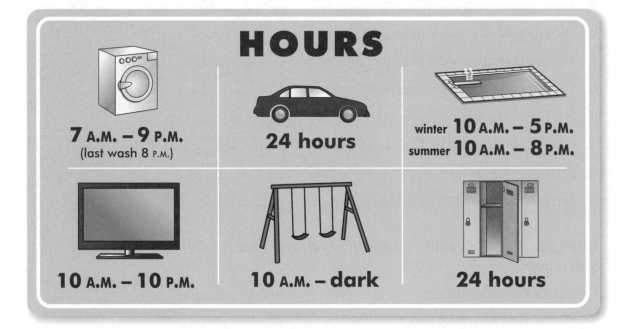

a. The swimming pool is always open until 8:00 p.m.   *false*

b. You can use the washer and dryer all night.   _____

c. The garage is always open.   _____

d. The playground closes at different times each day.   _____

e. You can use the storage lockers at midnight.   _____

f. The recreation room is open twenty-four hours.   _____

g. You can watch a movie on the big-screen TV at 9:00 p.m.   _____

3. **Look in your dictionary. *True* or *False*? Correct the underlined words in the false sentences.**

   a. Each apartment has a ~~fire escape~~. _{balcony}   _____false_____

   b. The apartment complex has a <u>swimming pool and courtyard</u>. _____

   c. The <u>trash chute</u> is in the alley. _____

   d. The emergency exit is in the <u>hallway</u>. _____

   e. The landlord is talking about a <u>lease</u>. _____

   f. A tenant is using her <u>peephole</u>. _____

4. **Complete the signs. Use the words in the box.**

buzzer	elevator	~~emergency exit~~	intercom
mailbox	tenants	trash bin	trash chute

   a.
   IN CASE OF FIRE use the
   emergency exit
   DO NOT use the
   _____

   b.
   NEW _____:
   Please put your name on your
   _____ .

   c.
   NOTICE Do not throw...
   ...down the _____ .
   Put them in the _____ in the alley.

   d.
   ATTENTION ALL TENANTS:
   Do not allow strangers into the building.
   Always use the _____
   BEFORE you use the _____ !

5. **What about you? Check (✓) the items in your home.**

   ☐ fire escape   ☐ security camera   ☐ laundry room

   ☐ garage   ☐ balcony   ☐ smoke detector

   ☐ lobby   ☐ third floor   ☐ security gate

   ☐ door chain   ☐ dead-bolt lock   ☐ peephole

Challenge Look at Exercise 5. Which three items are most important to you? Why? Tell a classmate.

Different Places to Live

1. Look in your dictionary. Where are they?

a. students   _college dormitory_

b. an elderly, physically-challenged woman   _____

c. a man with a newspaper   _____

2. Look at the chart. Circle the words to complete the sentences.

Based on information from: *Population Profiles of the United States:* 2000 Internet Release (U.S. Census) and *American Housing Survey 2003* (U.S. Census).

a. Most people live in the city / (suburbs).

b. Only 24% of people live in the city / country.

c. About 30% live in the city / suburbs.

d. Most people live in houses and apartments, but there are almost nine million mobile homes / condominiums.

e. There are more townhouses than condominiums / mobile homes.

f. The chart does NOT have information about the number of nursing homes / townhouses.

3. What about you? Check (✓) the places you've lived.

☐ city   ☐ country   ☐ college dorm

☐ suburbs   ☐ farm   ☐ townhouse

☐ small town   ☐ ranch   ☐ mobile home

☐ senior housing ☐ condo   ☐ Other: _____

Challenge Take a class survey. Where do your classmates live? Write the results.
Example: *Ten students live in the suburbs.*

          See page 270 for listening practice.

1. **Look in your dictionary. Check (✓) the locations.**

	On the Lawn	On the Patio
a. patio furniture	☐	✓
b. hose	☐	☐
c. hammock	☐	☐
d. grill	☐	☐
e. compost pile	☐	☐
f. garbage can	☐	☐
g. sliding glass door	☐	☐

2. **Look at the house.** *True* or *False*? **Correct the <u>underlined</u> words in the false sentences.**

                  steps

a. There are three <s><u>mailboxes</u></s> in front of the front door.   *false*

b. The <u>doorbell</u> is to the right of the doorknob.   _____

c. The <u>storm</u> door is open.   _____

d. The <u>porch light</u> is on.   _____

e. There's a <u>vegetable garden</u> in the front lawn.   _____

f. The <u>chimney</u> is blue.   _____

g. The satellite dish is near the <u>driveway</u>.   _____

h. The <u>front walk</u> stops at the steps.   _____

3. **What about you? Do you like this house? Check (✓)** *Yes* **or** *No.*

    ☐ Yes   ☐ No   Why? _____

Challenge Draw a picture of your "dream house." Describe it to a partner.

See page 270 for listening practice.

1. Look in your dictionary. Where can you find the . . . ? Use *on* or *under*.

a. paper towels   *under the cabinet*

b. dish rack   _____

c. coffeemaker   _____

d. pot   _____

e. broiler   _____

f. garbage disposal   _____

2. Look at the bar graph. How long do things last? Put the words in the correct columns.

How Long Things Last

Years

20

15

10

5

Based on information from: *Consumer Reports Buying Guide* (2000).

1–5 Years	6–10 Years	11–15 Years	16–20 Years
_____	*blender*	_____	_____
	_____	_____	

3. What about you? Check (✓) the items you have.

		Where is it?	How long have you had it?
☐	blender	*on the counter*	*two years*
☐	electric can opener	_____	_____
☐	coffeemaker	_____	_____
☐	electric mixer	_____	_____
☐	food processor	_____	_____
☐	microwave	_____	_____
☐	teakettle	_____	_____
☐	toaster oven	_____	_____

Challenge Look at the kitchen appliances in your dictionary. List the five you think are the most important. Compare your list with a partner's list.

1. Look in your dictionary. *True* or *False*?

    a. There's a teapot on the tray.   _____true_____

    b. The fan has two light fixtures.   _____

    c. The tablecloth is blue.   _____

    d. There's a vase on the buffet.   _____

    e. The salt shaker is on the table.   _____

    f. There's a coffee mug on the dining room table.   _____

    g. The sugar bowl and creamer are in the hutch.   _____

2. Look at the table setting. Complete the sentences.

    a. The _____plate_____ is light blue.

    b. It's on a dark blue _____.

    c. A white _____ is on the plate.

    d. There are two _____ to the left of the plate.

    e. They're on the yellow _____.

    f. There are two _____. They're to the right of the plate.

    g. There's also a _____ to the right of the plate.

    h. There's a _____ above the spoons.

3. What about you? What does *your* table setting look like? Draw a picture on your own paper. Then, complete the charts.

Item	How Many?	Where?
knife		
fork		
spoon		
plate		
bowl		

Item	How Many?	Where?
teacup		
placemat		
napkin		
Other: _____		

Challenge   Describe your table setting to a partner. Your partner will draw it. Does it look the same as your picture in Exercise 3?

See page 271 for listening practice.

1. Look in your dictionary. How many . . . can you see?

a. paintings __2__

b. walls ___

c. throw pillows ___

d. fireplaces ___

e. windows ___

f. end tables ___

2. Look at the Millers' new living room. Cross out the items they already have.

To Buy

~~throw pillows~~	DVD player	houseplant
love seat	couch	basket
armchair	candle holder	drapes
entertainment center	carpet	fire screen
TV	floor lamp	coffee table
stereo system	magazine holder	end table
		candles

3. What about you? Look at the list in Exercise 2. List the items you have.

Challenge Write six sentences about the Millers' living room.

Example: *They have a couch, but they don't have a love seat.*

1. Look in your dictionary. Check (✓) the locations.

	Sink	Bathtub	Wall
a. hot and cold water	✓	✓	☐
b. towel racks	☐	☐	☐
c. shower curtain	☐	☐	☐
d. faucets	☐	☐	☐
e. tiles	☐	☐	☐
f. drains	☐	☐	☐
g. grab bar	☐	☐	☐
h. toilet paper	☐	☐	☐

2. Look at the ad. Circle the words to complete the sentences.

THE **BIG** SPLASH
The Place for Big Bath Buys

$18.99 $8.99 $9.99 $6.99

$44.99 $7.99 $5.99 $3.99 $4.99 $1.99

$.99 $4.99 $2.99 $37.99 $6.99

a. The bath mat / rubber mat is $9.99.

b. The hamper / wastebasket is $6.99.

c. The bath towel / hand towel is $5.99.

d. The soap dish / soap is $2.99.

e. The toilet brush / toothbrush is $4.99.

f. The showerhead / washcloth is $3.99.

g. The mirror / scale is $37.99.

h. The toothbrush holder / soap dish is $4.99.

Challenge What items do people put in a medicine cabinet? Make a list.

See page 272 for listening practice.   57

1. Look in your dictionary. What color is the . . . ?

a. pillow ___white___   b. mattress _____   c. dust ruffle _____

2. Cross out the word that doesn't belong.

a. They're electric.	~~mirror~~	outlet	light switch	lamp
b. They're soft.	pillowcase	quilt	headboard	blanket
c. They're part of a bed.	mattress	alarm clock	box spring	bed frame
d. They're on the wood floor.	dresser	lampshade	rug	night table
e. They make the room dark.	light switch	curtains	mini-blinds	flat sheet
f. You put things in them.	closet	drawer	photos	picture frame

3. Complete the conversations. Use words from Exercise 2.

a. **Lee:**   What time is it?

   Mom: I don't know. There's an _alarm clock_ on the night table.

b. **Tom:**   I'm cold.

   Ana: Here's an extra _____.

c. **Ray:**   The bed's uncomfortable.

   Mia: The _____ is too soft.

d. **Amir:**   There are no curtains.

   Marwa: No, but there are _____.

e. **Bill:**   My sweater isn't in the drawer.

   Molly: Look in the _____.

4. What about you? Check (✓) the items that are on your bed.

☐ fitted sheet   Color: _____

☐ flat sheet   Color: _____

☐ quilt   Color: _____

☐ pillow(s)   How many? _____   Hard or soft? _____

☐ mattress   Hard or soft? _____

☐ blankets   How many? _____

Challenge Write a paragraph describing your bedroom.

1. **Look in your dictionary. Which three items are for safety?**

    a. ___bumper pad___

    b. _____

    c. _____

2. **Look at Olivia and Emma's room. There are ten dolls. Find and circle nine more.**

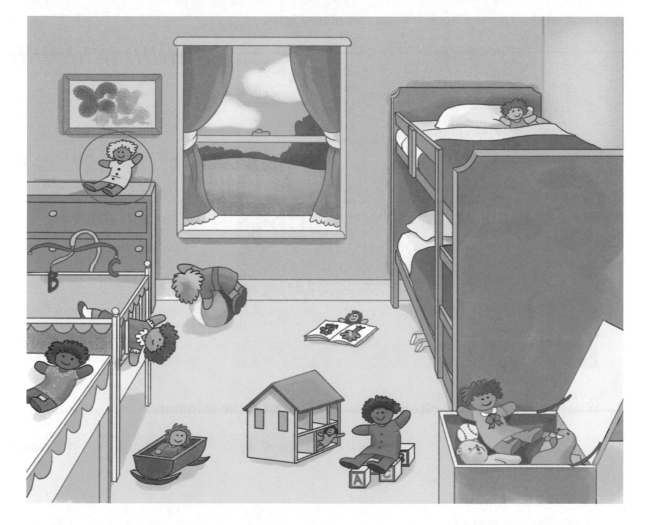

3. **Write the locations of the dolls. Use *on*, *under*, and *in*. Use your own paper.**

    Example: *on the chest of drawers*

4. **What about you? Check (✓) the things you had when you were a child.**

    ☐ dolls   ☐ mobile   ☐ crayons   ☐ Other: _____

    ☐ stuffed animals ☐ balls   ☐ puzzles

    Challenge Look at the toys you checked in Exercise 4. Write a paragraph about your favorite one.

1. **Look in your dictionary. What are the people doing? Circle the words.**

   a. "Can we do this with magazines, too?"   (recycling newspapers) / taking out the garbage

   b. "Dad, does this truck go here?"   dusting the furniture / putting away the toys

   c. "I like this new blanket."   making the bed / sweeping the floor

   d. "Is this the last plate, Dad?"   cleaning the oven / drying the dishes

2. **Look at the room. Check (✓) the completed jobs.**

To Do

✓	wash the sheets
☐	change the sheets
☐	sweep the floor
☐	empty the trash
☐	polish the dresser
☐	scrub the sink
☐	mop the bathroom floor
☐	take out the newspapers

3. **What about you? How often do you . . . ? Check (✓) the columns.**

	Every Day	Every Week	Every Month	Never
dust the furniture				
polish the furniture				
recycle the newspapers				
wash the dishes				
vacuum the carpet				
wipe the counter				
scrub the sink				
put away the toys				
Other: _____				

Challenge Write a To Do list of your housework for this week.

See page 273 for listening practice.

1. **Look in your dictionary. What can you use to clean the . . . ? There may be more correct answers than you can write here.**

Windows	Floor	Dishes
glass cleaner		

2. **Match each item with the correct coupon.**

TO BUY

_4_ a. feather duster
___ b. steel-wool soap pads
___ c. sponges
___ d. pail
___ e. cleanser
___ f. trash bags
___ g. dishwashing liquid
___ h. rubber gloves
___ i. vacuum cleaner bags
___ j. disinfectant wipes

1. 50-33 gal. $2.99 Strongy 50 lg Strongy Strongy 50 lg
2. 22 oz. SPARKLE $1.89
3. 9 qt. $1.99
4. $1.99
5. 3/ $1.00 Cleanest
6. 99¢/pair
7. $3.29
8. pk of 12 $1.99
9. $1.59 SCRUB EZ
10. 2-pack $3.19

3. **What about you? Look at the cleaning supplies in Exercise 2. Which ones do you have? What do you use them for?**

Example: *feather duster—dust the desk*

Challenge Look in a store, online, or at newspaper ads. Write the prices of some cleaning supplies that you use.

1. **Look in your dictionary. Who said . . . ?**

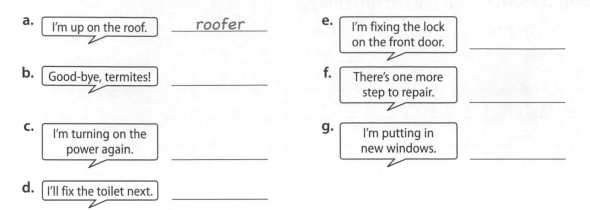

a. I'm up on the roof. <u>roofer</u>

b. Good-bye, termites! _____

c. I'm turning on the power again. _____

d. I'll fix the toilet next. _____

e. I'm fixing the lock on the front door. _____

f. There's one more step to repair. _____

g. I'm putting in new windows. _____

2. **Look at John's bathroom. There are seven problems. Find and circle six more.**

3. **Look at Exercise 2. *True* or *False*? Correct the <u>underlined</u> words in the false sentences.**

       bathtub
a. The ~~sink~~ faucet is dripping. <u>*false*</u>

b. The <u>window</u> is broken. _____

c. There are <u>ants</u> near the sink. _____

d. The <u>light</u> isn't working. _____

e. The <u>sink</u> is overflowing. _____

f. The <u>wall</u> is cracked. _____

4. Look at Exercise 2 and the ads below. Who should John call? Include the repair person, the problem(s), and the phone number on the list. (Hint: John will use some companies for more than one problem.)

224   YELLOW PAGES

ABC
ELECTRIC CORP.
- Licensed Electricians
- Free Estimates
555-2656

Free estimates
HAMPTON CARPENTERS INC.
- closets
- shelves
- cabinets
- wall units
- shutters
- bookcases
555-7367

JACK O. TRADES
GENERAL REPAIRS
No job is too small.
555-8356

Keys Made
While-U-Wait
UNIVERSITY LOCKSMITHS
Your one-stop security shop
555-9946

EXTERMINALL PEST CONTROL
Fast and Safe
Residential and Commercial
555-4789

Affordable Home Remodeling
HARMON ROOFING REPAIRS
- *All types of roofing*
- *leaders & gutters*
- *Licensed & Insured*
555-758
"We care about y

Tell the Advertisers you found them in the **Yellow Pages**

EMERGENCY SERVICES
24 HOURS
7 DAYS A WEEK
Free Flow Plumbing Co.
555-2233

Let your fing
the walking i
Yellow Pa

Why wonder
buy it?
The **Yellow**
tell you *where*

CALL	
1. __exterminator__	555-4789
a. __cockroaches__	
2. _____	
a. __The faucet is dripping.__	
b. _____	
c. _____	
3. _____	555-2656
a. _____	
4. __repair person__	
a. _____	
b. _____	

Challenge   Look at the problems in Exercise 2. Who fixes them in your home? Make a list.
Example: *toilet stopped up—my son*

1. Look in your dictionary. *True* or *False*?

   a. Sally and Tina are roommates.   *true*

   b. They had a party in Apartment 3B.   _____

   c. A DJ played music.   _____

   d. Some people danced.   _____

   e. Sally and Tina were irritated by the noise.   _____

   f. The neighbors cleaned up the mess in the hallway.   _____

   g. Sally and Tina gave an invitation to the woman in Apartment 2C.   _____

2. Look at the pictures. Check (✓) the answers.

Friday Night   Saturday Night

	Friday Night	Saturday Night
a. The party was in the rec room.	✓	☐
b. There was a DJ at the party.	☐	☐
c. The music was loud.	☐	☐
d. There was a mess on the floor.	☐	☐
e. People danced.	☐	☐
f. There was a lot of noise.	☐	☐
g. The roommates were at the party.	☐	☐
h. A neighbor was irritated.	☐	☐

3. **Look at the top picture on page 65 in your dictionary. Circle the words to complete the sentences.**

   a. The man is Sally and Tina's (neighbor)/ roommate.

   b. He's at the party / in his bedroom.

   c. He's happy / irritated.

   d. It's before / after midnight.

   e. Sally and Tina didn't give him an invitation / the rules to the party.

   f. He can't sleep because of the mess / noise.

4. **Complete the sign. Use the words in the box.**

   | dance | DJs | mess | music | noise | parties | ~~Rules~~ |

   # Building ___Rules___
   a.

   - No loud _____ after 10:00 p.m.
     b.

   - Large _____ in rec room only.
     c.

   - Please be quiet in the hallways. No _____!
     d.

   - Please clean up your _____ in public areas.
     e.

   - You can _____ in your apartment, but you must have carpet.
     f.

   - No _____ at apartment parties.
     g.

   Thank you,
   The Manager

Challenge Look at the rules in Exercise 4 and the parties in Exercise 2. Did the people follow the rules? Talk about it with a partner.

1. **Look in your dictionary. Where's the . . . ? Check (✓) the answers.**

a. fish	✓	☐	☐
b. rice	☐	☐	☐
c. butter	☐	☐	☐
d. meat	☐	☐	☐
e. bread	☐	☐	☐
f. pasta	☐	☐	☐
g. milk	☐	☐	☐

2. **Complete Shao-fen's shopping list. Use your dictionary for help.**

✓ **a.** e _g_ _g_ s
☐ **b.** ___ r ___ i t
☐ **c.** v ___ g e ___ a ___ l ___ s
☐ **d.** r ___ ___ e
☐ **e.** c ___ ___ ___ e ___ e
☐ **f.** ___ r e ___ d
☐ **g.** ___ a ___ ___ ___ a
☐ **h.** ___ h ___ c k ___ n

Shao-fen

3. **Look at the food that Shao-fen bought at the market. Check (✓) the items she bought on the shopping list in Exercise 2.**

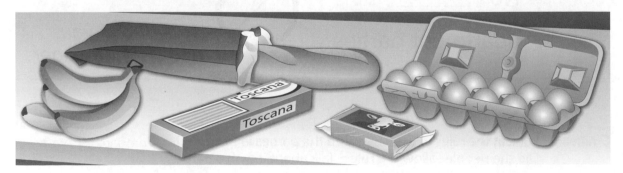

4. Look in your dictionary. *True* or *False*?

a. There are four grocery bags in the kitchen. _____false_____

b. There's a shopping list on the table. _____

c. The word *butter* is on the shopping list. _____

d. There are coupons on the table. _____

e. There are eggs on the table. _____

f. There are vegetables in the refrigerator. _____

g. There's fruit in the refrigerator. _____

5. Complete the coupons. Write the names of the foods.

a.

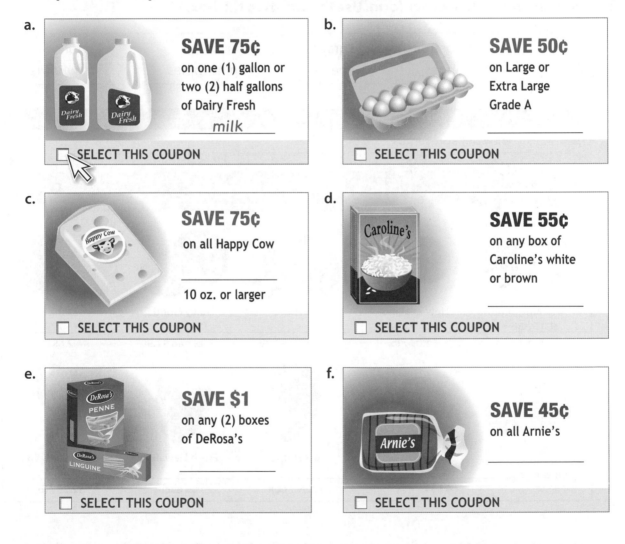

SAVE 75¢
on one (1) gallon or
two (2) half gallons
of Dairy Fresh
_____milk_____

☐ SELECT THIS COUPON

b.

SAVE 50¢
on Large or
Extra Large
Grade A
_____

☐ SELECT THIS COUPON

c.

SAVE 75¢
on all Happy Cow

_____

10 oz. or larger

☐ SELECT THIS COUPON

d.

Caroline's

SAVE 55¢
on any box of
Caroline's white
or brown
_____

☐ SELECT THIS COUPON

e.

DeRosa's
PENNE

DeRosa's
LINGUINE

SAVE $1
on any (2) boxes
of DeRosa's

_____

☐ SELECT THIS COUPON

f.

Arnie's

SAVE 45¢
on all Arnie's

_____

☐ SELECT THIS COUPON

6. What about you? Do you use store coupons?

☐ Yes   ☐ No   If *yes*, for what items? _____

Challenge Look in your dictionary. Which foods do you like? Make a list. Compare lists with
a classmate. Do you and your classmate like the same things?

1. Look in your dictionary. Write the name of the fruit.

a. They're to the right of the figs.   _____dates_____

b. They're to the left of the tangerines.   _____

c. They're below the peaches.   _____

d. They're above the mangoes.   _____

e. They're to the right of the raspberries.   _____

f. One is ripe, one is unripe, and one is rotten.   _____

2. Complete the online order form. Use the words in the box.

| ~~apples~~ | grapefruit | grapes | kiwi | lemons |
| limes | oranges | pears | pineapples | strawberries |

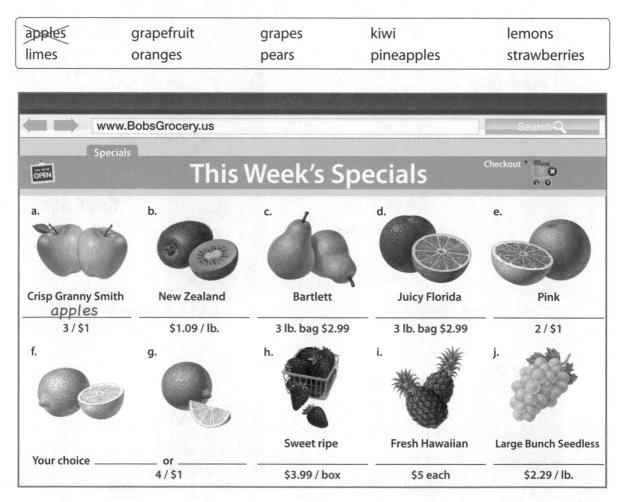

www.BobsGrocery.us   Search

Specials

This Week's Specials   Checkout

a. Crisp Granny Smith
_____apples_____
3 / $1

b. New Zealand
_____
$1.09 / lb.

c. Bartlett
_____
3 lb. bag $2.99

d. Juicy Florida
_____
3 lb. bag $2.99

e. Pink
_____
2 / $1

f. Your choice _____ or _____
4 / $1

g.

h. Sweet ripe
_____
$3.99 / box

i. Fresh Hawaiian
_____
$5 each

j. Large Bunch Seedless
_____
$2.29 / lb.

3. What about you? Make a shopping list using the fruit in Exercise 2. How much or how many will you buy? How much will it cost?

Example: *6 apples—$2.00*

Challenge   Make a list of fruit from your native country.

   See page 275 for listening practice.

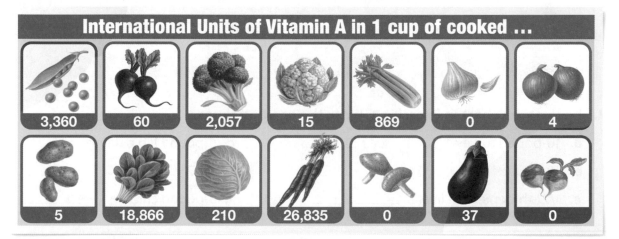

1. Look in your dictionary. Which vegetables are . . . ? Put them in the correct columns.

Yellow / Orange	Green	Red
sweet potatoes	_____ _____	_____
_____	_____ _____	_____
_____	_____ _____	_____
_____	_____ _____	_____
_____	_____ _____	_____
	_____ _____	
	_____ _____	
	_____ _____	

2. Look at the chart. Which has more vitamin A? Circle the correct answer.

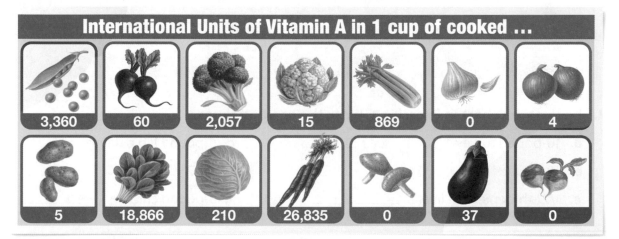

International Units of Vitamin A in 1 cup of cooked ...

3,360	60	2,057	15	869	0	4
5	18,866	210	26,835	0	37	0

Based on information from: U.S. Department of Agriculture, Agricultural Research Service. 2007. USDA National Nutrient Database for Standard Reference, Release 20.

a. cabbage / (spinach)

b. beets / turnips

c. mushrooms / onions

d. carrots / celery

e. garlic / potatoes

f. turnips / eggplant

g. broccoli / cauliflower

h. spinach / celery

i. beets / peas

3. What about you? How often do you eat these vegetables in a week? Circle the numbers.

carrots	0	1	2	3	4	more than 4 times a week
broccoli	0	1	2	3	4	more than 4 times a week
spinach	0	1	2	3	4	more than 4 times a week

Challenge Make a list of vegetables from your native country.

See page 275 for listening practice.

1. Look in your dictionary. Label the foods in the chart.

		Size	Cooking time	Method
	a. ___lamb___	5–8 pounds	30 min./pound	oven
	b. _____	1/2" thick	3 min.*	broiler
	c. _____	1 1/2" thick	10 min.*	broiler
	d. _____	8–20 pounds	20 min./pound	oven
	e. _____	8–12 pounds	3–4 hours	oven
	f. _____	2 1/2 –3 pounds	1 1/4 hours	oven
*each side				

2. Look at the chart in Exercise 1. Write the cooking times.

a. 10-pound turkey   _3–4 hours_   **d.** 6-pound leg of lamb _____

b. 10-pound ham   _____   **e.** 1-1/2" thick steak _____

c. 1/2"-thick piece of liver   _____   **f.** 3-pound chicken _____

3. Label the chicken parts.

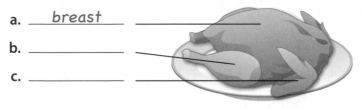

a. ___breast___ _____

b. _____

c. _____

4. What about you? Check (✓) the meat and poultry you eat.

☐ veal cutlets   ☐ bacon   ☐ duck   ☐ lamb chops

☐ tripe   ☐ beef ribs   ☐ pork chops   ☐ sausage

Challenge Take a survey. Ask five people which meats and poultry they eat.

See page 275 for listening practice.

1. Look in your dictionary. Write the names of the seafood.

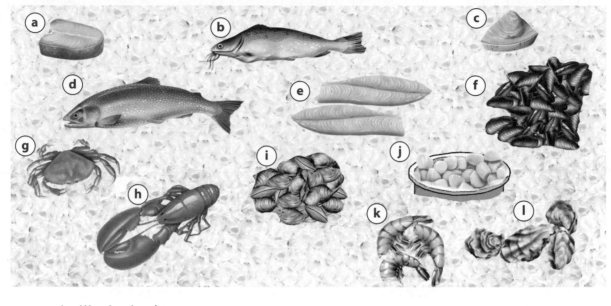

a. _halibut steak_   e. _____   i. _____

b. _____   f. _____   j. _____

c. _____   g. _____   k. _____

d. _____   h. _____   l. _____

2. Look at the sandwich. Complete the order form. Check (✓) the correct boxes.

Sandwich Order		
Meat	**Cheese**	**Bread**
✓ smoked turkey	☐ American	☐ white
☐ roast beef	☐ mozzarella	☐ wheat
☐ corned beef	☐ Swiss	☐ rye
☐ salami	☐ cheddar	
☐ pastrami		

3. What about you? Complete your order with the food on the form in Exercise 2.

I'd like a _____ sandwich with _____ cheese on _____ bread.

Challenge Ask five classmates what they want from the deli. Write their orders.

See page 276 for listening practice.

1. Look in your dictionary. *True* or *False*?

a. A customer is buying pet food. _____true_____

b. The manager is in aisle 3A. _____

c. The grocery clerk is in the produce section. _____

d. There's a scale in the dairy section. _____

e. There are five customers in line. _____

f. You can get frozen vegetables in aisle 2B. _____

g. The bagger is near the cashier. _____

h. The self-checkout doesn't have a cash register. _____

2. Complete the conversations. Use the words in the box.

| Bagger | bottle return | cart | checkstands |
| ~~Customer~~ | manager | scale | self-checkout |

___Customer___ : Excuse me. Where do I take these empty soda bottles?
     a.

Grocery Clerk: To the _____. Near aisle 1.
                              b.

Amy: I'll get a shopping basket.

Jason: Get a _____. We have a lot on our list!
                    c.

Jason: We need two pounds of potatoes. Is this enough?

Amy: There's a _____ over there. We can weigh them.
                      d.

Jason: Look at the dates on these frozen dinners.

Amy: They're all too old. Let's tell the _____.
                                            e.

Amy: Wow! Look at the lines at the _____.
                                        f.

Jason: I see. But I don't like to use the _____. I like to talk to a person.
                                              g.

Amy: Can we have four bags, please?

_____: Sure. Paper or plastic?
     h.

3. Look at the things Amy and Jason bought. Check (✓) the items on the shopping list.

Grocery List

☑ potatoes	☐ soup	☐ plastic wrap
☐ tuna	☐ cookies	☐ apple juice
☐ aluminum foil	☐ nuts	☐ sour cream
☐ bagels	☐ margarine	☐ coffee
☐ yogurt	☐ sugar	☐ cake
☐ potato chips	☐ ice cream	☐ candy bars
☐ beans	☐ oil	

4. Put the items from the list in Exercise 3 in the correct category. Use your dictionary for help.

Canned Foods	Dairy	Snack Foods
_____	_____	_____
_____	_____	_____
_____	_____	_____

Baking Products	Beverages	Baked Goods
_____	_____	_____
_____	_____	_____
		_____

Grocery Products	Produce	Frozen Foods
_____	*potatoes*	_____
_____		

Challenge Make a shopping list for yourself. Write the section for each item.
Example: *scallops—seafood section*

See page 276 for listening practice.

1. Look at <u>pages 72 and 73</u> in your dictionary. What is the container or packaging for . . . ?

a. pinto beans   *can*   c. sour cream   _____

b. plastic storage bags _____   d. potato chips _____

2. Complete these coupons. Use the words in the box.

bag	bottle	carton	loaf
six-pack	package	roll	~~tube~~

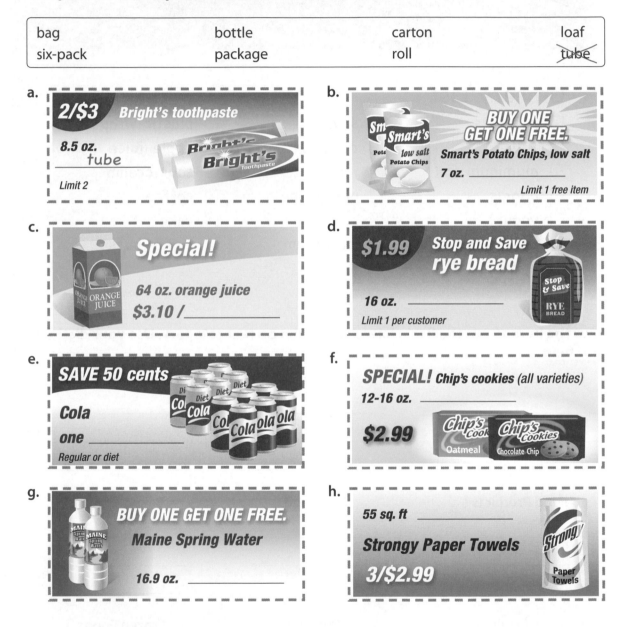

a.
2/$3 **Bright's toothpaste**
8.5 oz.
_____tube_____
Bright's
Bright's Toothpaste
Limit 2

b.
BUY ONE GET ONE FREE.
Smart's Potato Chips, low salt
7 oz. _____
Limit 1 free item
Smart's Pota... low salt Potato Chips

c.
Special!
64 oz. orange juice
$3.10 / _____
ORANGE JUICE

d.
$1.99 **Stop and Save rye bread**
16 oz. _____
Limit 1 per customer
Stop & Save RYE BREAD

e.
SAVE 50 cents
Cola
one _____
Regular or diet
Diet Cola

f.
SPECIAL! Chip's cookies (all varieties)
12-16 oz. _____
$2.99
Chip's Cookies Oatmeal Chocolate Chip

g.
BUY ONE GET ONE FREE.
Maine Spring Water
16.9 oz. _____
MAINE Spring Water

h.
55 sq. ft _____
Strongy Paper Towels
3/$2.99
Strongy Paper Towels

3. Write a shopping list. Use all the coupons in Exercise 2.

Example: *2 tubes of toothpaste*

Challenge   Which foods do you think are in your refrigerator? Make a list. Then check your answers at home. **Example:** *a bottle of soda*

💿   **See page 277 for listening practice.**

1. Look in your dictionary. Write the words.

a. oz. <u>ounce</u>

b. lb. _____

c. pt. _____

d. qt. _____

e. c. _____

f. tsp. _____

g. TBS. _____

h. gal. _____

2. Write the weight or measurement.

a. <u>1 1/2 pounds of potatoes</u>

b. _____

c. _____

d. _____

e. _____

f. _____

3. What about you? How much . . . do you eat or drink every week?

a. cheese _____

b. water _____

c. fish _____

d. sugar _____

Challenge Look at page 254 in this book. Follow the instructions.

1. **Look in your dictionary. *True* or *False*? Correct the <u>underlined</u> words in the false sentences.**

   counters
   a. Clean the kitchen ~~windows~~.   *false*   d. Cook <u>meat</u> to 165°.   _____

   b. Separate carrots and <u>meat</u>.   _____   e. Chill leftovers in the <u>refrigerator</u>.   _____

   c. Cook <u>chicken</u> to 160°.   _____

2. **Look at the pictures. Which preparation has the most calories? Number them in order. (1 = the most calories)**

Calories in 3 oz. Chicken Breast

| 150 | 161 | 222 |
| 172 | 168 | 175 |

   ___ **a.** boiled   ___ **c.** grilled   _1_ **e.** fried

   ___ **b.** broiled   ___ **d.** roasted   ___ **f.** stir-fried

3. **What about you? Label the preparations and check (✓) the ways you like to eat eggs.**

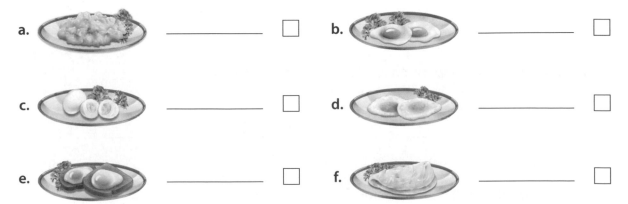

a. _____ ☐   b. _____ ☐

c. _____ ☐   d. _____ ☐

e. _____ ☐   f. _____ ☐

4. **Look in your dictionary. Read the recipe. <u>Underline</u> all the food preparation words.**

🍳 Baked Carrots   email ✉   print 🖨   ★★★★

Ingredients:
1 lb. (450 g.) carrots
3 TBS. butter
1 small onion
salt and pepper
1/8 tsp. nutmeg
1 tsp. sugar
1/2 cup water

Method:
<u>Preheat</u> the oven to 350°F (180°C). <u>Dice</u> the onion. <u>Peel</u> and <u>grate</u> the carrots. <u>Grease</u> a small pan. <u>Add</u> the onion and <u>sauté</u> until soft. <u>Stir</u> in the carrots. <u>Add</u> the sugar, salt, pepper, nutmeg, and water. <u>Bake</u> in a covered casserole until soft, about 30–40 minutes, or <u>microwave</u> on high for 7–10 minutes. <u>Stir</u> after half the cooking time.

---

5. **Look at the recipe in Exercise 4. Number the pictures in order.**

___ a.   ___ b.   ___ c.   ___ d.

___ e.   ___ f.   ___ g.   ___ h.

6. **Look at the pictures. Circle the words to complete the recipe.**

Potatoes and Sauteed Onions   Ingredients: potatoes, onions, butter, salt, pepper

a.

Step 1: (Boil) / Beat the potatoes until soft.

b.

Step 2: Slice / Dice the cool potatoes.

c.

Step 3: Grate / Chop the onion.

d.

Step 4: Saute / Bake the onion in butter until brown. Add the potatoes.

e.

Step 5: Stir / Simmer the ingredients.

f.

Step 6: Saute / Steam until potatoes are brown. Add salt.

Challenge Write the recipe for one of your favorite foods. Share it with a classmate.

1. **Look in your dictionary. *True* or *False*?**

   a. The grater is below the steamer and the plastic storage container.   *false*

   b. The eggbeater is between the spatula and the whisk.   _____

   c. The vegetable peeler, tongs, strainer, and saucepan are on the wall.   _____

   d. The ladle and the wooden spoon are in the pot.   _____

   e. There are lids on the double boiler and casserole dish.   _____

   f. The frying pan is next to the roasting pan.   _____

   g. The kitchen timer is near the colander and the paring knife.   _____

2. **Complete the two-part words. Use the words in the box.**

bowl	holders	knife	opener
~~pan~~	pin	press	sheet

   a. cake   *pan*

   b. mixing   _____

   c. garlic   _____

   d. pot   _____

   e. rolling   _____

   f. cookie   _____

   g. can   _____

   h. carving   _____

3. **Which kitchen utensils do you need? Use words from Exercise 2.**

   a.   *garlic press*   b. _____   c. _____

   d. _____   e. _____   f. _____

   Challenge List the three most important kitchen utensils. Why are they important?
   Example: *pot—to cook spaghetti, soup, and vegetables*

1. **Look in your dictionary. *True* or *False*? Correct the underlined words in the false sentences.**

   a. There are muffins and ~~onion rings~~ *donuts* on the counter.   _____false_____

   b. The restaurant has <u>pizza</u>.   _____

   c. The <u>counterperson</u> is talking to a woman.   _____

   d. The <u>plastic utensils</u> are next to the salad bar.   _____

   e. A woman is drinking <u>a milkshake</u> with a straw.   _____

   f. A man is using <u>sugar substitute</u>.   _____

2. **Look at the orders. Write the food.**

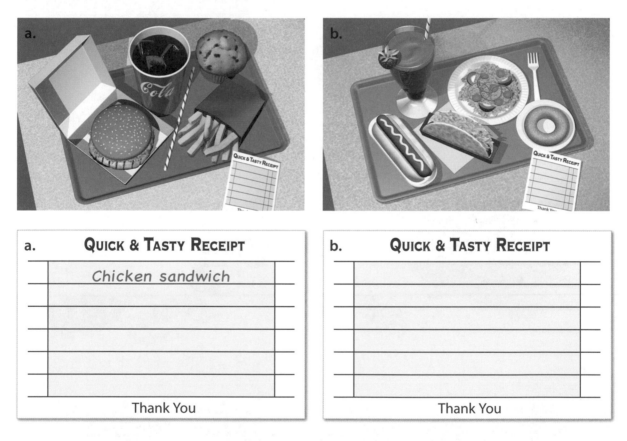

a.   **QUICK & TASTY RECEIPT**
Chicken sandwich
Thank You

b.   **QUICK & TASTY RECEIPT**
Thank You

3. **What about you? Look at the fast food in your dictionary. Tell a classmate your order.**

   Example: *I'd like a cheeseburger.*

   Challenge   Look at the fast food in your dictionary. Which foods are the most healthy? Make a list.

See page 278 for listening practice.

1. Look in your dictionary. Complete the chart. Do not include sandwiches or salads.

meat	vegetables	breads	hot beverages
bacon			

2. Look at the ingredients. Write the food.

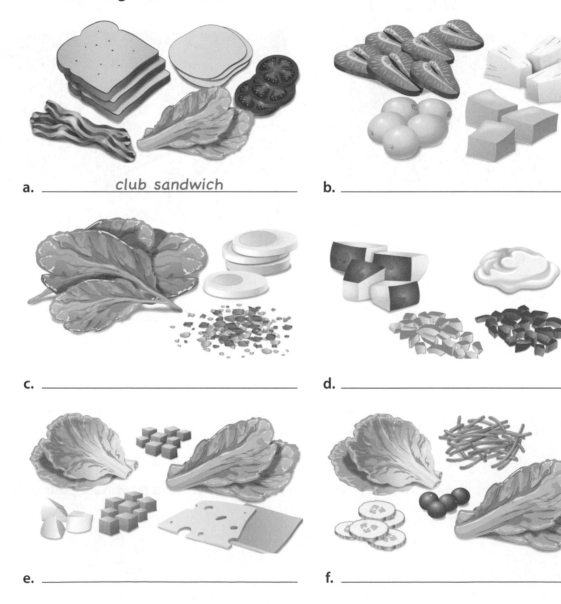

a. _____club sandwich_____

b. _____

c. _____

d. _____

e. _____

f. _____

3. Cross out the word that doesn't belong.

a. Potatoes	baked potato	hash browns	mashed potatoes	~~rice~~
b. Breads	garlic bread	roll	pie	toast
c. Beverages	soup	coffee	low-fat milk	tea
d. Breakfast food	biscuits	layer cake	pancakes	waffles
e. Side salads	chef's salad	coleslaw	pasta salad	potato salad
f. Desserts	cheesecake	layer cake	pie	hot cereal

4. Look at the food. Complete the orders.

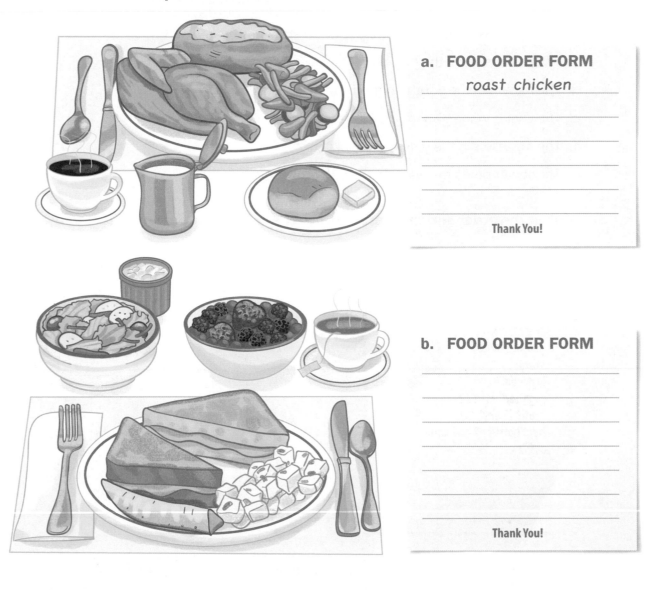

a. **FOOD ORDER FORM**

roast chicken

_____

_____

_____

_____

Thank You!

b. **FOOD ORDER FORM**

_____

_____

_____

_____

_____

_____

_____

Thank You!

5. What about you? What's your favorite . . . ?

soup _____   dessert _____   hot beverage _____

Challenge Show five people the coffee shop menu in your dictionary. Write their orders.

See page 279 for listening practice.

1. Look in your dictionary. Who . . . ?

    a. washes dishes   _dishwasher_

    b. leaves a tip   _____

    c. takes the orders   _____

    d. cooks food   _____

    e. seats the customers   _____

    f. orders from the menu   _____

2. Look in your dictionary. Circle the answers.

    a. The patrons are in the dish room / (dining room).

    b. The baby is in the booth / high chair.

    c. The chef is in the dish room / kitchen.

    d. The hostess is in the dining room / kitchen.

    e. The server pours the water in the dish room / dining room.

3. Look at the order and the place setting. Check (✓) the items the diner needs.

GUEST CHECK

Date	Table	Guests	Server	410121

onion soup
house salad
steak
broccoli
mashed potatoes
garlic bread
half bottle of red wine
coffee

Total

Thank you! Please come again.

☐ dinner plate	☐ wine glass	☐ dinner fork
✓ salad plate	☐ cup	☐ steak knife
☐ soup bowl	☐ saucer	☐ knife
☐ bread-and-butter plate	☐ napkin	☐ teaspoon
☐ water glass	☐ salad fork	☐ soupspoon

4. Look at the menu. Complete the check.

The Bistro
❧ MENU ❧

Soup of the day	$4.50
House salad	$3.50
Fish of the day	$15.50
Chicken á l'orange	$12.50
Sirloin steak	$19.00
Vegetables	$2.50
Potatoes	$2.50
Cherry pie	$4.00
with ice cream	$5.00
Coconut cake	$4.50
Coffee or tea	$1.50

The Bistro
242 West Street 555-0700
GUEST CHECK

				832000

black bean soup	$4.50
house salad	_____
grilled salmon	_____
peas	_____
french fries	_____
cherry pie w/vanilla ice cream	_____
coffee	_____
Subtotal	_____
Tax (5%)	_____
Total	_____

THANK YOU!

5. In the United States, most restaurant patrons leave a tip for the server when they pay the check. The tip is often 15% of the subtotal. Look at the check in Exercise 4. Circle the answers and complete the sentences.

a. The subtotal is ___$35.00___ .   (($35.00)) $36.75 $40.25

b. A 15% tip is _____ . $1.75 $5.25 $4.72

c. Diners leave the tip on the _____ .   menu   table   dinner plate

6. What about you? Do restaurant patrons leave tips for the server in your

native country? _____

If *yes*, how much? _____

Where do they leave it? _____

Challenge Look at the menu in Exercise 4. Order a meal. Figure out the subtotal, 5% tax, the total, and a 15% tip.

1. Look in your dictionary. *True* or *False*?

a. There's live music at the farmers' market.   _____true_____

b. The avocados are with the fruit.   _____

c. A vendor is counting watermelons.   _____

d. You can find the herb *dill* at the farmers' market.   _____

e. There are free samples of vegetables.   _____

f. The avocados are organic.   _____

g. The lemonade is sweet.   _____

2. Look at the signs. Match.

1. *Sweet!*

2. TAKE ONE!

3. USDA

4. *FRESH!*

5. *Basil*

_____ **a.** herb   _____ **c.** samples   _____ **e.** vegetables

_____ **b.** organic   _1_ **d.** strawberries

3. Complete the chart. Use the words in the box.

| ~~avocados~~ | dill | Herbs | lemonade | Vegetables | Vendors | watermelon | zucchini |

Fruit			Beverages				
avocados	peppers				Green Farms		parsley
strawberries			soda		Cara's Bakery		
	onions		milk		Hot Food		basil

4. Look in your dictionary. Circle the words to complete the flyer.

Welcome to
Greenview (Farmers)/ Fish *Market*
a.

Right now we have fresh:
- vegetables (<u>tomatoes / turnips</u>, lettuce, zucchini)
  b.
- fruits (<u>avocados / apples</u>, strawberries, apricots,
  c.
  <u>peaches / pineapples</u>)
  d.
- <u>fish / herbs</u> (basil, dill, parsley, chives)
  e.
- <u>local cheese / ice cream</u> (Swiss, cheddar, mozzarella)
  f.

We also have USDA <u>organic / sour</u> produce.
g.

Free <u>samples / vendors</u> of many items! (Take one, you'll like it!)
h.

Some of our <u>samples / vendors</u>:
i.
- Green Farms (fresh <u>fruits / vegetables</u>)
  j.
- The <u>Lemonade / Live Music</u> Stand (<u>sweet / sour</u>, but good!)
  k.   l.
- Cara's Bakery (freshly baked <u>apple pies / pancakes</u>, donuts, and
  m.
  cupcakes: <u>sweet / sour</u> and delicious!)
  n.
- Hot Food (<u>sandwiches / tacos</u> and much more!)
  o.

Listen to <u>live music / vendors</u> (featuring The Two-Step Band)!
p.

Time: Saturdays 8:00 a.m. – 2:00 p.m.
Place: Union Square, 4th and Park

5. What about you? Imagine you are at the farmers' market. Check (✓) the things you will do there. Then, compare answers with a classmate.

- ☐ listen to live music
- ☐ have lunch
- ☐ buy sweets
- ☐ buy organic vegetables
- ☐ speak to the vendors
- ☐ meet friends
- ☐ drink lemonade
- ☐ eat samples

Challenge Make a shopping list for the farmers' market in your dictionary.

See page 280 for listening practice.

Everyday Clothes

1. **Look in your dictionary. Which clothing items are . . . ?**

   a. green ___*dress*___ and _____

   b. dark blue _____, _____, and _____

   c. red _____

   d. yellow _____ and _____

   e. white _____, _____, _____, _____, and _____

   f. pink _____

   g. orange _____

   h. beige _____

2. **Look at the picture of Courtney and Nicholas. Read the school clothing rules. Complete the sentences.**

Courtney

Nicholas

CLOTHING RULES

Wear…	Don't wear…
shirts	T-shirts
blouses	jeans
slacks	baseball caps
skirts	athletic shoes
dresses	
socks	

What's OK?

a. Courtney is wearing a ___*blouse*___.

b. Nicholas is wearing _____.

c. He's also wearing _____.

What's NOT OK?

d. Courtney is wearing _____ and _____.

e. Nicholas is wearing a _____ and a _____.

3. **What about you? What are you wearing today?**

   _____

4. Look in your dictionary. *True* or *False*?

a. The man in the blue shirt is wearing jeans. _____true_____

b. The woman with white shoes is wearing socks. _____

c. The girl with the baseball cap is tying her shoes. _____

d. The woman in the skirt is putting on a sweater. _____

e. The woman with the sweater has a handbag. _____

f. The man in the green shirt and slacks has tickets. _____

5. Look in your dictionary. Circle the words to complete the conversation.

Nina: Clio? I'm in front of the theater. Where are you? It's 7:45!

Clio: Sorry. I'm still getting dressed. What are you wearing?

Nina: A blue (blouse)/ T-shirt and a white baseball cap / skirt.
                              a.   **b.**

Clio: Is it cold out? Do I need a handbag / sweater?
                                                        c.

Nina: Maybe. It *is* a little cool. What are you wearing?

Clio: Right now I'm wearing a dress / pants, but maybe I'll put on slacks / socks.
                                            d.   **e.**

Nina: OK. But hurry! The concert starts at 8:15!

6. Cross out the word that doesn't belong.

a. You wear it on top.   ~~handbag~~   T-shirt   sweater

b. They're for your feet.   shoes   socks   pants

c. It's only for women.   dress   blouse   suit

d. You wear it on bottom.   jeans   shirt   slacks

7. What about you? Complete the checklist. Do you wear . . . ?

	Yes	No	If *yes*, where?
jeans	☐	☐	_____
athletic shoes	☐	☐	_____
a T-shirt	☐	☐	_____
a suit	☐	☐	_____
a sweater	☐	☐	_____
a baseball cap	☐	☐	_____

Challenge Look in your dictionary. Imagine you have tickets for the concert. What are you going to wear? Tell a partner.

See page 280 for listening practice.

1. **Look in your dictionary. Circle the words to complete the sentences.**

   a. The woman's (business suit) / briefcase is purple.

   b. The cardigan / pullover sweater is green.

   c. The evening gown / uniform is turquoise.

   d. The tank top / sweatshirt is gray.

   e. The overalls / sweatpants are red.

   f. The knit top / sports shirt is blue and white.

   g. The cocktail / maternity dress is orange.

2. **Which clothes do women or men usually wear? Which clothes can both wear? Put the words from the box in the correct spaces in the circles.**

business suit	vest	shorts	cardigan sweater
uniform	tie	evening gown	sweatpants
pullover sweater	sandals	sports jacket	tuxedo
maternity dress	tank top	cocktail dress	capris

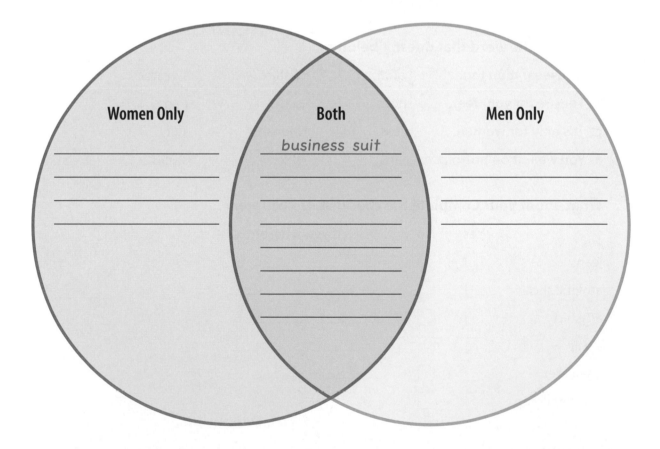

Women Only

Both

business suit

Men Only

3. **Look at the picture. Write the names of the clothing items on the list. Write the color, too.**

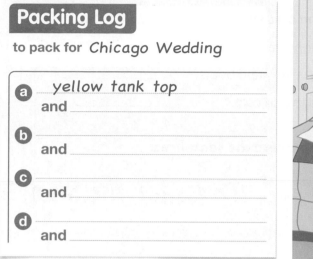

Packing Log

to pack for *Chicago Wedding*

- **a** _yellow tank top_
  and _____
- **b** _____
  and _____
- **c** _____
  and _____
- **d** _____
  and _____

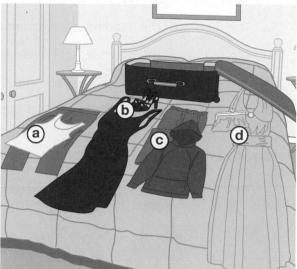

4. **Match the activity with the clothes from Exercise 3.**

HOTEL CHICAGO
ALEXANDRA PLACE
CHICAGO

SATURDAY

_c_	1. Meet Nina in exercise room	7:30 a.m.
___	2. Lunch near swimming pool	12:00 p.m.
___	3. Formal dinner at the Grill	6:00 p.m.
___	4. Wedding party at the Grand Hotel Ballroom	9:00 p.m.

5. **What about you? Where do you wear these clothes? Check (✓) the columns.**

	At School	At Work	At Home	At a Party	Never
pullover sweater					
vest					
sweatpants					
tuxedo or gown					
uniform					
cap					

Challenge What casual clothes do you have? Work clothes? Formal clothes? Exercise wear? Give two examples for each type of clothes.

See page 280 for listening practice.

1. Look in your dictionary. *True* or *False*?

a. The man with the headwrap is wearing a jacket.   _____true_____

b. The man with the down jacket is wearing earmuffs.   _____

c. The woman in the poncho is wearing yellow rain boots.   _____

d. The man with sunglasses is wearing a trench coat.   _____

2. Look at the ad. Circle the words to complete the sentences.

Dress for the Snow

Jessica is wearing a dark green down vest / (parka,)
                                             a.

white earmuffs / headband, and green
                   b.

gloves / mittens. Justin is wearing a blue
      c.

down jacket / coat, black ski hat / ski mask, and
      d.   **e.**

a light blue winter scarf / hat.
               f.

DRESS FOR THE SUN

Kimberly is wearing a headwrap / straw hat,
                g.

black swimming trunks / swimsuit, and a white
          h.

cover-up / windbreaker. Her raincoat / umbrella
     i.   **j.**

and leggings / sunglasses protect her from the sun.
      k.

3. What about you? Circle the words to complete the sentences.

a. I am / am not wearing a jacket or coat today.

b. I wear / don't wear sunglasses.

c. I sometimes / never wear a hat.

Challenge Look at the clothes in your dictionary. List eight items you have. When do you wear
them? **Example:** *gloves—for cold weather*

     See page 281 for listening practice.

1. **Look in your dictionary. Circle the words to complete the sentences.**

   a. The pajamas / tights are pink.

   b. The slippers / crew socks are gray.

   c. The thermal undershirt / blanket sleeper is yellow.

   d. The robe / nightshirt is blue and white.

   e. The body shaper / nightgown is beige.

2. **Look at the ad. Complete the bill.**

Underneath It All
Semi-annual Sale
Hours: M – F 10:00 – 6:00 ◆ Weekends 10:00 – 8:00

3 / $10.00	3 / $12.00	$6.50	4 / $18.00	$7.00

2 / $6.00	$3.50	3 / $13.50	$5.00	$25.00

$2.50	$9.00	$18.00	$15.00

230 Green St. Tel.: 555-5431 Fax: 555-6548
www.unia.us

```
       UNDERNEATH
         IT ALL
-------------------------------
2  _____bras_____    $50.00

1  _____    $ 9.00

2  _____    $36.00

3 PR. _____    $12.00

2 PR. _____    $ 6.00

8 PR. _____    $36.00

         TOTAL $149.00
```

Challenge Choose clothes from the ad in Exercise 2. Write a bill. Figure out the total.

1. Look in your dictionary. Put the words in the correct column.

For Your Head	For Your Face	For Your Hands
hard hat		

For Your Feet

2. Look at the online catalog. Write the names of the workplace clothing. Use the words on the left side of the catalog page.

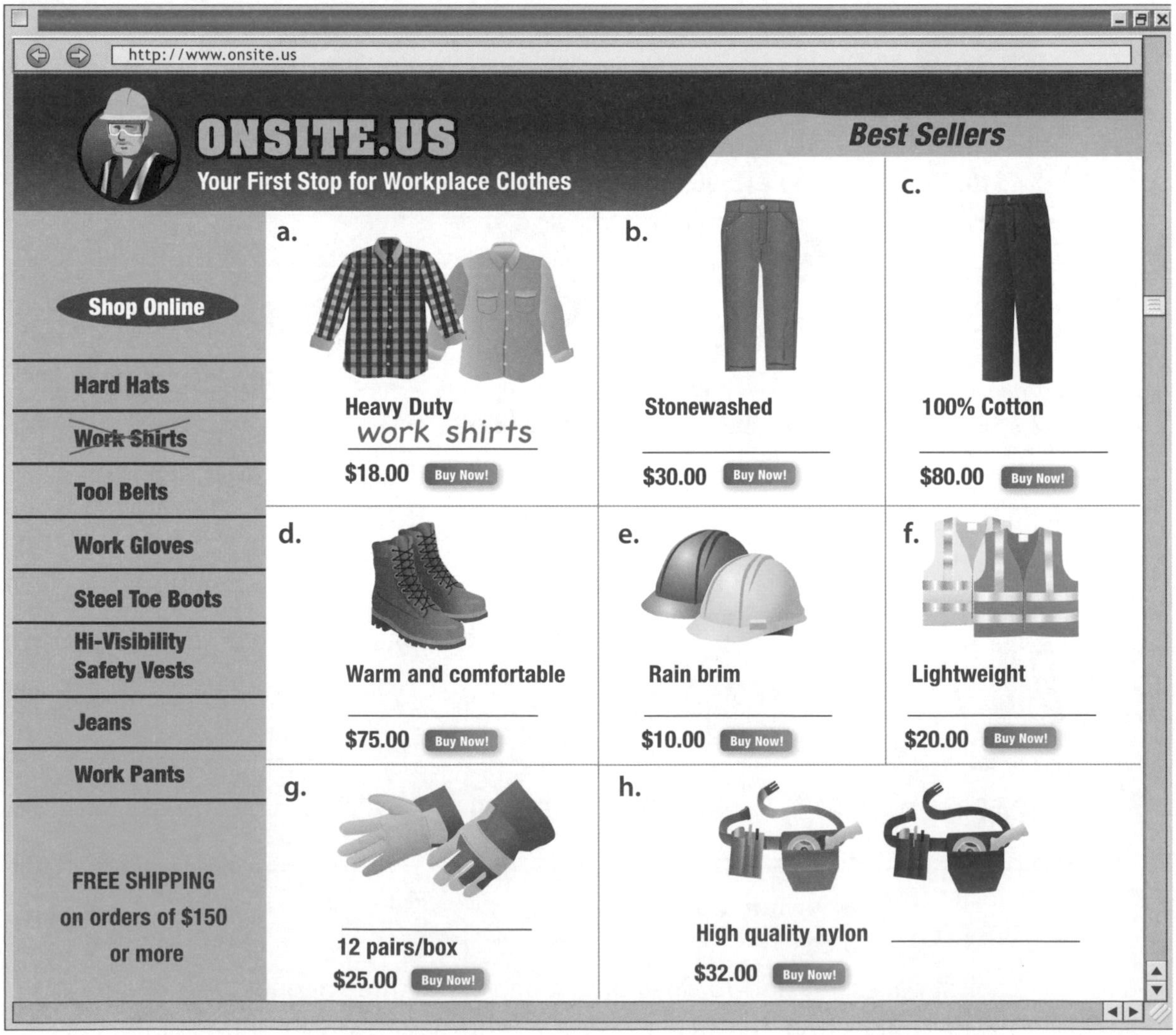

http://www.onsite.us

ONSITE.US
Your First Stop for Workplace Clothes

Best Sellers

Shop Online

Hard Hats
Work Shirts
Tool Belts
Work Gloves
Steel Toe Boots
Hi-Visibility Safety Vests
Jeans
Work Pants

FREE SHIPPING
on orders of $150
or more

a. Heavy Duty
work shirts
$18.00 Buy Now!

b. Stonewashed
$30.00 Buy Now!

c. 100% Cotton
$80.00 Buy Now!

d. Warm and comfortable
$75.00 Buy Now!

e. Rain brim
$10.00 Buy Now!

f. Lightweight
$20.00 Buy Now!

g. 12 pairs/box
$25.00 Buy Now!

h. High quality nylon
$32.00 Buy Now!

3. **Look in your dictionary. *True* or *False*? Correct the underlined words in the false sentences.**

   a. The construction worker is wearing a ~~polo~~ *work* shirt.   *false*

   b. The road worker is wearing <u>jeans</u>. _____

   c. The farmworker is wearing <u>work gloves</u>. _____

   d. The salesperson is wearing a <u>badge</u>. _____

   e. The manager is wearing a <u>blazer</u>. _____

   f. The counterperson is wearing a <u>chef's hat</u>. _____

   g. The nurse is wearing <u>scrubs</u>. _____

   h. The security guard has a <u>name tag</u>. _____

   i. The medical technician is wearing a <u>lab coat</u>. _____

   j. The surgeon is wearing a <u>surgical scrub cap</u>. _____

4. **Look at the online catalog in Exercise 2. What items will people buy? Complete the chart.**

Job	Quantity	Item	Item Price	Total
a. road worker	2 pairs	*steel toe boots*	$75	$150
	1 pair	_____	$80	_____
b. construction worker	1	_____	$32	_____
	2	safety vests	_____	_____
	1 box	_____	_____	_____

5. **What about you? Check (✓) the clothing you have. Do you wear the clothing for work?**

	For Work	Not for Work
☐ safety glasses	☐	☐
☐ waist apron	☐	☐
☐ blazer	☐	☐
☐ polo shirt	☐	☐
☐ work gloves	☐	☐
☐ helmet	☐	☐
☐ hairnet	☐	☐

Challenge Look at <u>pages 166 and 167</u> in your dictionary. List three people's work clothing.
Example: *the dental assistant—a face mask and disposable gloves*

See page 281 for listening practice.

1. Look at the top picture in your dictionary. How many . . . can you see?

a. salesclerks   __3__   d. customers trying on shoes   ___

b. customers waiting in line   ___   e. customers purchasing jewelry ___

c. hats   ___   f. display cases   ___

2. Look at the pictures. Label the items. Use the words in the box.

backpack	bracelet	pin	change purse	earrings	~~wallet~~
locket	cell phone holder	ring	shoulder bag	tote bag	watch

a. ___wallet___   b. _____   c. _____   d. _____

e. _____   f. _____   g. _____   h. _____

i. _____   j. _____   k. _____   l. _____

3. Look at the answers in Exercise 2. Put the words in the correct columns.

Jewelry Department		Other Accessories	
_____	_____	___wallet___	_____
_____	_____	_____	_____
_____	_____	_____	_____

4. Cross out the word that doesn't belong.

a. Things you wear around your neck   necklace   ~~belt~~   scarf   locket

b. Types of necklaces   beads   buckles   chain   string of pearls

c. Things you keep a change purse in   backpack   handbag   wallet   tote bag

d. Types of shoes   oxfords   boots   pumps   shoelaces

e. Parts of a shoe   sole   suspenders   heel   toe

5. Complete the ad. Use the words in the box.

~~pumps~~   flats   boots   hiking boots   loafers   oxfords   tennis shoes   high heels

SALE

The Good Sole

Save 20% on men's and women's shoes!

a. ___pumps___

b. _____

c. _____

d. _____

e. _____

f. _____

g. _____

h. _____

Located at the Lincoln Mall.
Route 65

6. What about you? Check (✓) the items you have.

☐ chain   ☐ watch   ☐ pierced earrings

☐ clip-on earrings   ☐ belt buckle   ☐ cell phone holder

Challenge List the kinds of shoes you have. When do you wear them?
Example: *boots—I wear them in cold or wet weather.*

See page 282 for listening practice.   95

1. Look at the T-shirts in your dictionary. *True* **or** *False***?**

a. They come in six sizes. _____true_____   d. They are short-sleeved. _____

b. They have a V-neck. _____   e. They are checked. _____

c. They are solid blue. _____   f. They are stained. _____

2. Look in your dictionary. Match the opposites.

_5_ **a.** big   **1.** plain

___ **b.** fancy   **2.** wide

___ **c.** heavy   **3.** long

___ **d.** loose   **4.** tight

___ **e.** narrow   **5.** small

___ **f.** high   **6.** print

___ **g.** short   **7.** low

___ **h.** solid   **8.** light

3. Look at the picture. Describe the problems.

a. His jeans are too ____baggy____ and too _____.

b. His sweater is too _____ and the sleeves are _____.

c. His jacket sleeve is _____ and a button _____.

4. Look at the order form. Circle the words to complete the statements.

ITEM #	PAGE #	DESCRIPTION	SIZE	COLOR	QUANTITY	ITEM PRICE	TOTAL
563218	3	CREWNECK SWEATER	S	RED AND BLACK STRIPED	3	$15.00	$45.00
962143	12	JACKET	M	BLACK	1	$62.00	$62.00
583614	8	3/4-SLEEVED SHIRT	L	PAISLEY	1	$18.00	$18.00
769304	15	MINI-SKIRT	S	RED	1	$50.00	$50.00
216983	10	LOOSE JEANS	8	DARK BLUE	1	$98.00	$98.00

Clothes Town — THE CATALOG STORE — toll free 1-800-000-4627 www.clothestown.us

a. The customer wants extra-small / ⟨small⟩ crewneck sweaters.

b. She's ordering a long / large paisley shirt.

c. It's a 3/4-sleeved / sleeveless shirt.

d. She also wants a plaid / medium jacket.

e. The skirt is short / long.

f. The jeans are expensive / tight.

5. What about you? Look at the ad. Choose two items to order. Add them to the order form in Exercise 4.

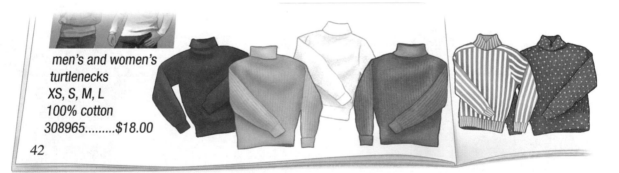

men's and women's
turtlenecks
XS, S, M, L
100% cotton
308965.........$18.00

42

6. What about you? Describe a problem you have or had with your clothes.

Example: *My jacket zipper is broken.*

_____

Challenge Describe the clothes you are wearing today. Include the color, style, and pattern.
Example: *I'm wearing tight black jeans, a red and white striped shirt, and a light jacket.*

See page 282 for listening practice.

1. Look at the garment factory in your dictionary. How many . . . are there?

a. women sewing by hand   _1_

b. women sewing by machine   ___

c. bolts of fabric   ___

d. shirts on the rack   ___

e. sewing machine needles   ___

2. Write the name of the material. Use the words in the box.

| cotton | ~~cashmere~~ | leather | linen | silk | wool |

a. ___cashmere___

b. _____

c. _____

d. _____

e. _____

f. _____

3. What about you? What materials are you wearing today? Write three sentences.

Example: _I'm wearing a cotton sweater._

_____

_____

_____

4. **Look in your dictionary. Cross out the word that doesn't belong.**

   a. Closures   zipper   snap   buckle   ~~ribbon~~

   b. Trim   thread   sequins   fringe   beads

   c. Material   cashmere   pattern   leather   nylon

   d. Sewing machine parts   bobbin   rack   needle   feed dog

5. **Look at the picture. Circle the words to complete the sentences.**

Vilma is wearing a (denim)/ wool jacket with buttons / snaps. Her jacket has beautiful
                      a.   **b.**

appliqués / sequins on it. Her husband, Enrique, is wearing a corduroy / suede jacket with
       c.   **d.**

fringe / ribbon. It's cold outside, but his jacket buckle / zipper is open. Their daughter,
   e.   **f.**

Rosa, is wearing a lace /velvet jacket with beads / thread. Her jacket is closed with
              g.   **h.**

hooks and eyes / buttons.
     i.

6. **What about you? What type of closures do your clothes have?**

   Example: *My shirt has buttons. My jeans have a zipper.*

Challenge Look at pages 86 and 87 in your dictionary. Describe two people's clothing. Include the fabric, material, closures, and trim. **Example:** *One man is wearing blue denim jeans with a zipper and button, a light blue cotton shirt with buttons, and brown leather loafers.*

See page 282 for listening practice.

1. **Look in your dictionary. Who is . . . ? Check (✓) the answers.**

	Dressmaker	Tailor
a. working in the alterations shop	✓	✓
b. working on a dress	☐	☐
c. using a sewing machine	☐	☐
d. using a dummy	☐	☐
e. using a tape measure	☐	☐
f. using thread	☐	☐

2. **Look at the pictures. Check (✓) the alterations the tailor made.**

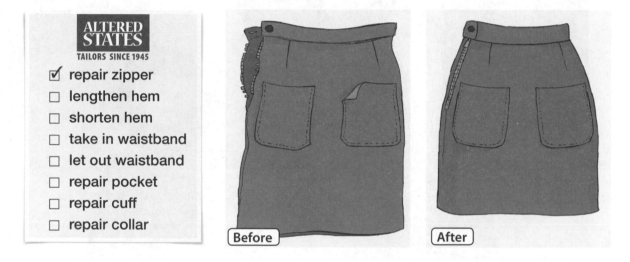

ALTERED STATES
TAILORS SINCE 1945

- ☑ repair zipper
- ☐ lengthen hem
- ☐ shorten hem
- ☐ take in waistband
- ☐ let out waistband
- ☐ repair pocket
- ☐ repair cuff
- ☐ repair collar

Before   After

3. **List the items in the sewing basket.**

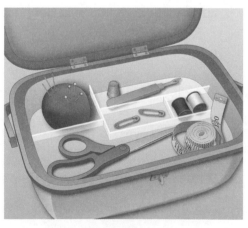

tape measure   _____

_____   _____

_____   _____

_____

Challenge Look at the boy on page 96 of this workbook. What alterations do his clothes need? Discuss them with a classmate. **Example:** *He needs to shorten his pants.*

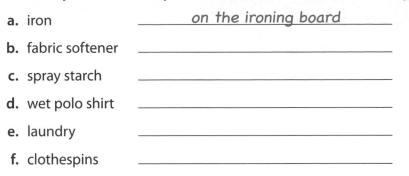

1. Look in your dictionary. Where is the . . . ? Use _in_ or _on_ in your answers.

a. iron _____on the ironing board_____

b. fabric softener _____

c. spray starch _____

d. wet polo shirt _____

e. laundry _____

f. clothespins _____

2. Look at the pictures. Write the instructions. Use the sentences in the box.

Clean the lint trap.	Fold the laundry.	Unload the washer.
~~Sort the laundry.~~	Load the washer.	Add the detergent.

a. _____Sort the laundry._____

b. _____

c. _____

d. _____

e. _____

f. _____

3. What about you? Do you do the laundry in your family? Check (✓) the items you use.

☐ iron   ☐ hanger   ☐ clothespins

☐ ironing board   ☐ spray starch   ☐ dryer sheets

☐ clothesline   ☐ fabric softener   ☐ bleach

Challenge Which clothes do you iron? Which clothes do you hang up?

Go to page 246 for Another Look (Unit 5). | **See page 283 for listening practice.**

1. Look in your dictionary. *True* or *False*?

a. You can buy new clothing at the garage sale.   *false*

b. The flyer has information about the prices.   _____

c. A woman is bargaining for an orange sweatshirt.   _____

d. The sweatshirt has a blue sticker on it.   _____

e. She buys the sweatshirt for $.75.   _____

f. Some customers are browsing.   _____

g. You can buy the folding card table and folding chair.   _____

h. The VCR is new.   _____

i. A customer buys the clock radio.   _____

2. Look at the price list and the item stickers. Complete the sentences.

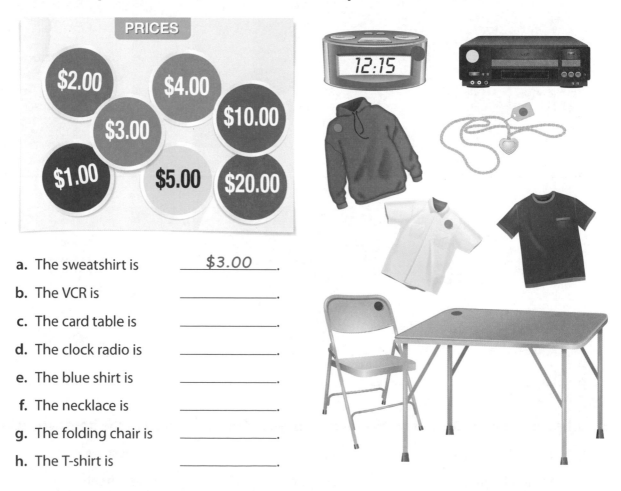

PRICES

$2.00 $4.00 $10.00 $3.00 $1.00 $5.00 $20.00

a. The sweatshirt is   *$3.00* .

b. The VCR is   _____.

c. The card table is   _____.

d. The clock radio is   _____.

e. The blue shirt is   _____.

f. The necklace is   _____.

g. The folding chair is   _____.

h. The T-shirt is   _____.

3. What about you? Look in your dictionary. Imagine you are at the garage sale. What will you buy? What price do you want to pay for it? Tell a partner.

4. Look in your dictionary. Check (✓) the items you can buy at the garage sale.

☐ belt	☐ socks	☐ necklace
✓ books	☐ sports jacket	☐ sewing machine
☐ bracelet	☐ straw hat	☐ shoes
☐ briefcase	☐ necklace	☐ sweatshirt
☐ clock radio	☐ hard hat	☐ T-shirt
☐ folding card table	☐ ironing board	☐ VCR
☐ purse	☐ jeans	☐ pin cushion

5. Complete the flyer. Use the words in the box.

bargain	browse	clock radios	folding card tables	folding chairs
~~Garage Sale~~	sweatshirts	sticker	Used Clothing	VCRs

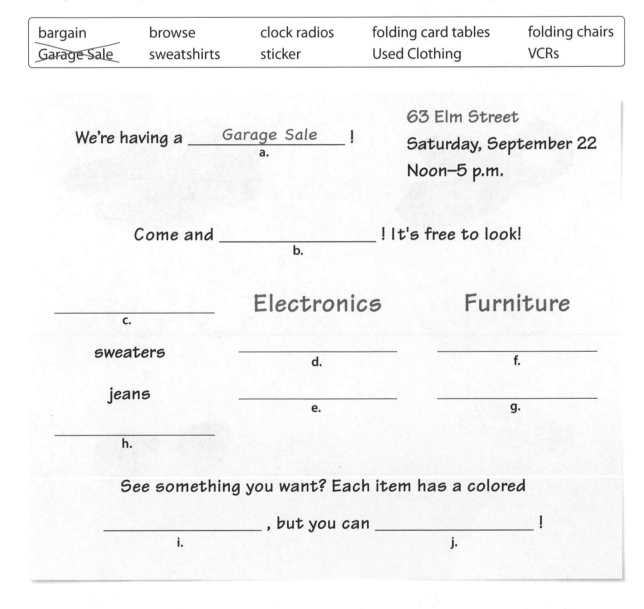

We're having a ___Garage Sale___ !
a.

63 Elm Street
Saturday, September 22
Noon–5 p.m.

Come and _____ ! It's free to look!
b.

_____   Electronics   Furniture
c.

sweaters   _____   _____
d.   f.

jeans   _____   _____
e.   g.

_____
h.

See something you want? Each item has a colored

_____ , but you can _____ !
i.   j.

Challenge   Work with a partner. Imagine you are going to have a garage sale. What items will you sell? Make a flyer. Use the flyer in Exercise 5 as an example.

1. Look in your dictionary. How many . . . do you see?

a. heads _11_   e. eyes ___

b. feet ___   f. ears ___

c. hands ___   g. shoulders ___

d. backs ___

2. Look at the pictures. Where on the body do you find them? Match.

1.

2.

3.

4.

5.

6.

7.

8.

___ a. hair   ___ e. eyes

___ b. neck   ___ f. nose

___ c. feet   _1_ g. hands

___ d. ears   ___ h. finger

3. How many . . . do people usually have? Put the words in the correct column.

One	Two	Ten
head		

4. Look at the medical chart. *True* or *False*?

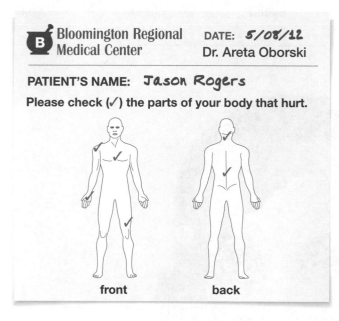

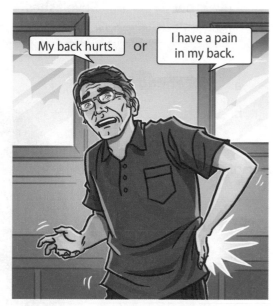

a. Jason's head hurts. _____false_____

b. His right hand hurts. _____

c. His left shoulder hurts. _____

d. He has a pain in his neck. _____

e. His leg hurts. _____

f. He has a pain in his chest. _____

g. His back hurts. _____

Challenge Which parts of the body do these doctors help? Look online or ask a classmate.

podiatrist _____ ophthalmologist _____ chiropractor _____

See page 284 for listening practice.

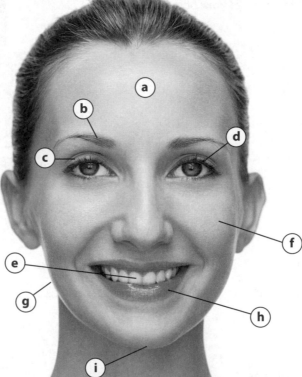

Inside and Outside the Body

1. Look in your dictionary. Cross out the word that doesn't belong.

a. The face	forehead	jaw	chin	~~toe~~
b. Inside the body	liver	intestines	abdomen	stomach
c. The leg and foot	knee	heel	ankle	tongue
d. The skeleton	pelvis	brain	skull	rib cage
e. The hand	thumb	shin	palm	wrist
f. The senses	taste	hear	lip	smell

2. Label the parts of the face. Use the words in the box.

eyebrow	eyelashes	eyelid	cheek	chin
~~forehead~~	jaw	lip	teeth	

a. _forehead_

b. _____

c. _____

d. _____

e. _____

f. _____

g. _____

h. _____

i. _____

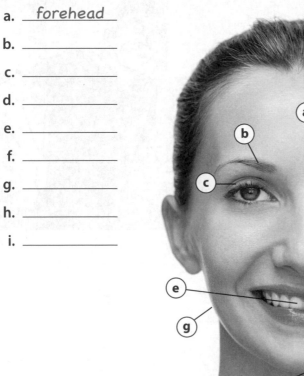

3. **Look at the picture. Check (✓) the parts of the body that are NOT covered by clothes.**

✓ arms	☐ buttocks	
☐ calves	☐ chest	
☐ elbows	☐ fingers	
☐ feet	☐ forearms	
☐ hands	☐ head	
☐ knees	☐ legs	
☐ lower back	☐ shins	
☐ shoulder blades	☐ jaw	

4. **Match.**

___4___ **a.** heart

_____ **b.** kidney

_____ **c.** lung

_____ **d.** liver

_____ **e.** gallbladder

_____ **f.** bladder

_____ **g.** throat

_____ **h.** stomach

_____ **i.** pancreas

_____ **j.** brain

_____ **k.** intestines

_____ **l.** artery

_____ **m.** vein

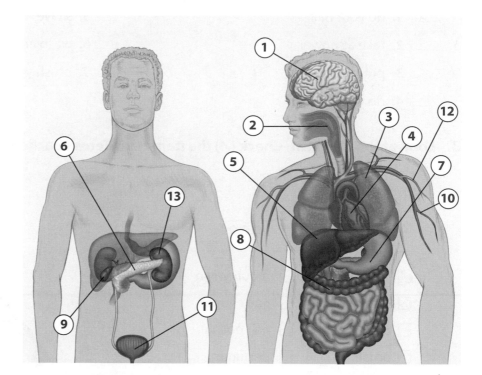

5. **What about you? <u>Underline</u> the words for parts of the body that are NOT OK for men to show on the street in your native country. Circle the words for parts of the body that are NOT OK for women to show.**

arms	abdomen	elbows	face	mouth
ankles	chest	knees	calves	feet

Challenge Choose five parts of the body. What are their functions?
Example: *brain—We use it to think.*

See page 284 for listening practice.

1. Look in your dictionary. Cross out the word that doesn't belong.

a.	shower cap	soap	~~hair spray~~	bath powder
b.	electric shaver	razorblades	aftershave	sunscreen
c.	hair clip	emery board	nail polish	nail clipper
d.	barrettes	eyebrow pencil	bobby pins	hair gel
e.	blush	foundation	eyeliner	deodorant
f.	body lotion	shampoo	blow dryer	conditioner
g.	toothbrush	comb	dental floss	toothpaste

2. Look at Exercise 1. Write the letter of the items that you need for these activities.

_d_ 1. do your hair

___ 2. take a shower

___ 3. put on makeup

___ 4. do your nails

___ 5. shave

___ 6. wash and dry your hair

___ 7. brush your teeth

3. Look at the checklist. Check (✓) the items that Teresa packed.

Travel Packing List

to pack for San Diego

- ☑ bath powder
- ☐ blow dryer
- ☐ bobby pins
- ☐ brush
- ☐ comb
- ☐ conditioner
- ☐ curling iron
- ☐ dental floss
- ☐ deodorant
- ☐ emery board
- ☐ lipstick
- ☐ mascara
- ☐ mouthwash
- ☐ nail clipper
- ☐ nail polish
- ☐ perfume
- ☐ razor
- ☐ shampoo
- ☐ shaving cream
- ☐ shower cap
- ☐ soap
- ☐ sunscreen
- ☐ toothbrush
- ☐ toothpaste

4. Teresa is at the hotel. Go back to the checklist in Exercise 3. Check (✓) the additional items that Teresa has now.

5. What does Teresa still need? Complete her shopping list.

HOTEL KENT

| TO BUY |
| bobby pins |
| |
| |
| |
| |
| |

6. What about you? How often do you use . . . ? Check (✓) the columns.

	Every Day	Sometimes	Never
sunblock			
shower gel			
perfume or cologne			
hair spray			
dental floss			
body lotion or moisturizer			
mouthwash			
Other: _____			

Challenge List the personal hygiene items you take with you when you travel.

See page 285 for listening practice.

Symptoms and Injuries

1. Look in your dictionary. *True* or *False*?

a. The man in picture 11 has an insect bite on his right arm.   <u> true </u>

b. The man in picture 13 has a cut on his thumb.   <u>   </u>

c. The man in picture 15 has a blister on his hand.   <u>   </u>

d. The woman in picture 16 has a swollen toe.   <u>   </u>

e. The woman in picture 18 has a sprained ankle.   <u>   </u>

2. Look at Tania's medicine. Complete the form. Look at <u>page 113</u> in your dictionary for help.

DATE: *3/5/12*

PATIENT'S NAME: *Tania Zobor*

Please check (✓) all your symptoms.

I OFTEN GET. . . .

☐ headaches	☐ sore throats
☐ earaches	☐ nasal congestion
☑ toothaches	☐ fevers
☐ stomachaches	☐ bruises
☐ backaches	☐ rashes
☐ bloody noses	☐ chills

I OFTEN. . . .

☐ cough	☐ feel nauseous	☐ vomit
☐ sneeze	☐ feel dizzy	

3. What about you? Complete the form. Use your own information or information about someone you know.

PATIENT'S NAME: _____   Please check (✓) all your symptoms.

I OFTEN GET. . . .			I OFTEN. . . .	
☐ headaches	☐ backaches	☐ fevers	☐ cough	☐ feel dizzy
☐ earaches	☐ bloody noses	☐ bruises	☐ sneeze	☐ vomit
☐ toothaches	☐ sore throats	☐ rashes	☐ feel nauseous	
☐ stomachaches	☐ nasal congestion	☐ chills		

Challenge Choose four health problems in Exercise 3. What can you do for them? Look at <u>page 113</u> in your dictionary for help. **Example:** *headaches—Take pain reliever.*

110   See page 285 for listening practice.

1. Look at the bottom picture in your dictionary. Write the illness or medical condition.

   a. lungs   _____*TB*_____ and _____

   b. heart and arteries   _____ and _____

   c. pancreas   _____

   d. brain   _____

   e. blood   _____

   f. joints   _____

2. Look at the photos of Mehmet when he was a child. Complete the form.

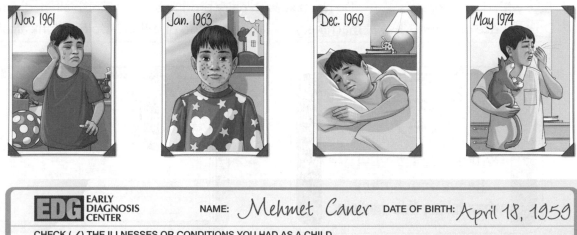

EDG EARLY DIAGNOSIS CENTER	NAME: *Mehmet Caner*	DATE OF BIRTH: *April 18, 1959*
CHECK (✓) THE ILLNESSES OR CONDITIONS YOU HAD AS A CHILD.		
☐ DIABETES	☐ CHICKEN POX	☐ MUMPS
☐ INTESTINAL PARASITES	☐ ASTHMA	☐ ALLERGIES
☑ EAR INFECTIONS	☐ STREP THROAT	

3. What about you? Complete the form. Use your own information or information about someone you know.

EDG EARLY DIAGNOSIS CENTER	NAME:	DATE OF BIRTH:
CHECK (✓) THE ILLNESSES OR CONDITIONS YOU HAD AS A CHILD.		
☐ DIABETES	☐ CHICKEN POX	☐ MUMPS
☐ INTESTINAL PARASITES	☐ ASTHMA	☐ ALLERGIES
☐ EAR INFECTIONS	☐ STREP THROAT	

Challenge List the things you do when you have a cold or flu. **Example:** *drink hot water with lemon*

1. Look in your dictionary. *True* or *False*? Correct the underlined words in the false sentences.

a. The pharmacist is giving a customer a ~~prescription~~.   *false*   prescription medication

b. The humidifier is above the heating pad.   _____

c. The hot water bottle is next to the air purifier.   _____

d. There is a pair of crutches and three wheelchairs.   _____

e. A customer is wearing a sling and a cast.   _____

2. Complete the medical warning labels. Use the sentences in the box.

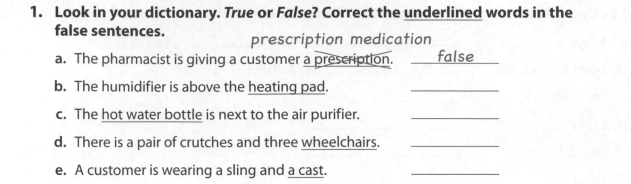

Take with dairy products.   Do not take with dairy products.   Finish all medication.

~~Do not drive or operate heavy machinery.~~   Take with food or milk.   Do not drink alcohol.

a.

Do not drive or operate heavy machinery.
when taking this medicine

b.

_____

_____

c.

_____

_____

d.

IMPORTANT

_____

_____

e.

_____

f.

_____

when taking this medicine

3. Look at the picture. Circle the words to complete the sentences.

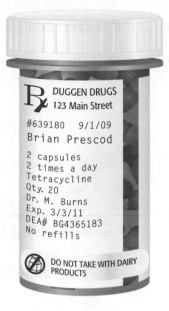

a. Brian got over-the-counter /(prescription)
medication.

b. The name of the pharmacist / pharmacy
is Duggen Drugs.

c. The bottle contains capsules / tablets.

d. The prescription number is 20 / 639180.

e. The prescription / warning label says,
"Do not take with dairy products."

f. Brian can't drink water / eat cheese
with this medicine.

g. The medicine isn't good after
September 2009 / March 2011.

h. The dosage is two / four capsules every day.

**4. What about you? Check (✓) the items you think are in your medicine cabinet.
Then, check your answers at home.**

☐ pain reliever
☐ cold tablets
☐ antacid
☐ cream
☐ cough syrup
☐ throat lozenges
☐ nasal spray
☐ ointment
☐ eye drops
☐ vitamins

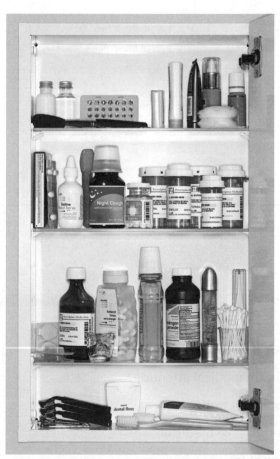

Challenge Look at some prescription or over-the-counter medication in your medicine cabinet.
What's the dosage? The expiration date? Is there a warning label? Make a list.

See page 286 for listening practice.

1. Look in your dictionary. Complete the poster.

For Good Health...

a. ___*Eat*___ a healthy diet.

b. _____ lots of fluids.

c. _____ fit.

d. _____

e. _____ immunized.

f. _____ regular checkups.

2. Look at the doctor's notes. *True* or *False*?

a. The patient sought* medical attention. ___*true*___

b. The patient should get bed rest. _____

c. She doesn't need to take medicine. _____

d. She must stop smoking. _____

e. She should drink more fluids. _____

*sought = past tense of seek

From the desk of Dr. Mary Burns

Stay in bed.

Fill prescription for antibiotics.

Drink a lot of water or juice.

<u>NO</u> more smoking!!

Call for Appointment in __2 weeks__.

3. Look in your dictionary. Complete the chart.

Problem	Doctor	Help
a. vision problems		glasses or contact lenses
b.		hearing aid
c. stress or		talk therapy or
d. knee pain		

4. Match.

_7_ **a.** I see my doctor every January.

____ **b.** I'd like some more vegetables, please.

____ **c.** I exercise every day.

____ **d.** No cigarettes for me, thanks.

____ **e.** I always get a flu vaccination.

____ **f.** I'll have another glass of water, please.

____ **g.** I need to see the doctor today.

____ **h.** It's time for my pills.

1. Eat a healthy diet.

2. Seek medical attention.

3. Get immunized.

4. Don't smoke.

5. Take medicine

6. Drink fluids.

7. Have regular checkups.

8. Stay fit.

5. What about you? Check (✓) the things you do. Explain.

Example: *stay fit—I exercise four times a week.*

☐ stay fit _____

☐ eat a healthy diet _____

☐ get immunized _____

☐ drink fluids _____

☐ have regular checkups _____

☐ follow medical advice _____

☐ Other: _____

Challenge List three other kinds of doctors. What problems do they treat?
Example: *orthopedist—for problems with bones*

See page 286 for listening practice.

Medical Emergencies

1. **Look in your dictionary. *True* or *False*?**

   a. A paramedic is helping an unconscious woman. _____true_____

   b. The woman in the red sweater is in shock. _____

   c. The man near the bookcase is hurt. _____

   d. The boy in the dark blue shirt is having an allergic reaction. _____

   e. The child in the swimming pool is getting frostbite. _____

   f. The woman at the table is choking. _____

   g. The boy in the doctor's office broke a leg. _____

   h. The man holding his chest is having a heart attack. _____

2. **Look at the chart. How did the people injure themselves? Circle the words.**

Number of Injuries in the United States in a Year		
Product	Estimated Injuries	People probably . . . .
a. Stairs	2,074,047	had an allergic reaction / (fell)
b. Bikes	535,100	overdosed / fell
c. Bathtubs / Showers	304,880	broke bones / got frostbite
d. TVs	53,471	were in shock / got an electric shock
e. Razors	36,612	bled / couldn't breathe
f. Stoves / Ovens	43,356	burned themselves / choked
g. Irons	12,818	drowned / burned themselves

Based on information from: *Consumer Product Safety Review*, 2003. www.cpsc.gov.

3. **What about you? Check (✓) the emergencies that have happened to you. When or where did they happen?**

   Emergency | When or Where

   ☐ I had an allergic reaction to _____. _____

   ☐ I fell. _____

   ☐ I broke my _____. _____

   ☐ Other: _____. _____

Challenge Write a paragraph about an emergency in Exercise 3. What treatment did you (or someone you know) get? Look at <u>page 117</u> in your dictionary for help.

See page 286 for listening practice.

1. Look in your dictionary. Write the first aid item for these conditions.

a. rash on hand <u>antihistamine cream</u>

b. broken finger _____

c. swollen foot _____ or _____

d. infected cut _____ or _____

2. Look at Chen's first aid kit. Check (✓) the items he has.

> **FAMILY FIRST AID AND EMERGENCY PREPAREDNESS**
>
> | | |
> |---|---|
> | ✓ adhesive bandages | ☐ first aid manual |
> | ☐ antihistamine cream | ☐ antibacterial ointment |
> | ☐ elastic bandage | ☐ hydrogen peroxide |
> | ☐ splint | ☐ ice pack |
> | ☐ sterile pad | ☐ sterile tape |
> | ☐ gauze | ☐ tweezers |

3. What about you? Check (✓) the first aid items you have at home. Then, check (✓) the things you can do.

At home I have		I can do . . . .
☐ adhesive bandages	☐ first aid manual	☐ CPR
☐ antihistamine cream	☐ antibacterial ointment	☐ rescue breathing
☐ elastic bandages	☐ hydrogen peroxide	☐ the Heimlich maneuver
☐ splints	☐ ice packs	
☐ sterile pads	☐ sterile tape	
☐ gauze	☐ tweezers	

Challenge Look at the items in Exercise 3. What can you use them for?
Example: *adhesive bandages—cuts*

1. Look in your dictionary. Who . . . ? Check (✓) the columns.

	Patient	Receptionist	Doctor	Nurse
a. has an appointment	✓			
b. checks blood pressure				
c. has a thermometer				
d. examines the throat				
e. has a health insurance card				
f. is on the examination table				
g. is holding a health history form				
h. has a stethoscope				

2. Look at the doctor's notes. Which medical instrument did the doctor use? Match.

⊕ **MEDICAL CENTER**

Dr. D. Ngoc Huynh

DATE: 3/5/12

PATIENT'S NAME: Carla Vega

1. checked BP—120/80
2. took temp.—98.6°
3. listened to lungs—clear
4. gave flu immunization

_4_ a. syringe

___ b. thermometer

___ c. blood pressure gauge

___ d. stethoscope

3. What about you? Think of the last time you saw the doctor. How long were you . . . ?

in the waiting room _____

in the examining room _____

on the examination table _____

Did the doctor or nurse . . . ? Check (✓) the answers.

☐ check your blood pressure   ☐ draw blood

☐ examine your eyes   ☐ take your temperature

Challenge Find out about health insurance in other countries. Which countries have national health insurance? Who can get it?

See page 287 for listening practice.

1. Circle the words to complete the sentences.

a. A dental assistant / orthodontist helps the dentist.

b. A dental hygienist uses dental instruments / fillings to clean teeth.

c. An orthodontist / A dentist gives people braces.

d. A crown / Plaque causes gum disease.

e. The dentist takes x-rays to help find cavities / dentures.

f. The dentist uses a syringe to drill a tooth / numb the mouth.

g. The dentist numbs your mouth before taking x-rays / pulling a tooth.

2. Label the pictures. Use the words in the box.

| clean teeth | ~~drill a tooth~~ | fill a cavity | numb the mouth | pull a tooth | take x-rays |

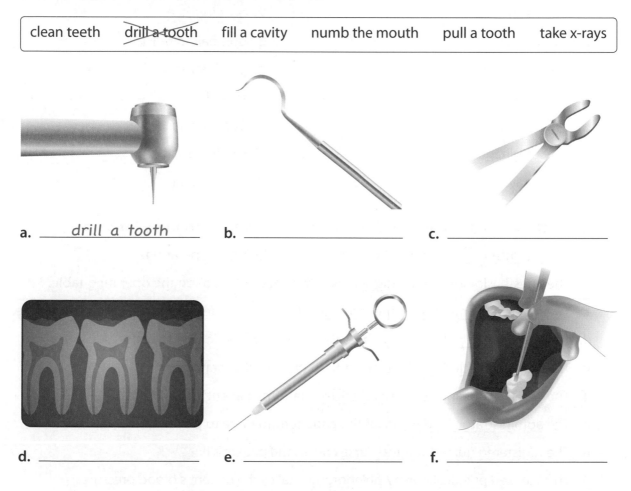

a. _drill a tooth_   **b.** _____   **c.** _____

d. _____   **e.** _____   **f.** _____

Challenge How can you try to prevent gum disease? Write three sentences.
Example: *Go to the dentist two times a year.*

1. Look in your dictionary. Match.

_5_ **a.** general health problems

___ **b.** heart

___ **c.** cancer

___ **d.** depression

___ **e.** eyes

___ **f.** children

___ **g.** pregnant women

___ **h.** x-rays

1. radiologist

2. oncologist

3. ophthalmologist

4. psychiatrist

5. internist

6. pediatrician

7. cardiologist

8. obstetrician

2. Circle the words to complete the sentences. Use your dictionary for help.

a. The internist / ⟨surgical nurse⟩ helps the surgeon during an operation.

b. The anesthesiologist / radiologist makes the patient "sleep" on the operating table.

c. The emergency medical technician / pediatrician takes the patient out of the ambulance.

d. The oncologist / phlebotomist takes the patient's blood for blood tests.

e. The admissions clerk / volunteer works in the hospital for no pay.

f. The certified nursing assistant / dietician plans the patient's food.

g. The administrator / orderly takes the patient from place to place.

h. The registered nurse / surgical nurse checks the patient's IV.

i. The licensed practical nurse / phlebotomist takes the patient's blood pressure.

3. Write the full forms. Use your dictionary for help.

a. IV ___intravenous drip___

b. EMT _____

c. CNA _____

d. LPN _____

e. RN _____

4. **Look at the hospital room in your dictionary.** *True* **or** *False***?**

   a. The patient is on a stretcher.   _false_

   b. There's a bed pan near the bed.   _____

   c. The volunteer is carrying medication.   _____

   d. The nurse is wearing a hospital gown.   _____

   e. There's medication on the bed table.   _____

   f. The vital signs monitor is near the hospital bed. _____

   g. The patient is using the call button now.   _____

5. **Look at the picture and the supply list. Match.**

Supplies

a. __3__ intravenous drip

b. ____ surgical gloves

c. ____ medical charts

d. ____ medical waste disposal

e. ____ surgical caps

f. ____ surgical gowns

Challenge Find out the names of an internist, an ophthalmologist, and a pediatrician in your community. Make a list.

Go to page 247 for Another Look (Unit 6). | See page 288 for listening practice.

1. Look in your dictionary. How many people are . . . ? Write the number.

a. doing aerobic exercise   <u>4</u>

b. doing yoga now   ____

c. getting acupuncture   ____

d. waiting to get a free eye exam   ____

e. listening to the nutrition lecture   ____

f. taking people's blood pressure   ____

g. watching the Healthy Cooking demonstration   ____

h. getting a low-cost exam   ____

2. Look in your dictionary. Match the people with the booths.

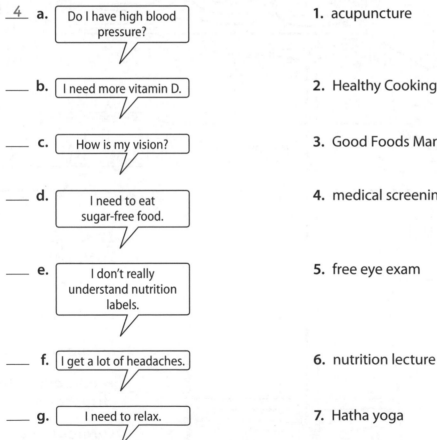

Booth

<u>4</u> a. Do I have high blood pressure?

1. acupuncture

____ b. I need more vitamin D.

2. Healthy Cooking

____ c. How is my vision?

3. Good Foods Market

____ d. I need to eat sugar-free food.

4. medical screenings

____ e. I don't really understand nutrition labels.

5. free eye exam

____ f. I get a lot of headaches.

6. nutrition lecture

____ g. I need to relax.

7. Hatha yoga

3. What about you? Look in your dictionary. Imagine you are at the health fair. Where will you go? Why? Tell a partner.

4. Look in your dictionary. *True* or *False*? Correct the underlined words in the false sentences.

                clinic

a. The health fair is at a ~~hospital~~.   _____*false*_____

b. A nurse is checking a woman's <u>temperature</u>.   _____

c. People pay $5.00 for <u>a medical screening</u>.   _____

d. Four people are doing <u>yoga</u>.   _____

e. They sell <u>sugar-free</u> food at Healthy Cooking.   _____

f. The woman in line at the eye exam booth uses a <u>walker</u>.   _____

g. The acupuncture doctor is going to put a needle in the man's <u>hand</u>.   _____

5. Complete the flyer. Use the words in the box.

Acupuncture	aerobic exercise	demonstration	Health Clinic	Free
~~Health Fair~~	lecture	Low-cost	nurse	
nutrition label	pulse	Sugar-free	yoga	

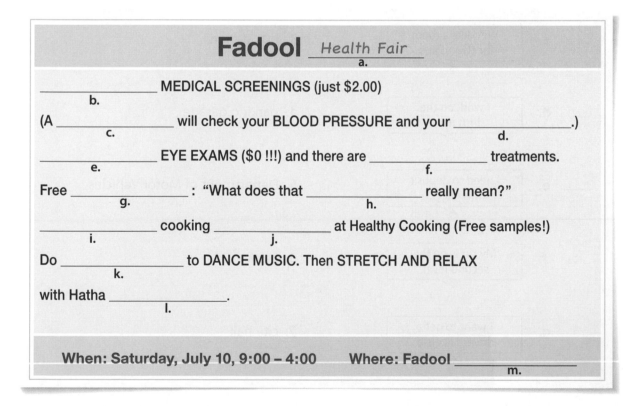

Fadool <u>*Health Fair*</u>
a.

_____ MEDICAL SCREENINGS (just $2.00)
       b.

(A _____ will check your BLOOD PRESSURE and your _____.)
       c.   d.

_____ EYE EXAMS ($0 !!!) and there are _____ treatments.
       e.   f.

Free _____ : "What does that _____ really mean?"
            g.   h.

_____ cooking _____ at Healthy Cooking (Free samples!)
     i.   j.

Do _____ to DANCE MUSIC. Then STRETCH AND RELAX
         k.

with Hatha _____.
            l.

When: Saturday, July 10, 9:00 – 4:00   **Where: Fadool _____**
                                                                            m.

Challenge   Look at three nutrition labels. How much sugar does the food have? How much salt?
           Example: *La Rosa spaghetti sauce has 6 grams of sugar and 310 milligrams of salt in a half cup serving.*

See page 288 for listening practice.

Downtown

1. Look at page 124 in your dictionary. _True_ or _False_?

a. The parking garage is next to the office building. ___true___

b. The bank is on the corner of Main and Grand. _____

c. The Department of Motor Vehicles is on 5th Street. _____

d. There's a bus station across from the hotel. _____

e. There's a clock on the city hall building. _____

2. Match.

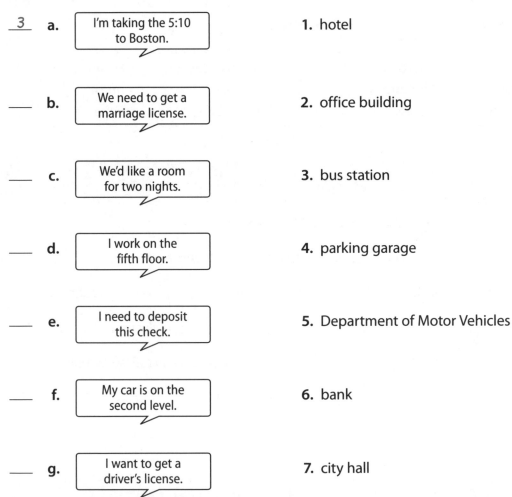

__3__ a. | I'm taking the 5:10 to Boston. |

1. hotel

____ b. | We need to get a marriage license. |

2. office building

____ c. | We'd like a room for two nights. |

3. bus station

____ d. | I work on the fifth floor. |

4. parking garage

____ e. | I need to deposit this check. |

5. Department of Motor Vehicles

____ f. | My car is on the second level. |

6. bank

____ g. | I want to get a driver's license. |

7. city hall

3. What about you? Write the street locations for these places in your community.

bus station _____Broadway and West 10th Street_____

bank _____

office building _____

city hall _____

4. **Look in your dictionary. Complete the sentences.**

a. The _____hospital_____ is on 6th Street.

b. The _____ is next to the fire station.

c. There's a Chinese _____ on Main Street.

d. The _____ is on the corner of Main and Grand Avenue.

e. The _____ is to the right of the restaurant.

f. There's a _____ across from the hospital.

5. **Look at the pictures. Where should the people go? Use the words in the box.**

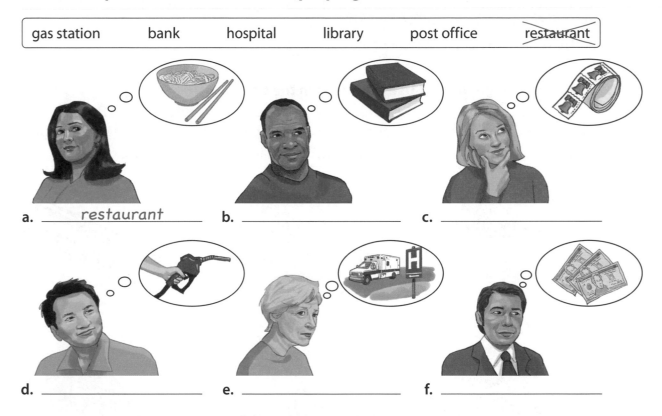

| gas station | bank | hospital | library | post office | ~~restaurant~~ |

a. _____restaurant_____   b. _____   c. _____

d. _____   e. _____   f. _____

6. **What about you? How often do you go to the . . . ? Check (✓) the columns.**

	Often	Sometimes	Never
gas station			
library			
post office			
hospital			
courthouse			

Challenge Look in your dictionary. Choose four places. Why do you go there? Write sentences.
Example: *I go to the post office to buy stamps.*

1. Look in your dictionary. Circle the words to complete the sentences.

a. There's a (furniture store)/ coffee shop on Second and Oak.

b. There's a school / factory on Third near Elm.

c. The mosque / synagogue is on Second and Oak.

d. There's a car dealership / construction site on Oak and First.

e. The garbage truck is in front of the home improvement store / office supply store.

f. The shopping mall is next to the movie theater / theater.

g. There's a bakery / cemetery near the church.

h. There are two people in front of the bakery / gym.

2. Where do you go for . . . ? Use the words in the box.

| home improvement store | car dealership | ~~coffee shop~~ | furniture store | gym |
| office supply store | movie theater | bakery | shopping mall | |

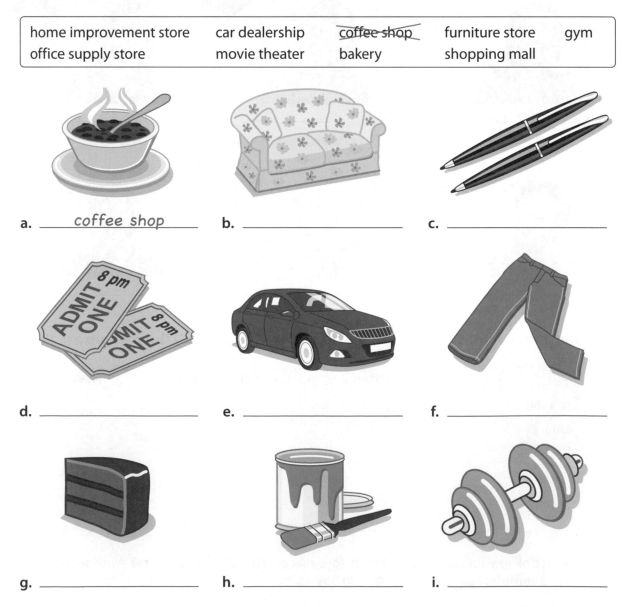

a. ___coffee shop___   b. _____   c. _____

d. _____   e. _____   f. _____

g. _____   h. _____   i. _____

126

3. Look at the map. Complete the notes.

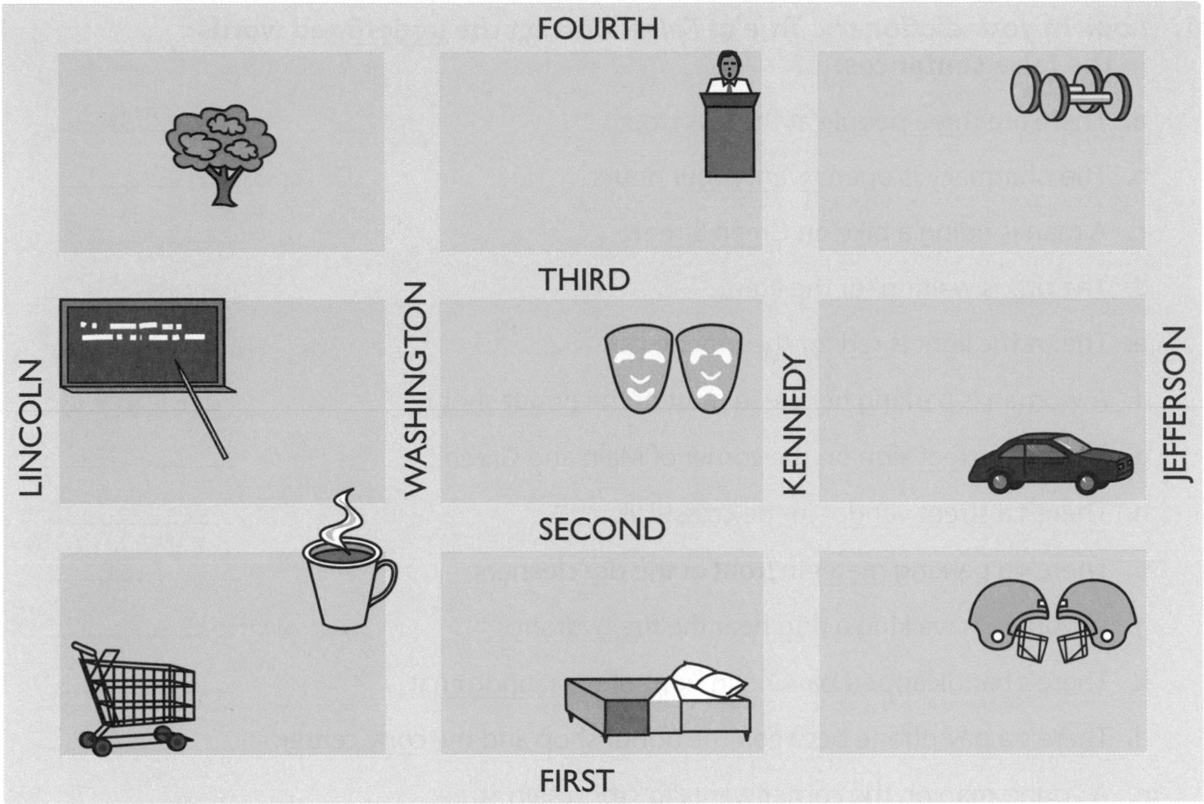

FOURTH

THIRD

SECOND

FIRST

LINCOLN

WASHINGTON

KENNEDY

JEFFERSON

LOCATIONS

a. gym _Fourth and Jefferson_

b. theater _____

c. stadium _____

d. convention center _____

e. community college _____

f. car dealership _____

g. supermarket _____

h. coffee shop _____

i. motel _____

4. What about you? Does your community have . . . ? Check (✓) the boxes.

☐ a stadium

☐ a movie theater

☐ a convention center

☐ skyscrapers

☐ factories

☐ a motel

☐ a community college

☐ a cemetery

Challenge Draw a street map of an area you know. Use some of the places in Exercises 2, 3, and 4.

See page 289 for listening practice.

1. Look in your dictionary. *True* or *False*? Correct the underlined words in the false sentences.

a. There are ~~three~~ (two) people at the bus stop.   *false*

b. The pharmacy is open <u>twenty-four</u> hours.   _____

c. A man is riding a bike on <u>Green Street</u>.   _____

d. The <u>bus</u> is waiting for the light.   _____

e. The traffic light is <u>red</u> for the orange car.   _____

f. A woman is parking her car in front of the <u>donut shop</u>.   _____

g. There's a <u>street sign</u> on the corner of Main and Green.   _____

h. There's a <u>street vendor</u> in the crosswalk.   _____

i. There's a parking <u>meter</u> in front of the dry cleaners.   _____

j. A woman is walking a dog near the <u>fire hydrant</u>.   _____

k. There's handicapped parking in front of the <u>laundromat</u>.   _____

l. There's a pay phone between the donut shop and the <u>copy center</u>.   _____

m. A young man on the corner wants to cross Main Street. He's <u>waiting for the light</u>.   _____

2. Match.

____ **a.** video store

____ **b.** pay phone

____ **c.** dry cleaners

____ **d.** copy center

____ **e.** pharmacy

____ **f.** childcare center

____ **g.** laundromat

_1_ **h.** convenience store

____ **i.** barbershop

____ **j.** fast food restaurant

____ **k.** newsstand

____ **l.** mailbox

3. Cross out the word that doesn't belong.

a. **People** pedestrian street vendor ~~corner~~

b. **Stores** donut shop mailbox pharmacy

c. **Services for clothes** street sign laundromat dry cleaners

d. **Transportation** drive-thru window bus bike

e. **Parts of the street** curb sidewalk cart

f. **Things you put coins in** pay phone parking meter fire hydrant

g. **Things that move** bus cart crosswalk

4. Write the location of these signs.

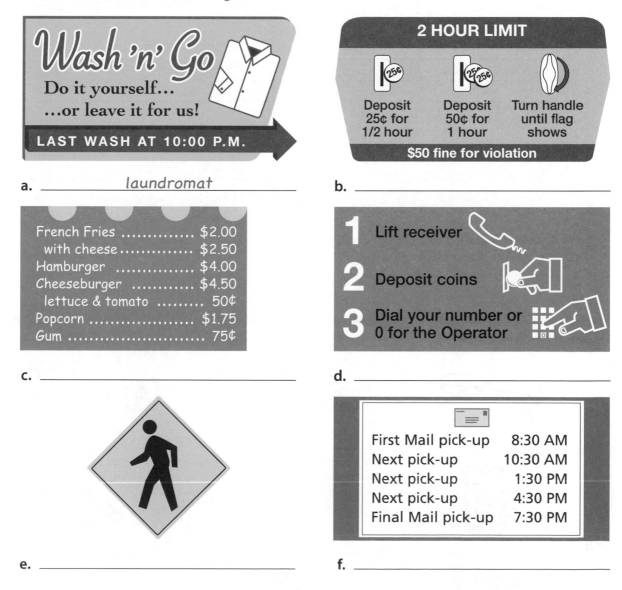

a. _____laundromat_____

b. _____

c. _____

d. _____

e. _____

f. _____

Challenge Look in your dictionary. Write the locations of five stores. **Example:** *The donut shop is on the corner of Main and Green.*

See page 289 for listening practice.

1. Look in your dictionary. Complete the mall directory. Use the words in the box.

florist	jewelry store	nail salon	food court
travel agency	maternity store	hair salon	candy store
~~cell phone kiosk~~	ice cream shop	optician	~~pet store~~
toy store	electronics store	music store	shoe store

MALL DIRECTORY

	Floor
Department Store	1, 2
Entertainment / Music	
Food	

*Services are stores that do jobs for people or help people.

Services*	Floor
cell phone kiosk	1
Shoes / Accessories	
Specialty Stores	
pet store	1

2. Look at the mall directory in Exercise 1. Where can you buy these items (other than a department store)?

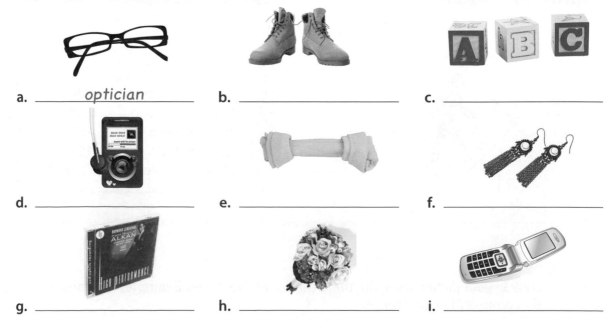

a. _____optician_____

b. _____

c. _____

d. _____

e. _____

f. _____

g. _____

h. _____

i. _____

3. **Look at this mall directory and map. Circle the words to complete the conversations.**

NEWPORT MALL
DIRECTORY—SECOND FLOOR

Books / Cards
The Book Market **6**
Cards Galore **8**

Department Store
L.R. Nickel's—See Map

Entertainment / Music
Music World **9**
Eli's Electronics **3**

Food / Restaurants
Candy Corner **2**
The Ice Cream Cart **12**
Food Court—See Map

Services
Eye Shop **13**
Hair's Where **1**
Nan's Nails **14**
Travel Smart **10**

Shoes
Walkrite **7**

Specialty Shop
The New Mom **4**
Flower Bud **5**
Toy with Us **11**

L.R. Nickel's
Food Court

(?) Guest Services
Escalator
Restrooms
Telephone
Play area

Customer 1:   Excuse me. Where's the card store?

Guest Services: It's next to the nail salon / shoe store.
                                        a.

Customer 2:   Can you tell me where the hair salon is?

Guest Services: Sure. It's across from the department store / guest services.
                                                                            b.

Customer 3:   I'm looking for the elevator / escalator.
                                            c.
Guest Services: It's next to Nickel's.

Customer 4:   Hi. Where's the travel agency, please?

Guest Services: It's right over there. Next to the toy / music store.
                                                                    d.

Customer 5:   Excuse me. I'm looking for the candy store.

Guest Services: It's between the music / electronics store and the
                                                        e.

                            hair salon / maternity store.
                                        f.

Customer 6:   Excuse me. Is there an optician in this mall?

Guest Services: Yes. There's one across from the florist / bookstore.
                                                                    g.

Challenge Look at the map in Exercise 3. Write the locations of Flower Bud, The Ice Cream Cart,
and Guest Services.

See page 289 for listening practice.

The Bank

1. Look in your dictionary. Circle the words to complete the sentences.

a. The security guard /(teller)is speaking to a customer.

b. The customer is making a deposit / withdrawing cash.

c. The ATM / vault is near the security guard.

d. The account manager / customer is holding a form.

e. The two customers on the left are cashing a check / opening an account.

2. Look at the ATM receipt. *True* or *False*?

a. This is a bank statement.   *false*

b. The customer banked online.   _____

c. Her ATM card ends in 6434.   _____

d. She withdrew cash.   _____

e. She withdrew $100 from her checking account.   _____

f. Her savings account number is 056588734.   _____

g. Her balance is $623.40.   _____

```
----------------------------------------
            FIRST BANK
          54 CHURCH STREET
          LIBERTYVILLE, IL
----------------------------------------

DATE: 05/06/09          TIME: 11:51
ATM: 045-3
CARD NUMBER:    ************6434

TRANSACTION:           WITHDRAWAL
SERIAL NUM.:                  345
AMOUNT:                      $100
FROM SAVINGS:           056588734
BALANCE:                   $6,234
```

3. How do you use an ATM? Number these steps in order. (1 = the first thing you do)

___ a. enter your PIN

___ b. withdraw cash

___ c. remove your card

_1_ d. insert your ATM card

4. What about you? Check (✓) the things you did last month.

☐ bank online   ☐ withdraw cash

☐ cash a check   ☐ make a deposit

☐ use an ATM   ☐ open an account

☐ use a passbook   ☐ read a bank statement

Challenge Which documents and valuables do people keep in a safety deposit box? Make a list.

1. Look in your dictionary. Where can you find . . . ?

a. titles and locations of library books _____online catalog_____

b. magazines and newspapers _____

c. maps _____

d. DVDs, videocassettes, and audiobooks _____

e. the library clerk _____

2. Circle the words to complete the sentences.

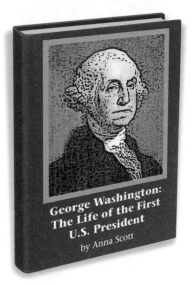

JEFFERSON PUBLIC LIBRARY
CENTRAL BRANCH

CHECK OUT DATE: APRIL 15
DUE DATE: MAY 06
----
1 GEORGE WASHINGTON:
THE LIFE OF THE FIRST
U.S. PRESIDENT

LATE FINE: $.10 A DAY

TOTAL ITEMS: 1

a. The (author)/ reference librarian is Anna Scott.

b. The headline / title of the book is *George Washington: The Life of the First U.S. President*.

c. This book is a biography / novel.

d. You need a library card to check out / return the book.

e. You return the book on May 16. The book is / is not late.

f. The book is ten days late. The late fine is $.10 / $1.00.

3. What about you? Check (✓) the items you would like to borrow from a library.

☐ novels   ☐ videocassettes

☐ DVDs   ☐ picture books

☐ audiobooks   ☐ Other: _____

Challenge Find out about your school library or a public library in your community. For how long can you borrow the items in Exercise 3? Ask at the library or check online.

See page 290 for listening practice.

1. Look in your dictionary. Match.

<u>6</u> **a.** Certified Mail™

1. for delivery tomorrow

____ **b.** airmail

2. for packages

____ **c.** Express Mail®

3. for CDs

____ **d.** ground post

4. for two- to three-day delivery

____ **e.** Media Mail®

5. for mail to other countries

____ **f.** Priority Mail®

6. for very important mail

2. Circle the words to complete the sentences.

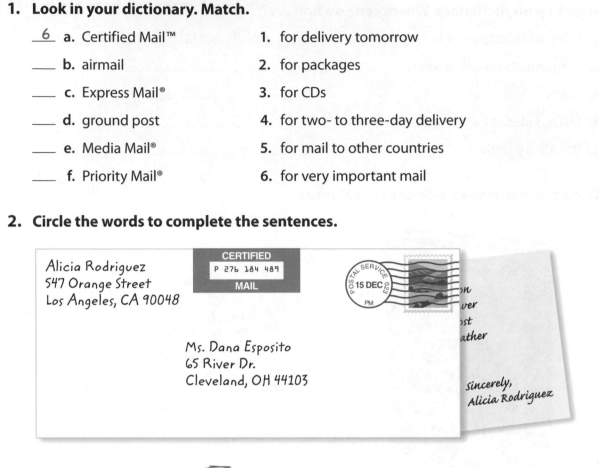

a. This is a <u>greeting card</u> /(letter.)

b. The <u>envelope / letter</u> is white.

c. The <u>mailing / return</u> address is 65 River Dr., Cleveland, OH 44103.

d. The <u>postal form / postmark</u> is December 15.

e. Alicia sent this <u>Priority Mail® / Certified Mail™</u>.

3. What about you? Address this envelope to your teacher. Use your school's address. Don't forget your return address.

4. Look in your dictionary. *True* or *False*?

a. A postal clerk is using a scale. ___true___

b. Letter carriers deliver packages and letters. _____

c. You can mail a letter in a PO box. _____

d. A postal clerk is using the automated postal center. _____

e. A United States mailbox is yellow. _____

f. Sonya wrote her return address on the envelope. _____

g. Cindy received a post card from Sonya. _____

5. Put the sentences in order. Use your dictionary for help. (1 = the first thing you do)

___ a. Write a note in the card.

___ b. Put on a stamp.

___ c. Go to the stamp machine.

___ d. Find the mailbox.

_1_ e. Buy a greeting card.

___ f. Buy a book of stamps.

___ g. Mail the card.

___ h. Go to the post office.

___ i. Address the envelope.

6. What about you? Check (✓) the things you did last month.

☐ go to the post office   ☐ buy stamps

☐ receive a card   ☐ speak to a postal clerk

☐ address an envelope   ☐ read a letter from a friend

☐ mail a post card   ☐ write back to a friend

☐ speak to the letter carrier   ☐ receive a package

☐ complete a postal form   ☐ use an APC

Challenge Find out how much it costs to send a Priority Mail ® letter.

See page 291 for listening practice.

1. **Look at page 136 in your dictionary. How many . . . do you see?**

   a. people in the testing area   _3_

   b. DMV clerks   ____

   c. DMV handbooks   ____

   d. open windows   ____

   e. closed windows   ____

   f. people taking a vision exam   ____

2. **Circle the words to complete the sentences.**

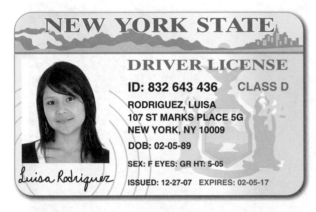

   a. This is a ⟨driver's license⟩ / license plate.

   b. The driver's license number is
      020589 / 832643436.

   c. There's a fingerprint / photo
      of Luisa Rodriguez.

   d. The expiration date is 12-27-07 / 02-05-17.

   e. This is a driver's license / license plate.

   f. It has two driver's license numbers /
      registration tags.

   g. The expiration date / license number
      is August 2010.

3. **What about you? Check (✓) the things you have.**

   ☐ driver's license

   ☐ license plate

   ☐ registration tags

   ☐ proof of insurance

4. Look at page 137 in your dictionary. *True* or *False*?

a. Miguel wants to get a driver's license.   _____true_____

b. He needs a learner's permit to take a driver's training course.   _____

c. He takes two tests.   _____

d. He takes three courses.   _____

e. He shows two forms of identification.   _____

f. He pays the application fee with cash.   _____

g. He passes the written test.   _____

h. He studies the DMV handbook.   _____

i. He passes the driving test.   _____

5. Which happens first? Bubble in the first event.

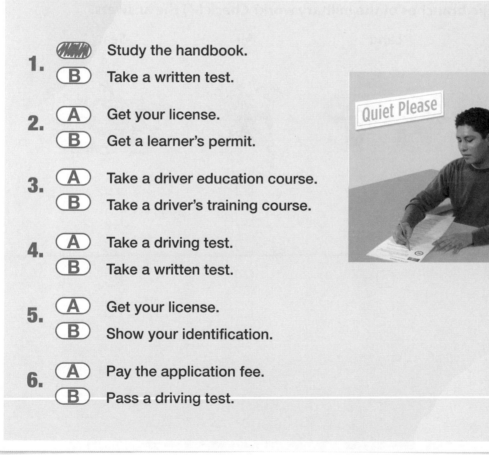

1. (A) Study the handbook.
   (B) Take a written test.

2. (A) Get your license.
   (B) Get a learner's permit.

3. (A) Take a driver education course.
   (B) Take a driver's training course.

4. (A) Take a driving test.
   (B) Take a written test.

5. (A) Get your license.
   (B) Show your identification.

6. (A) Pay the application fee.
   (B) Pass a driving test.

Challenge Answer these questions about your community.

a. Where is the DMV?   _____

b. How much is the application fee?   _____

See page 291 for listening practice.

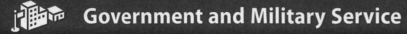
1. Look in your dictionary. Put the words in the correct column. Use the words in the box.

Supreme Court	congressperson	vice president	White House
chief justice	Senate	senator	~~president~~
justices	cabinet	House of Representatives	

Executive Branch	Legislative Branch	Judicial Branch
president	_____	_____
_____	_____	_____
_____	_____	_____
_____	_____	

2. Where do the branches of the military work? Check (✓) the answers.

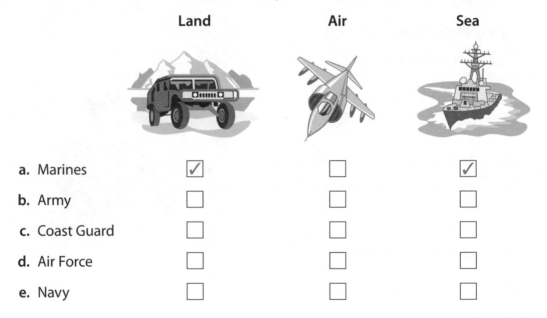

	Land	Air	Sea
a. Marines	✓	☐	✓
b. Army	☐	☐	☐
c. Coast Guard	☐	☐	☐
d. Air Force	☐	☐	☐
e. Navy	☐	☐	☐

3. Look in your dictionary. *True* or *False*? Correct the underlined words in the false sentences.

                city

a. Dan Chen wants a job in ~~state~~ government.   *false*

b. He wants to be a <u>state senator</u>.   _____

c. Chen <u>runs for office</u>.   _____

d. Chen debates <u>his opponent</u>.   _____

e. Chen is happy with the <u>election results</u>.   _____

f. Chen <u>gets elected</u>.   _____

g. He now works in the <u>state capital</u>.   _____

h. Chen is <u>an elected official</u>.   _____

4. Cross out the word that doesn't belong.

a. Branches of government	~~Congress~~	Executive	Judicial	Legislative
b. Branches of the military	Army	Air Force	Legislature	Navy
c. People	councilperson	justice	president	Senate
d. Buildings	Cabinet	Supreme Court	U.S. Capitol	White House
e. State officials	assemblyperson	governor	president	state senator

5. What about you? Answer the quiz questions.

Quiz: U.S. Government

Name: _____

1. Who is the President of the United States?

_____

2. Who is the Vice President?

_____

3. What is your state capital?

_____

4. Who is the governor of your state?

_____

5. How many state senators does your state have?

_____

6. Who is the mayor of your city?

_____

Challenge   How long can the . . . serve? Use an encyclopedia or the Internet to find the answers.

President of the United States   _____

Chief Justice of the Supreme Court   _____

governor of your state   _____

See page 291 for listening practice.

1. Look in your dictionary. Check (✓) the civic responsibilities.

- ✓ pay taxes
- ☐ serve on a jury
- ☐ vote
- ☐ free speech
- ☐ obey the law
- ☐ peaceful assembly

2. Label the pictures. Use the words in the box.

> fair trial   free speech   freedom of the press   freedom of religion   ~~peaceful assembly~~

a. _peaceful assembly_

b. _____

c. _____

d. _____

e. _____

3. Look at the forms. Who . . . ?

Name: Hassan Al Bahraini	**Date of Birth:** 8/13/97
Address: 25 Colony St.	**Lived there** 8 years
Houston, Texas 77036	**Gender: M** ☑ **F** ☐

Name: Yoko Tanaka	**Date of Birth:** 2/9/71
Address: 209 Gorham St.	**Lived there** 4 years
Los Angeles, CA 90049	**Gender: M** ☐ **F** ☑

Name: Ana Suarez	**Date of Birth:** 5/6/82
Address: 38 Opechee Dr.	**Lived there** 10 years
Miami, Florida 33133	**Gender: M** ☐ **F** ☑

Name: Chen Lu	**Date of Birth:** 11/11/88
Address: 47 Bleecker St.	**Lived there** 3 years
New York, N.Y. 10005	**Gender: M** ☑ **F** ☐

a. lived in the U.S. for five or more years   _Hassan_ and _Ana_

b. is 18 years or older   _____, _____, and _____

c. can take a U.S. citizenship test   _____

d. must register with the Selective Service   _____

Challenge List the ways people can be informed. **Example:** *read the paper*

1. **Look in your dictionary. Circle the words to complete the sentences.**

   a. The guard / (police officer) arrested the suspect.

   b. The suspect / witness wears handcuffs.

   c. The defense attorney / prosecuting attorney is a man.

   d. The court reporter / judge says, "Guilty."

   e. There are ten / twelve people on the jury.

   f. The judge is in the courtroom / prison.

   g. The convict / bailiff is in prison.

2. **Complete the sentences with the words in the box. Then, number the events in order. (1 = the first event)**

court	defendant	~~jail~~	lawyer	released	suspect	trial	verdict

   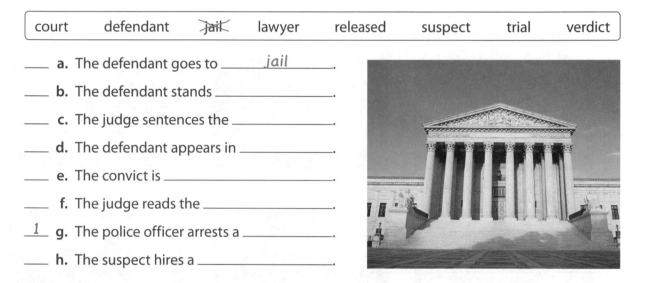

   ____ **a.** The defendant goes to _____ *jail* _____.

   ____ **b.** The defendant stands _____.

   ____ **c.** The judge sentences the _____.

   ____ **d.** The defendant appears in _____.

   ____ **e.** The convict is _____.

   ____ **f.** The judge reads the _____.

   _1_ **g.** The police officer arrests a _____.

   ____ **h.** The suspect hires a _____.

3. **Label the pictures. Use the words in the box.**

bail	evidence	handcuffs

   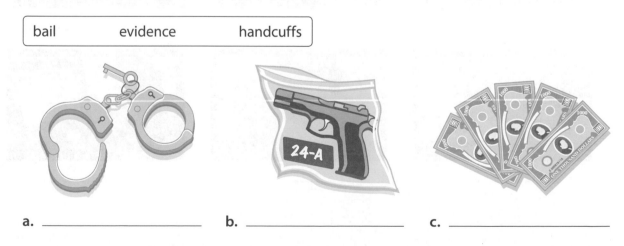

   a. _____   **b.** _____   **c.** _____

Challenge Look in your dictionary. Tell the story. Begin: *The police officer arrested the suspect....*

1. Look in your dictionary. Read the TV movie descriptions. Circle the crime words.

	8:00 P.M.	**TELEVISION GUIDE** ◀▶ ▼▲
2	**UNDER THE INFLUENCE** ('05) (Drunk driving) destroys two families.	
4	**THE BREAK-IN** ('02) A burglary changes life in a small, quiet town.	
5	**CRIMES AGAINST PROPERTY** ('09) Teenage boys commit vandalism.	
7	**THE VICTIM** ('00) A man fights back after a mugging.	
9	**THE FIVE-FINGER DISCOUNT** ('07) A young woman can't stop shoplifting.	
11	**IT'S MY LIFE!** ('09) Identity theft causes big problems.	
13	**KEEP THE CHANGE** ('05) An assault changes a man's life.	
28	**EAST SIDE SAGA** ('09) A story of gang violence.	
41	**WITH HIS GUN** ('99) A doctor tries to hide her husband's murder.	

2. Match the TV movies with the descriptions in Exercise 1. Write the channel numbers.

a. _____28_____   b. _____   c. _____

d. _____   e. _____   f. _____

g. _____   h. _____   i. _____

Challenge Look at the movies in Exercise 1. Which do you want to see? Which don't you want to see? Why?

  See page 292 for listening practice.

1. **Look in your dictionary. Put the public safety tips in the correct columns.**

At Home

Lock your doors.

_____

_____

_____

_____

On the Street

_____

_____

_____

_____

At the Airport

_____

At the Bank

BANK

_____

2. **Give these people advice. Use the information from Exercise 1.**

a. _Be aware of your_
   surroundings.

b. _____

_____

c. _____

_____

d. _____

_____

e. _____

_____

f. _____

_____

Challenge Make a list of things you do to be safe in public.

See page 293 for listening practice.

Emergencies and Natural Disasters

1. Look in your dictionary. Circle the emergency or disaster.

a. It covered almost half the house! — earthquake / <u>mudslide</u>

b. It's going to hit the farm! — tornado / volcanic eruption

c. We need rain. — drought / famine

d. Don't move. We're coming to get you! — flood / forest fire

e. The light was red! You didn't stop. — airplane crash / car accident

f. There's almost a foot of snow! — blizzard / explosion

2. Match.

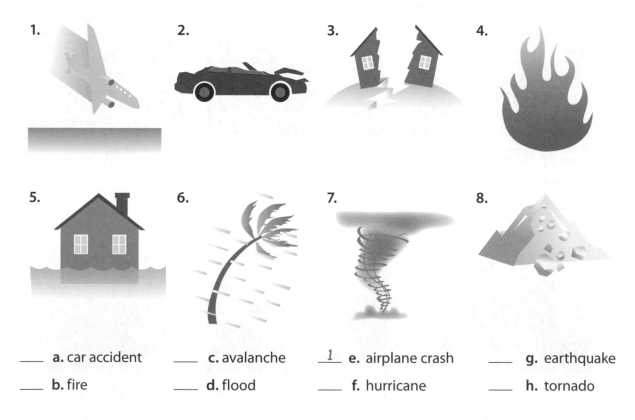

_____ **a.** car accident   _____ **c.** avalanche   _1_ **e.** airplane crash   _____ **g.** earthquake

_____ **b.** fire   _____ **d.** flood   _____ **f.** hurricane   _____ **h.** tornado

3. Match.

a. _____3_____

b. _____

c. _____

d. _____

e. _____

f. _____

1. **EXTRA**
EXPLOSION ROCKS CITY CENTER

2. **Strongville Chronicle**
SEARCH AND RESCUE TEAM SAVES FLOOD VICTIMS

3. **SUNDAY EDITION**
TIDAL WAVE HITS JAPAN

4. **Boston Global**
Lost Child Home Safe

5. **Town Spirit**
Firefighters Fight Forest Fires

6. **EARTH MAGAZINE**
VOLCANIC ERUPTION AT MT. ST. HELENS

4. What about you? Check (✓) the natural disasters your state has experienced. Complete the chart.

Disaster	Which city?	When?
earthquake		
blizzard		
hurricane		
tornado		
flood		
Other: _____		

Challenge Find information about a natural disaster. Look online or in an almanac, encyclopedia, or newspaper. What kind of disaster was it? Where and when was it?

See page 293 for listening practice.

1. Look in your dictionary. Match.

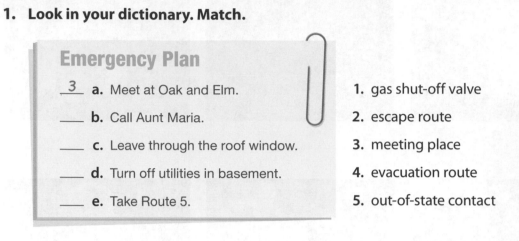

Emergency Plan

_3_ **a.** Meet at Oak and Elm.

___ **b.** Call Aunt Maria.

___ **c.** Leave through the roof window.

___ **d.** Turn off utilities in basement.

___ **e.** Take Route 5.

1. gas shut-off valve
2. escape route
3. meeting place
4. evacuation route
5. out-of-state contact

2. Carlos is starting a disaster kit. Check (✓) the items he has.

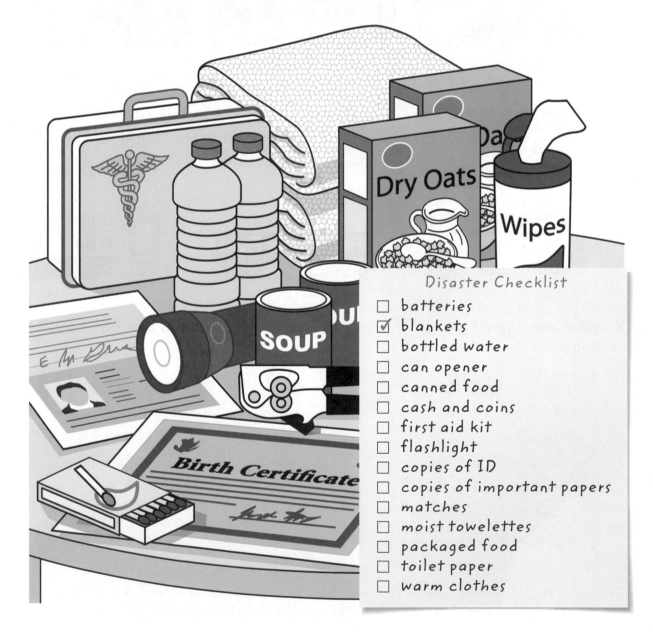

Disaster Checklist

- ☐ batteries
- ☑ blankets
- ☐ bottled water
- ☐ can opener
- ☐ canned food
- ☐ cash and coins
- ☐ first aid kit
- ☐ flashlight
- ☐ copies of ID
- ☐ copies of important papers
- ☐ matches
- ☐ moist towelettes
- ☐ packaged food
- ☐ toilet paper
- ☐ warm clothes

3. Look in your dictionary. Circle the answers.

a. Stay under the table.

Seek shelter. / (Take cover.)

b. Aunt Maria? It's me—Rosa!

Call out-of-state contacts. / Help people with disabilities.

c. The radio says we need to go to a shelter.

Clean up debris. / Follow directions.

d. How does it look outside? Did it start raining yet?

Evacuate the area. / Watch the weather.

e. There are a lot of cars on the road.

Evacuate the area. / Stay away from windows.

f. Don't worry. We're almost at the shelter.

Help people with disabilities. / Remain calm.

g. The radio says there's a hurricane watch.

Pay attention to warnings. / Seek shelter.

4. What about you? Are you ready? Check (✓) the things you have for an emergency.

☐ can opener   ☐ first aid kit   ☐ flashlight

☐ copies of important papers   ☐ batteries   ☐ Other: _____

Challenge Make a list of other items for a disaster kit. **Example:** *medicine*

Go To Page 248 For Another Look (Unit 7). | **See Page 293 For Listening Practice.**

1. **Look in your dictionary. *True* or *False*?**

   a. Marta's street has problems.   _____true_____

   b. There's graffiti on the stores.   _____

   c. There's litter in front of the pharmacy.   _____

   d. The hardware store is between the donut shop and the florist.   _____

   e. The man in the hardware store is upset.   _____

2. **Look at the pictures. Check (✓) the changes. Then, write sentences about each item on the list.**

OAK STREET ASSOCIATION	✓ repair street sign	☐ clean up graffiti
	☐ repair curb	☐ repair streetlight
	☐ repair sidewalk	☐ repair windows
	☐ clean up litter	☐ paint stores

   a. *They repaired the street sign.*   e. _____

   b. *They didn't* _____   f. _____

   c. _____   g. _____

   d. _____   h. _____

3. **Look in your dictionary. Who . . . ? Check (✓) the columns.**

	Marta Lopez	City Council	Volunteers	Citizens of City Center	Hardware store manager
a. is upset	✓				✓
b. gives a speech					
c. signs the petition					
d. applauds Marta					
e. votes *yes*					
f. cleans up the street					
g. donates donuts					
h. donates paint					
i. changes Main Street					

4. **Complete the letter to the City Center City Council. Use the words in the box.**

street	change	~~hardware store~~	graffiti	litter	volunteers

5/6/08

Dear Councilperson:

I live in City Center, and I am the owner of Hammers & More ___hardware store___.
a.
I am very upset about the problems on my _____. There is _____
b.   c.
on the buildings and _____ in the street. The streetlight in front of my store
d.
is broken, too. We have many _____ ready to help clean up the street, but
e.
we need your help. Please repair the streetlights. Together we can _____
f.
Main Street.

Sincerely yours,

Tom Lee

Tom Lee

5. **What about you? Imagine you live in City Center. How can you volunteer to help Main Street?**

Challenge Imagine you own the florist on Main Street. Write a letter to the City Center City Council about the problems on your street.

Basic Transportation

1. **Look in your dictionary. How many . . . do you see?**

   a. cars   _2_

   b. bicycles   ___

   c. trucks   ___

   d. airplanes   ___

   e. helicopters   ___

   f. motorcycles   ___

   g. people at the bus stop   ___

   h. passengers leaving the subway station   ___

2. **Look at the graph. Complete the sentences.**

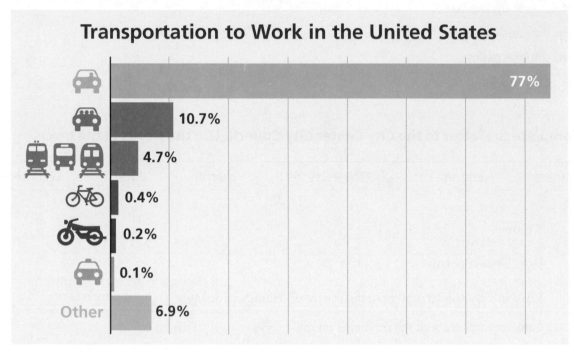

Transportation to Work in the United States

- 77%
- 10.7%
- 4.7%
- 0.4%
- 0.2%
- 0.1%
- Other 6.9%

Based on information from: *2005 American Community Survey*, U.S. Census Bureau.

   a. Almost 80% of Americans get to work alone in a _____ *car* _____.

   b. Almost 11% go to work in a _____ with other people.

   c. Only 0.1% take a _____.

   d. Only 0.2% ride a _____ to work.

   e. Only 0.4% ride a _____ to work.

   f. Almost 5% take a _____, _____, or _____ to work.

3. **What about you? How do you get to . . . ?**

   a. school   _____

   b. work   _____

   c. the supermarket   _____

   d. Other: _____   _____

4. Look in your dictionary. *True* or *False*?

a. A passenger is getting into a taxi. _____true_____

b. There is a bus at the bus stop. _____

c. Two people are entering the subway station. _____

d. There's a train near the airport. _____

e. There's a helicopter over the bus. _____

f. There are bicycles on the street. _____

g. The motorcycle is with the bicycles. _____

h. The bus stop is in front of Mario's Italian Deli. _____

5. Look at the pictures. Match.

1.
Hummingbird Air
FLIGHT **128** GATE B27
Date 6-28-08 SEAT 10C
Origin   Atlanta
Destination   NYC
Boarding Pass

Hummingbird Air
Boarding Pass
Date 6-28-08
FLIGHT 128
SEAT 10C
Origin: Atlanta
Destination: NYC

2.
MTA
MetroCard
◄◄◄ Insert the way/This side facing you

3.
GJ16098203A
J10 FEDERAL RESERVE NOTE
THE UNITED STATES OF AMERICA
We the People
GJ16098203A
TEN DOLLARS

4.
CALIFORNIA
DRIVER LICENSE
M06188
MARTIN PEREZ

5.
1
NOVAK/ANNA
RALEIGH, NC   NEWTON, NC
2V   276   17 OCT 10
NEWTON, NC   RALEIGH, NC
2V   276   22 OCT 10
$18   M XXXX939979   COACH CL

____ a. car   _1_ b. plane   ____ c. taxi   ____ d. train   ____ e. subway

6. What about you? How often do you take or ride a . . . ? Check (✓) the columns.

	Often	Sometimes	Never
car			
taxi			
motorcycle			
truck			
train			
plane			
subway			
bus			
bicycle			
Other: _____			

Challenge Take a survey. How do your classmates come to school? **Example:** *Five students take the bus, two students . . . .*

1. Look in your dictionary. Circle the words to complete the sentences.

a. There are three <u>conductors</u> /(<u>riders</u>)on the bus.

b. The girl on the bus has the <u>fare / transfer</u> in her hand.

c. The man at the subway vending machine is buying a <u>fare card / token</u>.

d. The woman <u>at the subway turnstile / in the subway car</u> is paying the fare.

e. The ticket to Boston is for a <u>one-way trip / round trip</u>.

f. The woman on the <u>platform / track</u> in the train station has a ticket.

g. The airport <u>shuttle / town car</u> is bright blue.

h. The taxi license has a photo of the <u>taxi driver / meter</u>.

2. Cross out the word that doesn't belong.

a. **Types of transportation**	bus	shuttle	subway	~~track~~
b. **People**	rider	driver	transfer	conductor
c. **Forms of payment**	fare	track	token	fare card
d. **Places to wait for transportation**	subway car	platform	bus stop	taxi stand
e. **Things with words**	schedule	turnstile	transfer	fare card
f. **Things with numbers**	taxi license	ticket	meter	rider

3. Look at the ticket. *True* or *False*?

a. This is a train ticket. _____true_____

b. It shows the fare. _____

c. It's for a one-way trip. _____

d. It shows the track number. _____

```
YORK RAIL

CLASS          TICKET TYPE        ADULT    CHILD
COACH          ROUND TRIP         ONE      NONE
START DATE     NAME OF PASSENGER  PRICE
02 NOV 10      FOX/STEVE MR.      $16.88
FROM           VALID UNTIL        BAGGAGE
19TH AVE       10 NOV10
TO             DATE OF PURCHASE
SHEPPARD/YOUNG  10 AUG10

ROUND TRIP/SPECIAL FARE
PASSENGER RECEIPT 13303  1226058975
```

4. What about you? Check (✓) the items you have or use.

☐ bus transfer   ☐ train ticket   ☐ taxi license

☐ token   ☐ train schedule   ☐ Other: _____

☐ fare card   ☐ bus schedule

Challenge What public transportation can you take to the nearest airport? How much does it cost?

1. Look in your dictionary. _True_ or _False_?

a. A man is going under the bridge.   _false_

b. There are two people walking down the steps.   _____

c. A woman is getting into a taxi.   _____

d. A man is getting out of a taxi.   _____

e. A red car is getting on the highway.   _____

f. A yellow car is getting off the highway.   _____

g. A taxi is driving through the tunnel.   _____

2. Look at the map. Circle the words to complete the directions.

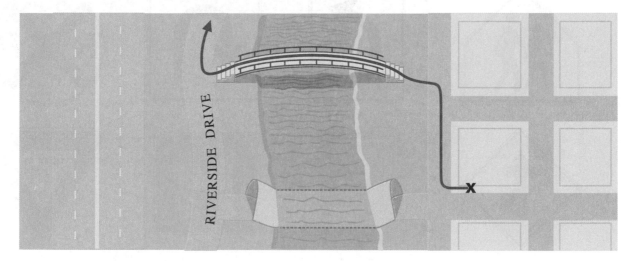

RIVERSIDE DRIVE

Man: Excuse me. How do I get to Riverside Drive?

Woman: Riverside Drive? Go around the ⟨corner⟩ / tunnel. Then go <u>down / up</u> the steps and
                                                       a.   **b.**

            <u>over / under</u> the <u>bridge / highway</u>. Go <u>down / up</u> the steps and you'll be right on
              c.   **d.**   **e.**
            Riverside Drive.

Man: Oh, so I have to go <u>across / around</u> the bridge?
                                                 f.

Woman: That's right.

3. Read the conversation in Exercise 2 again. Circle the answer.

The man is <u>driving / on a bus / walking</u>.

Challenge Write directions from your home to school.

See page 295 for listening practice.

1. Look at the intersection on <u>pages 128 and 129</u> in your dictionary. *True* or *False*?

a. There's a stop sign at the intersection.   *false*

b. There's a no parking sign near the fire hydrant.   _____

c. There's a pedestrian crossing sign at Main and Green Streets.   _____

d. The bus is on a one-way street.   _____

e. There's handicapped parking in front of Al's Mini Mart.   _____

f. There are no speed limit signs.   _____

2. Look at the traffic signs. Match.

____ **a.** yield

____ **b.** road work

____ **c.** U-turn OK

____ **d.** hospital

____ **e.** do not enter

____ **f.** pedestrian crossing

____ **g.** railroad crossing

____ **h.** no left turn

_1_ **i.** school crossing

____ **j.** right turn only

____ **k.** merge

____ **l.** handicapped parking

Challenge Draw three more traffic signs. Work with a partner. What do they mean?

1. **Look at <u>pages 128 and 129</u> in your dictionary. Circle the words to complete the sentences.**

    a. The bicycle is going <u>east</u> / <u>(west)</u> on Green Street.

    b. It just went past <u>Mel's / Print Quick</u>.

    c. The orange car is going <u>north / south</u>.

    d. To get to the bus stop, the bus must turn <u>right / left</u> at the intersection.

    e. Dan's Drugstore is on the <u>northwest / northeast</u> corner.

2. **Look at the map. Use your pen or pencil to follow the directions to a shoe store. Put an X on the shoe store.**

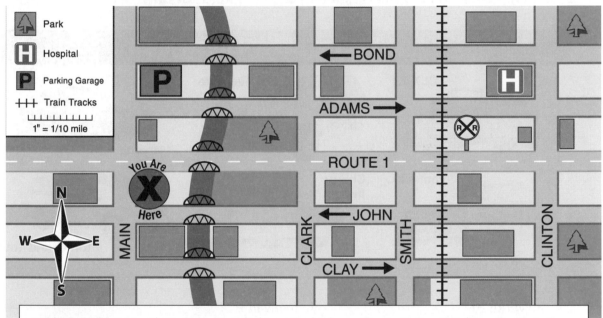

DIRECTIONS: Go north on Main. Turn right on the highway (Route 1). Go straight on Route 1. Cross the tracks and continue to Clinton. Turn left. The store is on the left side of Clinton, but you can't make a U-turn there. So, continue north on Clinton. Go past the hospital. Turn left on Bond, left on Smith, and left again on Adams. Then turn right on Clinton. The shoe store is in the middle of the block, on the west side.

3. **Look at the map in Exercise 2. *True* or *False*?**

    a. This is an Internet map.   *false*

    b. The map has a key.   _____

    c. There is a symbol for schools.   _____

    d. One inch equals 1/10 of a mile.   _____

Challenge Give directions to a place near your school. Draw a map.

1. Look in your dictionary. Circle the words to complete the sentences.

a. The 2-door / ④-door car is blue.

b. The <u>tank truck / cargo van</u> is light brown.

c. The <u>dump truck / tow truck</u> is white.

d. The <u>moving van / tractor trailer</u> has a red cab.

e. The <u>camper / school bus</u> is yellow.

f. The <u>limo / cargo van</u> is white.

g. The <u>hybrid / RV</u> uses gas and electricity.

2. Look at the chart. Match the car models with the kinds of car.

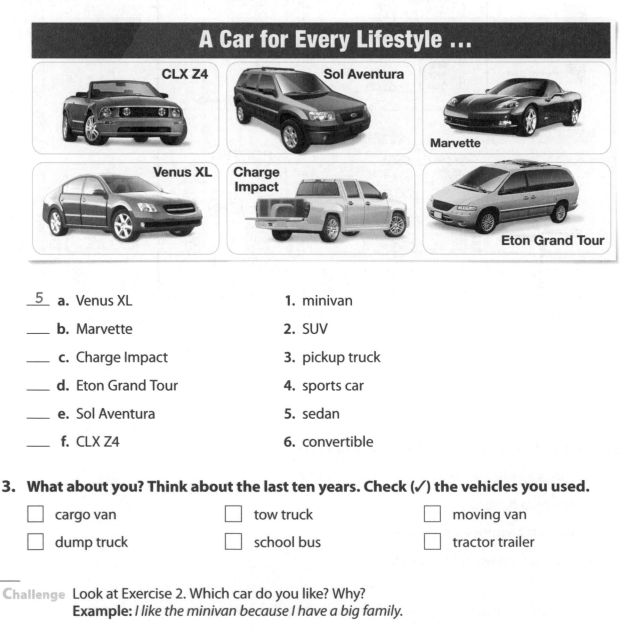

A Car for Every Lifestyle ...

CLX Z4 — Sol Aventura — Marvette — Venus XL — Charge Impact — Eton Grand Tour

_5_ **a.** Venus XL	**1.** minivan
___ **b.** Marvette	**2.** SUV
___ **c.** Charge Impact	**3.** pickup truck
___ **d.** Eton Grand Tour	**4.** sports car
___ **e.** Sol Aventura	**5.** sedan
___ **f.** CLX Z4	**6.** convertible

3. What about you? Think about the last ten years. Check (✓) the vehicles you used.

☐ cargo van   ☐ tow truck   ☐ moving van

☐ dump truck   ☐ school bus   ☐ tractor trailer

Challenge Look at Exercise 2. Which car do you like? Why?
Example: *I like the minivan because I have a big family.*

1. **Look in your dictionary. *True* or *False*?**

   a. Juan is looking at car ads on the Internet and in the newspaper. ___true___

   b. He buys the car. Then he takes the car to a mechanic. _____

   c. He asks the mechanic, "How many miles does it have?" _____

   d. He negotiates a price with the seller. _____

   e. He registers the car. Then he gets the title. _____

   f. He gets the title in the registration office. _____

2. **Match.**

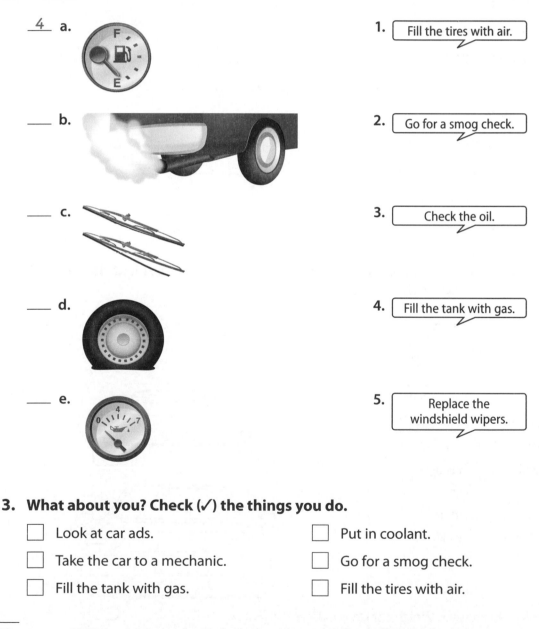

   __4__ a.

   ____ b.

   ____ c.

   ____ d.

   ____ e.

   1. Fill the tires with air.

   2. Go for a smog check.

   3. Check the oil.

   4. Fill the tank with gas.

   5. Replace the windshield wipers.

3. **What about you? Check (✓) the things you do.**

   ☐ Look at car ads. ☐ Put in coolant.

   ☐ Take the car to a mechanic. ☐ Go for a smog check.

   ☐ Fill the tank with gas. ☐ Fill the tires with air.

   Challenge What are other ways to buy a used car? **Example:** *from a friend*

1. Look in your dictionary. What does the person need to use or check?

Page 158

a. Turn left! _____turn signal_____

b. It's raining. _____

c. The battery is dead. _____

d. It's getting dark outside. _____

Page 159

e. It's hot in here. _____

f. Do we need gas? _____

g. That car doesn't see us! _____

h. You're going too slow. _____

i. Stop at the next traffic light. _____

j. It's cold in here. _____

k. Let's listen to some music, OK? _____

l. I forgot to charge my cell phone. _____

m. What's the weather report for tomorrow? _____

n. How fast are you going? _____

2. Look at the diagrams of the rental car. An X shows a problem. Look at the list and check (✓) all the car parts that have problems.

A&B RENTAL

☑ brake light	☐ sideview mirror
☐ bumper	☐ tail light
☐ headlight	☐ tail pipe
☐ hood	☐ tire
☐ hubcap	☐ trunk
☐ license plate	☐ windshield

3. Put the words in the correct column. Use your dictionary for help.

accelerator   brake pedal   clutch   gear shift   horn
ignition   seat belt   steering wheel   stick shift

Things you use with your hands

_____

_____

_____

_____

_____

_____

Things you use with your feet

_____*accelerator*_____

_____

_____

4. Cross out the word that doesn't belong.

a. **For problems**   lug wrench   jack   spare tire   ~~gas tank~~

b. **For safety**   air bag   hazard lights   front seat   seat belt

c. **To measure things**   oil gauge   speedometer   engine   temperature gauge

d. **To see other cars**   rearview mirror   windshield   muffler   sideview mirror

5. Circle the words to complete the sentences.

a. You can keep maps in the (glove compartment)/ power outlet.

b. The key is in the ignition / muffler.

c. You should always wear a clutch / seat belt in the car.

d. It's important to have a spare tire / steering wheel in the trunk.

e. The radiator is inside the trunk / under the hood.

f. Small children should sit in the front seat / backseat.

6. What about you? Check (✓) the items you would like in a car.

☐ CD player

☐ air conditioner

☐ child safety seat

☐ stick shift

☐ automatic transmission

☐ Other: _____

Challenge Explain your choices in Exercise 6. **Example:** *I would like an air conditioner because it's more comfortable.*

See page 296 for listening practice.

1. Look in your dictionary. Who . . . ?

a. works at the check-in kiosk   _ticket agent_

b. goes though security

c. examines your luggage in the screening area

d. helps passengers carry their baggage

e. is in the cockpit

f. helps passengers on the airplane

g. looks at your declaration form

2. Circle the words to complete the conversations. Then, write where the people are. Use the words in the box.

> ~~airplane~~   airplane   baggage carousel   boarding area   cockpit   customs

Passenger 1: Where's your carry-on bag?

Passenger 2: Up there, (in the overhead compartment)/ on the tray table.   _airplane_
                                              a.

Passenger 3: Is our flight still on time?

Passenger 4: Let's check the <u>arrival and departure monitors</u> / turbulence.
                                              b.

Customs Officer: Do you have anything to declare?

Passenger 1: Yes. Here's my <u>declaration form</u> / e-ticket.
                                 c.

Flight Attendant: You have a <u>boarding pass</u> / life vest under
                                     d.
          your seat in case of emergency. Please look for the

          nearest <u>emergency exit</u> / reclined seat now.
                              e.

Passenger 3: I don't see my e-ticket / <u>luggage</u>.
                            f.

Passenger 4: Don't worry. More bags are still coming out.

Pilot: I hope you enjoyed your flight. We will <u>land</u> / take off in about ten minutes,
                                            g.
     and we will be at the <u>check-in kiosk / gate</u> in about twenty minutes.
                                  h.

3. **Look at <u>page 160</u> in your dictionary. Match.**

<u>3</u> **a.** I just have this one bag.

____ **b.** Is this 14F?

____ **c.** Can I walk through now?

____ **d.** Now I just press PRINT.

____ **e.** OK. I'm pressing OFF. It won't ring now.

____ **f.** Here's my driver's license.

____ **g.** Here it is! The large red one.

____ **h.** I think I ate too much! It's a little too tight.

____ **i.** Oh, good. It fits in the overhead compartment.

1. Stow your carry-on bag.

2. Claim your baggage.

3. Check your bags.

4. Find your seat.

5. Check in electronically.

6. Go through security.

7. Show your ID.

8. Turn off your cell phone.

9. Fasten your seatbelt.

4. **Look at the picture. Check (✓) the things the passenger did.**

☑ got her boarding pass ☐ found her seat ☐ landed

☐ stowed her carry-on bag ☐ read the emergency card ☐ took off

☐ fastened her seat belt ☐ boarded the plane ☐ checked in

Challenge List the things you can do to make a plane trip more comfortable.
Example: *wear comfortable clothing*

Go to page 249 for Another Look (Unit 8). │ See page 297 for listening practice.

1. Look in your dictionary. *True* or *False*?

a. They pack their bags in New York.   *false*

b. They ask a gas station attendant for directions.   _____

c. They see beautiful scenery.   _____

d. The car breaks down in the middle of their trip.   _____

e. They get a speeding ticket in Seattle.   _____

f. They don't arrive at their destination.   _____

2. Look at the pictures. Match.

1.    2.

3.    4.

5.    6.

7.    8.

___ **a.** They get a speeding ticket.   ___ **e.** They see beautiful scenery.

___ **b.** The car breaks down.   ___ **f.** They run out of gas.

_1_ **c.** They pack their bags.   ___ **g.** They have a flat tire.

___ **d.** They arrive at their destination.   ___ **h.** They get lost.

3. **Look in your dictionary. Circle the words to complete the sentences.**

   a. Their (destination) / starting point is New York City.

   b. They put their bags <u>in the trunk / on the back seat</u>.

   c. They have a <u>4-door sedan / sports car</u>.

   d. Joe gives <u>the police officer / tow truck driver</u> his auto club card.

   e. There is a <u>flat / spare</u> tire in the trunk.

4. **Look at the pictures in Exercise 2. Complete the postcard. Use the words in the box.**

   | auto club card | broke down | ~~destination~~ | got | had | pack | ran out |

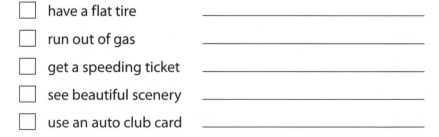

Well, we finally reached our <u>destination</u>. The trip was
                           a.
terrible. We got lost four times and we had a lot of
problems with the car. First, we _____ a speeding
                                            b.
ticket for driving over 65 mph. Then, we _____ a flat
                                          c.
tire. Next, we _____ of gas. Then, the
                      d.
car _____. I'm glad I had my _____ with me.
        e.   **f.**
We called a tow truck and the driver towed us all the
way to Los Angeles. We arrived at Mia's today—five days
late, and by taxi! Tomorrow our car will be ready, we'll
_____ our bags, and start for home. See you soon.
    g.

                                                        Amy

   Shaun Hensher
   45 Consumers Road
   Ann Arbor, MI
   48107

5. **What about you? Did you ever . . . ? Check (✓) the answers.**

                                       If *yes*, where?

   ☐ have a flat tire   _____

   ☐ run out of gas   _____

   ☐ get a speeding ticket   _____

   ☐ see beautiful scenery   _____

   ☐ use an auto club card   _____

Challenge   Work with a partner. Look in your dictionary. Plan a trip. What's your starting point?
How will you travel? What will you pack? What's your destination? Compare your
answers with those of your classmates.

See page 297 for listening practice.

1. Look in your dictionary. True or False?

a. Irina Sarkov is the receptionist.   *false*

b. The receptionist sits across from the entrance.   _____

c. The time clock shows 9:15.   _____

d. The safety regulations are in the office.   _____

e. There are two employees in the office.   _____

f. The employer is writing paychecks now.   _____

g. A customer is at the entrance.   _____

h. The employer is also the owner.   _____

2. Who said . . . ? Use the words in the box.

| employee | ~~employer~~ | payroll clerk | receptionist | customer | supervisor |

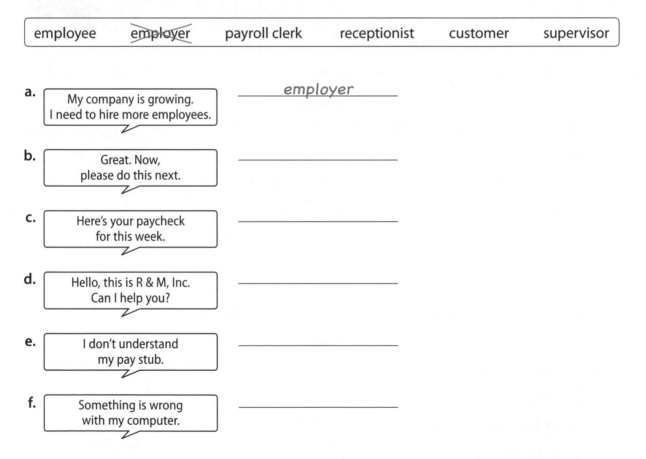

a. My company is growing. I need to hire more employees.   *employer*

b. Great. Now, please do this next.   _____

c. Here's your paycheck for this week.   _____

d. Hello, this is R & M, Inc. Can I help you?   _____

e. I don't understand my pay stub.   _____

f. Something is wrong with my computer.   _____

3. Look in your dictionary. Circle the answers to complete the sentences.

a. (An employee)/ The boss is fixing a computer.

b. Kate Babic is talking to the <u>payroll clerk / supervisor</u>.

c. Her <u>deductions / wages</u> are $800.

d. Irina Sarkov's signature is on the <u>paycheck / pay stub</u>.

e. The time clock is near the <u>receptionist / entrance</u>.

4. Look at the pay stub. *True* or *False*?

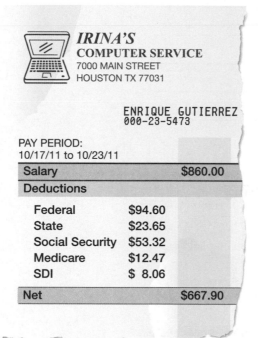

IRINA'S	
COMPUTER SERVICE	
7000 MAIN STREET	
HOUSTON TX 77031	

ENRIQUE GUTIERREZ
000-23-5473

PAY PERIOD:
10/17/11 to 10/23/11

Salary	$860.00
Deductions	
Federal	$94.60
State	$23.65
Social Security	$53.32
Medicare	$12.47
SDI	$ 8.06
Net	**$667.90**

a. Irina is Enrique's supervisor. _____*false*_____

b. Enrique is an employee at Irina's Computer Service. _____

c. This pay stub is for one month. _____

d. His wages are $667.90 after deductions. _____

e. Enrique pays five different deductions. _____

f. The pay stub shows the office phone number. _____

g. The Social Security deduction is $8.06. _____

Challenge Go to page 254 in this book. Follow the instructions.

1. Look in your dictionary. Who is . . . ?

a. putting together computer parts   _assembler_

b. making bread

c. repairing a refrigerator

d. working in a theater

e. planning a building

f. reading stories to children

g. taking notes at a meeting

h. using a computer on a plane

i. standing in front of a store

j. working at a table with children

2. Match.

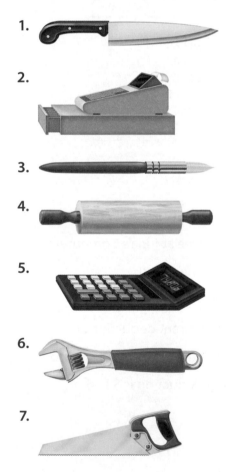

_4_ **a.** baker   1.

___ **b.** accountant   2.

___ **c.** mechanic   3.

___ **d.** butcher   4.

___ **e.** carpenter   5.

___ **f.** artist   6.

___ **g.** cashier   7.

Challenge Look in your dictionary. Choose one job. Would you like that job? Why or why not? Write three sentences.

1. Look in your dictionary. Where do they work? Check (✓) the columns.

	Inside	Outside
a. gardener		✓
b. electronics repair person		
c. customer service representative		
d. dockworker		
e. delivery person		
f. home health care aide		
g. graphic designer		
h. dental assistant		
i. hairdresser		

2. Look at the bar graph. Who works more hours? Circle the job.

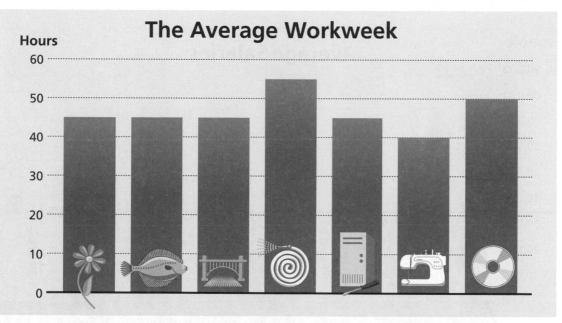

The Average Workweek

Hours
60
50
40
30
20
10
0

Based on information from: Krantz, L. *Jobs Rated Almanac.* (NJ: Barricade Books, 2002)

a. a computer technician or a ⟨computer software engineer⟩

b. a commercial fisher or a firefighter

c. an engineer or a computer software engineer

d. a garment worker or a commercial fisher

e. a florist or a garment worker

Challenge Go to page 255 in this book. Follow the instructions.

1. Look in your dictionary. *True* or *False*? **Write a question mark (?) if you don't know.**

a. The interpreter can speak Spanish. _____?_____

b. The manicurist is painting the woman's toenails. _____

c. The occupational therapist is helping a woman use a microwave. _____

d. The homemaker is in the kitchen. _____

e. The lawyer is in court. _____

f. The movers are carrying a table. _____

g. The physician assistant is talking to a patient. _____

h. The messenger rides a bicycle. _____

i. The medical records technician works in a hospital. _____

2. Look at the bar graph. Number the jobs in order of how much money people make. (1 = the most money)

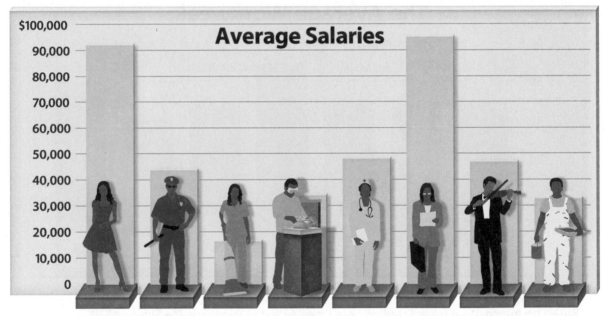

Based on information from: Krantz, L. *Jobs Rated Almanac*. (NJ: Barricade Books, 2002)

____ a. house painter

____ b. police officer

____ c. musician

____ d. model

_1_ e. lawyer

____ f. housekeeper

____ g. nurse

____ h. machine operator

Challenge What are the differences between a homemaker and a housekeeper? Write three sentences.

See page 299 for listening practice.

1. **Look in your dictionary. Circle the words to complete the sentences.**

   a. The (receptionist) / server sits at a desk all day.

   b. The <u>sanitation worker / security guard</u> works outside.

   c. The <u>stock clerk / writer</u> uses a computer.

   d. The <u>postal worker / printer</u> wears a uniform.

   e. The <u>truck driver / veterinarian</u> travels from place to place.

2. **Look at the job preference chart. Choose a job for each person.**

Likes to . . .	Ari	Luisa	Tom	Chris	Mia	Dave
work with people				✓		
speak on the phone	✓					
be inside	✓	✓	✓	✓		✓
be outside		✓	✓		✓	
sell things	✓					✓
be on TV			✓			
travel			✓		✓	
repair things		✓				
help people				✓		
wear a uniform					✓	
do physical work					✓	

   a. telemarketer ____Ari____   d. welder _____

   b. social worker _____   e. retail clerk _____

   c. soldier _____   f. reporter _____

3. **What about you? Look at <u>pages 166–169</u> in your dictionary. Write two jobs on each line.**

   Jobs I can do now: _____

   Jobs I can't do now: _____

   Jobs I would like to do: _____

   Jobs I wouldn't like to do: _____

Challenge Look at your answers in Exercise 3. Explain your choices.

See page 299 for listening practice.

Job Skills

1. Look in your dictionary. Circle the job skills in the job ads below. Then, write the name of the job. Use the words in the box.

Administrative Assistant	Assembler	Carpenter	Chef	Childcare Worker
Home Health Care Aide	Manager	~~Salesperson~~	Server	Garment Worker

	Job Title and Description	Company
a.	**Salesperson** needed part-time to (sell cars) at our new Route 29 location. Must have experience and be able to work weekends.	Herb Rupert
b.	_____ wanted to take care of small children. Part-time. Must speak English and Spanish. Experience and references required.	ChildCare
c.	_____ wanted to assist medical patients. Good income. Experience required.	Medical Homecare
d.	_____ needed to assemble telephone components in midtown factory. Immediate full-time employment.	Top Telecom
e.	_____ wanted to make tables and chairs in our small shop.	Woodwork Corner
f.	_____ wanted to supervise staff full-time at our small, friendly architecture company.	Nicolas Pyle, Inc.
g.	_____ needed for busy law office. Must type 50 words per minute.	DeLucca, Smith, & Rotelli
h.	_____ wanted to sew clothes in our downtown factory. Experience necessary.	L & H Clothing, Inc.
i.	_____ wanted to cook everything from hamburgers to duck à l'orange at our small neighborhood restaurant.	The Corner Bistro
j.	_____ needed to wait on customers at a busy downtown coffee shop. Part-time only. Experience preferred.	Kim's

2. What about you? Check (✓) the job skills you have. Circle the skills you want to learn.

☐ assemble components ☐ cook ☐ do manual labor
☐ drive a truck ☐ fly a plane ☐ make furniture
☐ operate heavy machinery ☐ program computers ☐ repair appliances
☐ sew clothes ☐ solve math problems ☐ speak another language
☐ supervise people ☐ teach ☐ use a cash register
☐ take care of children ☐ Other: _____ ☐ Other: _____

Challenge Choose two job ads from Exercise 1. Can you do the jobs? Why or why not?

**1. Look in your dictionary. For which skills do the employees need . . . ?
Put the words in the correct columns.**

A Computer	Paper	
type a letter	_type a letter_	_____
_____	_____	_____
_____	_____	_____
_____	_____	_____
_____	_____	_____
	_____	

2. Match.

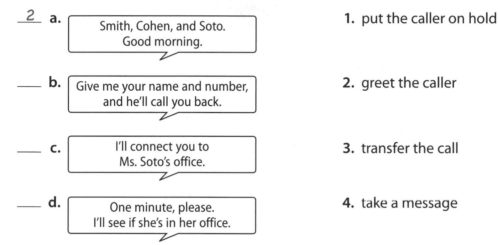

_2_ a. Smith, Cohen, and Soto. Good morning.

b. Give me your name and number, and he'll call you back.

c. I'll connect you to Ms. Soto's office.

d. One minute, please. I'll see if she's in her office.

1. put the caller on hold

2. greet the caller

3. transfer the call

4. take a message

3. What about you? Check (✓) the office skills you have.

☐ type a letter   ☐ collate papers

☐ enter data   ☐ staple

☐ transcribe notes   ☐ scan a document

☐ take dictation   ☐ fax a document

☐ organize materials   ☐ print a document

☐ make copies   ☐ take a message

Challenge Work with a partner. Role-play a phone call. Student A is a caller. Student B is a receptionist. Leave a message and take a message.

See page 300 for listening practice.

1. **Look in your dictionary. Cross out the word that doesn't belong.**

   a. **Forms**   interest inventory   ~~training~~   skill inventory

   b. **People**   career counselor   internship   recruiter

   c. **Job training**   online course   vocational training new job

   d. **Job information** entry-level job   job fair   recruiter

2. **Put the career planning steps in the correct order. Use your dictionary for help.**

   ___ **a.** promotion

   _1_ **b.** career counselor

   ___ **c.** entry-level job

   ___ **d.** interest and skill inventories

   ___ **e.** on-the-job training

3. **What about you? Complete the form.**

   ## jt TRAINING INSTITUTE

   Please check (✓) the job training you have had. For what job?

   ☐ vocational training   _____

   ☐ internship   _____

   ☐ on-the-job training   _____

   ☐ online course   _____

   ☐ Other: _____

   Which type of job training do you prefer? Why? _____

   _____

   _____

Challenge Look in your dictionary. Write about Ms. Diaz's career path. **Example:** *First, she had an entry-level job. She pushed a clothing rack. Then, . . .*

1. Look in your dictionary. Fill out Dan King's job application.

EMPLOYMENT APPLICATION   S&K GROCERY, INC.

NAME: Dan King	JOB APPLYING FOR: _____

1. HOW DID YOU HEAR ABOUT THIS JOB? (PLEASE CHECK (✓) ALL APPROPRIATE BOXES.)

☐ FRIENDS ☐ INTERNET JOB SITE ☐ HELP WANTED SIGN

☐ JOB BOARD ☐ CLASSIFIEDS ☐ EMPLOYMENT AGENCY

2. HOURS: ☐ PART-TIME ☐ FULL-TIME

3. HAVE YOU HAD ANY EXPERIENCE? ☐ YES ☐ NO	IF YES, WHAT? WHEN? _____

4. REFERENCES: Lily Wong , Manager, Zhou Market

FOR OFFICE USE ONLY

RESUME RECEIVED: 9/17	INTERVIEWED BY: Ron Hill 9/21
HIRED? ☐ YES ☐ NO	WAGES:

2. Look in your dictionary and at Exercise 1. *True* or *False*?

a. Dan filled out an application. _____true_____

b. Dan wrote a resume. _____

c. He didn't write a cover letter. _____

d. He sent in his resume before the interview. _____

e. He set up an interview for the job. _____

f. He went on an interview with Lily Wong at Zhou Market. _____

g. Dan didn't get hired. _____

3. What about you? What do you think are the best ways to find a job? Number them in order. (1 = the best)

____ look in the classifieds   ____ check Internet job sites

____ look for a help wanted sign   ____ go to an employment agency

____ network   ____ Other: _____

Challenge Survey four classmates. How did they find their jobs?

1. Look in your dictionary. When did Mr. Ortiz . . . ? Check (✓) the columns.

	Before the Interview	During the Interview	After the Interview
a. ask questions		✓	
b. dress appropriately			
c. prepare			
d. talk about his experience			
e. shake hands			
f. greet the interviewer			
g. write a thank-you note			

2. Look at the picture. Check (✓) Amy's interview skills.

Interview Skills Checklist

☑ be on time	☐ turn off cell phone
☐ dress appropriately	☐ make eye contact
☐ be neat	☐ listen carefully
☐ bring resume	☐ talk about job experience
☐ bring ID	

3. What about you? Check (✓) the things you do on a job interview.

Interview Skills Checklist

☐ be on time	☐ bring resume	☐ make eye contact
☐ dress appropriately	☐ bring ID	☐ listen carefully
☐ be neat	☐ turn off cell phone	☐ talk about job experience

Challenge Make a list of questions to ask on a job interview. **Example:** *What are the hours?*

See page 301 for listening practice.

1. **Look in your dictionary.** *True* or *False*?

   a. The factory manufactures lamps. _____true_____

   b. The factory owner and the designer are in the warehouse. _____

   c. A worker is operating a yellow forklift. _____

   d. The line supervisor is pushing a hand truck. _____

   e. There are three boxes on the pallet. _____

2. **Cross out the word that doesn't belong.**

   a. **People**   designer   shipping clerk   ~~forklift~~   packer

   b. **Places**   factory owner   warehouse   factory   loading dock

   c. **Machines**   hand truck   forklift   order puller   conveyor belt

   d. **Jobs**   ship   parts   assemble   design

3. **Complete the Lamplighter, Inc. job descriptions. Use the words in the box.**

~~designer~~   factory worker   line supervisor   order puller   packer   shipping clerk

   LAMPLIGHTER, Inc.

   a. design the lamp   _____designer_____

   b. watch the assembly line   _____

   c. assemble parts   _____

   d. count boxes on the loading dock   _____

   e. move boxes on a hand truck   _____

   f. put lamps in boxes on the conveyor belt   _____

4. **What about you? Look at the jobs in Exercise 3. Which one would you like? Which one wouldn't you like? Why?**

   Example: *I would like to be a line supervisor. I like to supervise people.*

   Challenge Rewrite the false sentences in Exercise 1. Make them true.

See page 301 for listening practice.   175

1. **Look in your dictionary. *True* or *False*?**

   a. The gardening crew leader is talking to the landscape designer.   _____true_____

   b. One of the gardening crew has a wheelbarrow.   _____

   c. The landscape designer is holding a leaf blower.   _____

   d. The shovel is between the lawn mower and the rake.   _____

   e. The pruning shears are to the right of the trowel.   _____

   f. The hedge clippers are to the left of the weed whacker.   _____

2. **Look at the Before and After pictures. Check (✓) the *completed* jobs.**

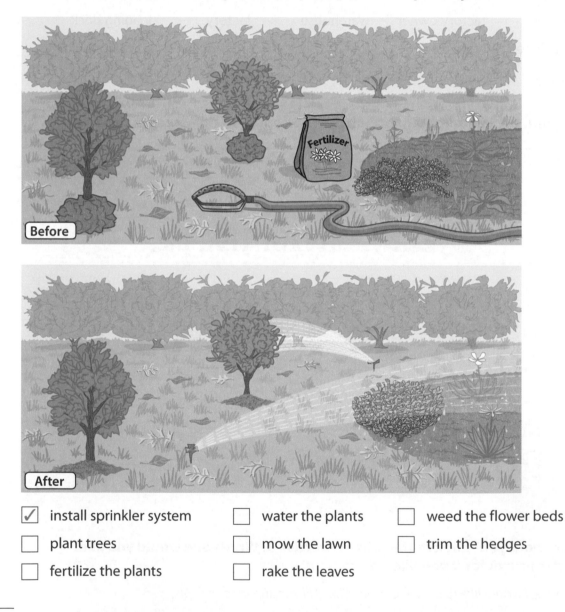

   Before

   After

✓ install sprinkler system	☐ water the plants	☐ weed the flower beds
☐ plant trees	☐ mow the lawn	☐ trim the hedges
☐ fertilize the plants	☐ rake the leaves	

   Challenge What can people use these tools for: shovel, hedge clippers, trowel, pruning shears?
   Example: *shovel—to plant a tree*

   See page 301 for listening practice.

1. **Look in your dictionary. Circle the words to complete the sentences.**

   a. A farmer / (rancher) is on a horse.

   b. In Picture C, a farmworker is <u>milking / feeding</u> a cow.

   c. There is <u>hay / alfalfa</u> near the fence of the corral.

   d. There is <u>farm equipment / livestock</u> next to the vegetable garden.

   e. A farmer is in the <u>orchard / vineyard</u>.

   f. In Picture B, two hired hands are <u>harvesting / planting</u> lettuce.

2. **Look at the bar graph. Number the crops in order. (1 = the biggest crop)**

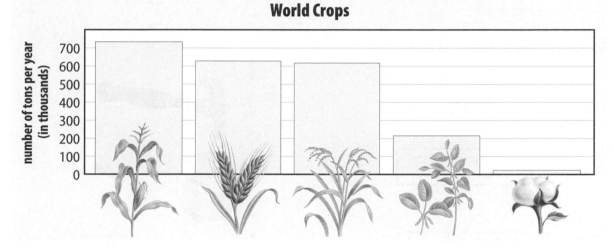

World Crops

Based on information from: *Food and Agricultural Organization Statistical Yearbook*, 2005–2006.
http://www.fao.org/statistics/yearbook

___ **a.** wheat   ___ **c.** cotton   ___ **e.** soybeans

_1_ **b.** corn   ___ **d.** rice

3. **What about you? Have you ever been in . . . ? Check (✓) *Yes* or *No*.**

	Yes	No	If *yes*, where?
a. a field	☐	☐	_____
b. an orchard	☐	☐	_____
c. a barn	☐	☐	_____
d. a vineyard	☐	☐	_____
e. a vegetable garden	☐	☐	_____

Challenge Work with a classmate. List products that are made from wheat, soybeans, corn, cotton, and cattle. **Example:** *wheat—bread*

1. Look in your dictionary. Put the words in the correct category.

Heavy Machines	Tools	Building Material	
cherry picker	jackhammer	concrete	_____
_____	_____	_____	_____
_____	_____	_____	_____
_____	_____	_____	_____

Things To Stand On _____ _____

ladder _____ _____

_____

_____

2. Look at the items. Match.

_3_ **a.** Install these tiles in the bathroom.

___ **b.** Lay the bricks for the south wall.

___ **c.** Hammer those nails into the wood.

___ **d.** Paint it green.

1.

2.

3.

4.

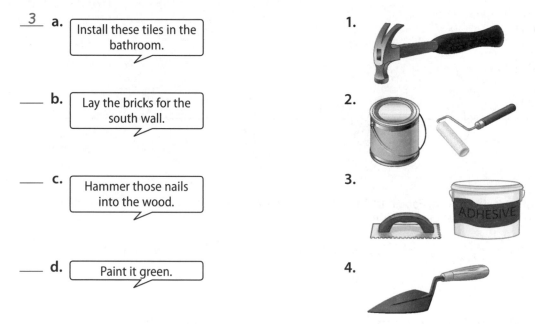

3. What about you? Check (✓) the materials your school building has.

- ☐ concrete
- ☐ shingles
- ☐ bricks
- ☐ stucco
- ☐ tile
- ☐ wood

Challenge Look in your dictionary. What are the construction workers doing? Write sentences.
Example: *One construction worker is using a jackhammer.*

See page 302 for listening practice.

1. Look in your dictionary. Match.

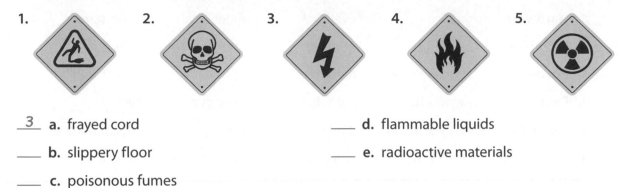

1.　　2.　　3.　　4.　　5.

__3__ **a.** frayed cord

_____ **b.** slippery floor

_____ **c.** poisonous fumes

_____ **d.** flammable liquids

_____ **e.** radioactive materials

2. Look at the worker. Check (✓) his safety equipment.

Super Safe Sam

Job Safety
Better safe than sorry!

☑ back support belt	☐ respirator
☐ earmuffs	☐ safety boots
☐ ear plugs	☐ safety glasses
☐ fire extinguisher	☐ safety goggles
☐ hard hat	☐ safety visor
☐ knee pads	☐ two-way radio
☐ particle mask	☐ work gloves

3. What about you? Which safety equipment do you use at work? At home? Write a list for each. Discuss your list with a classmate.

At Work

_____

_____

_____

_____

_____

At Home

_____

_____

_____

_____

_____

Challenge Imagine you work at the place in your dictionary. Which safety equipment will you wear or use?

See page 302 for listening practice.

Tools and Building Supplies

1. **Look in your dictionary. Cross out the word that doesn't belong.**

   a. **Hardware**   nail   eye hook   ~~outlet cover~~   wood screw

   b. **Plumbing**   C-clamp   plunger   pipe   fittings

   c. **Power tools** circular saw   hammer   router   electric drill

   d. **Paint**   wood stain   paint roller   spray gun   chisel

   e. **Electrical**   wire stripper plane   wire   extension cord

   f. **Hand tools**   hacksaw   work light   pipe wrench   mallet

2. **Look at the pictures. What do you need? Choose the correct tool from the box.**

drill bit	~~electrical tape~~	level	paintbrush
Phillips screwdriver	sandpaper	scraper	screwdriver

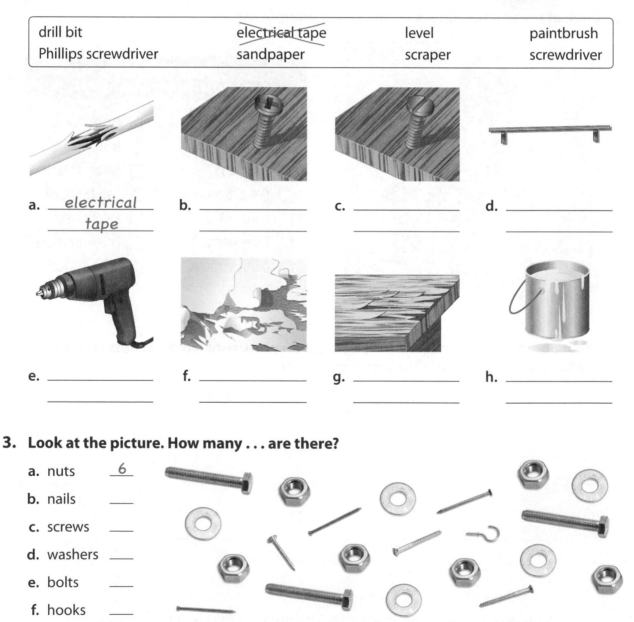

   a. ___electrical tape___   b. _____   c. _____   d. _____

   e. _____   f. _____   g. _____   h. _____

3. **Look at the picture. How many . . . are there?**

   a. nuts   6
   b. nails   ___
   c. screws   ___
   d. washers   ___
   e. bolts   ___
   f. hooks   ___

180

4. Look at the chart. *True* **or** *False*?

Multi-use Knife Features						
Deluxe	✓	✓	✓	✓	✓	✓
Traditional	✓	✓	✓		✓	
Micro	✓		✓			✓

a. The "Traditional" has a blade.   *false*

b. The "Micro" has a Phillips screwdriver. _____

c. All three models have screwdrivers.   _____

d. All three models have a tape measure.   _____

e. The "Deluxe" has pliers.   _____

f. Only the "Deluxe" has a wire stripper.   _____

5. What about you? Check (✓) the tools and supplies you have.

☐ hammer   ☐ plunger

☐ handsaw   ☐ vise

☐ power sander   ☐ ax

☐ electric drill   ☐ masking tape

☐ adjustable wrench   ☐ duct tape

☐ jigsaw   ☐ plane

☐ yardstick   ☐ chisel

☐ screwdriver   ☐ Other: _____

Challenge Look at the chart in Exercise 4. Which model would you buy? What can you use it for?

See page 303 for listening practice.

1. Look in your dictionary. *True* or *False*? Correct the underlined words in the false sentences.

    a. The receptionist is in the ~~conference room~~.   *reception area*   _____*false*_____

    b. The office manager is at his desk in a <u>cubicle</u>.   _____

    c. The <u>clerk</u> is cleaning the floor.   _____

    d. The computer technician is working on a <u>scanner</u>.   _____

    e. The <u>executive</u> is at a presentation.   _____

    f. The <u>file clerk</u> is at the file cabinet.   _____

2. Look at the pictures. What do the office workers need? Use the words in the box.

calculator	electric pencil sharpener	file folder	mailing label	~~staples~~
paper cutter	photocopier	fax machine	postal scale	

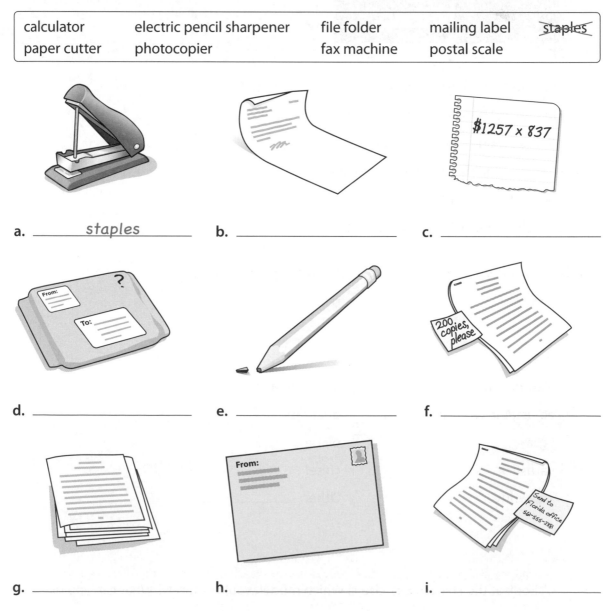

a. _____*staples*_____   b. _____   c. _____

d. _____   e. _____   f. _____

g. _____   h. _____   i. _____

3. Look at the supply cabinet. Complete the office inventory.

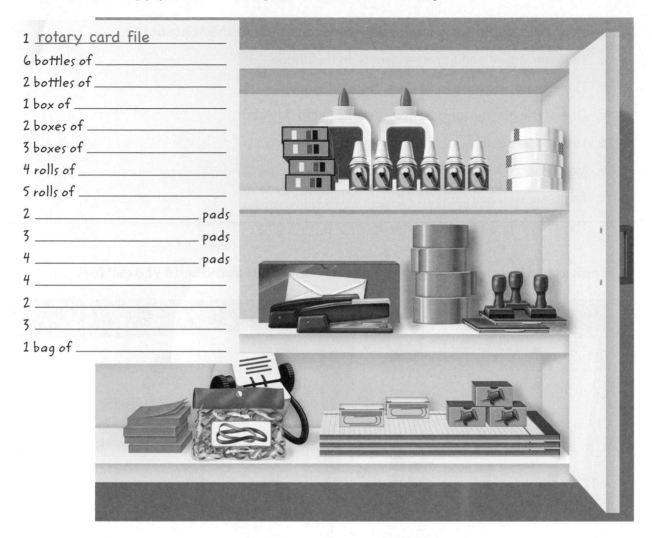

1 <u>rotary card file</u>
6 bottles of _____
2 bottles of _____
1 box of _____
2 boxes of _____
3 boxes of _____
4 rolls of _____
5 rolls of _____
2 _____ pads
3 _____ pads
4 _____ pads
4 _____
2 _____
3 _____
1 bag of _____

4. What about you? How often do you use . . . ? Check (✓) the columns.

	Often	Sometimes	Never
a fax machine			
sticky notes			
an inkjet printer			
a laser printer			
an organizer			
an appointment book			
a rotary card file			
a paper shredder			

Challenge Make a shopping list of office supplies you need for your home. What will you use them for? **Example:** *envelopes—to pay bills*. Discuss your list with a classmate.

See page 303 for listening practice.

1. Look in your dictionary. Circle the words to complete the sentences.

a. The (concierge) / parking attendant is on the phone.

b. The elevator is across from the gift shop / luggage cart.

c. One of the guest rooms has two double / king-size beds.

d. The housekeeping cart is in the hallway / ballroom.

e. Maintenance / The desk clerk is repairing the ice machine.

f. There are two bell captains / guests in the suite.

g. The doorman isn't opening the door / revolving door.

2. Look at the hotel directory in the guest room. What number do you call for . . . ?

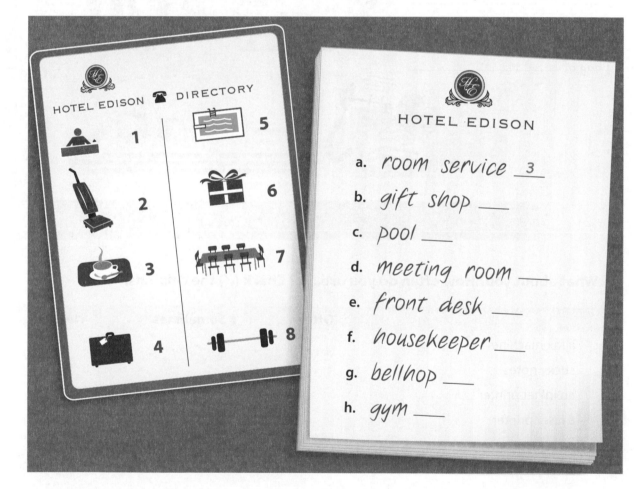

a. room service __3__
b. gift shop ___
c. pool ___
d. meeting room ___
e. front desk ___
f. housekeeper ___
g. bellhop ___
h. gym ___

3. What about you? Would you like to be a guest at the hotel in your dictionary?

☐ Yes   ☐ No   Why? _____

Challenge Look in your dictionary. Write five questions that you can ask the desk clerk about the hotel. **Example:** *What time does the pool open?*

See page 303 for listening practice.

1. Look in your dictionary. Who is . . . ?

a. leaving the walk-in freezer   _food preparation worker_

b. washing dishes   _____

c. sitting near the buffet   _____

d. talking to the bus person   _____

e. working in the banquet room   _____ and _____

f. carrying food to a diner   _____

g. seating a diner at a table   _____

2. Look in your dictionary. Where are they? Check (✓) all the correct columns.

	Dining Room	Banquet Room	Kitchen
a. servers	✓	✓	
b. diners			
c. short-order cook			
d. sous chef			
e. caterer			
f. bus person			
g. head chef			
h. maitre d'			
i. runner			

3. Look in your dictionary. Who said . . . ?

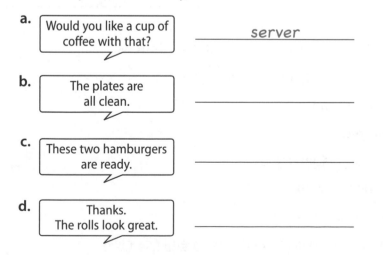

a. | Would you like a cup of coffee with that? | _server_

b. | The plates are all clean. | _____

c. | These two hamburgers are ready. | _____

d. | Thanks. The rolls look great. | _____

Challenge Imagine you own a hotel. Make a list of food to have at a breakfast buffet. Compare your list with a classmate's. Do you have any of the same items?

1. Look in your dictionary. *True* or *False*?

a. The contractor is holding a floor plan. _____false_____

b. Three bricklayers called in sick. _____

c. One construction worker is going to the clinic. _____

d. The man operating the crane is not being careful. _____

e. The wiring is dangerous. _____

f. The budget is three thousand dollars. _____

g. There's an electrical hazard in the office. _____

2. Look in your dictionary. Check (✓) the things at the construction site.

☐ ladder	☐ insulation	☐ bricks
✓ I beams	☐ hard hats	☐ pickax
☐ forklift	☐ shovel	☐ trowel
☐ scaffolding	☐ crane	☐ tiles
☐ tractor	☐ jackhammer	☐ sledgehammer
☐ cherry picker	☐ backhoe	☐ safety regulations
☐ bulldozer	☐ wheelbarrow	☐ wood

3. Look at the list in Exercise 2. Choose two items. What do people use them for?

Example: *You can use a ladder to reach high things.*

_____

_____

4. Look in your dictionary. Circle the words to complete the sentences.

a. There is an electrical hazard in the clinic / (at the construction site).

b. One worker isn't wearing a hard hat / shoes.

c. One worker fell into bricks / concrete.

d. Another worker dropped a hammer / jackhammer.

e. An I beam / Drywall is going to hit two workers.

f. A piece of tile / wood is going to fall on a worker.

g. The worker with the headphones and red hard hat is very careful / careless.

5. **Look in your dictionary. Answer the questions.**

   a. Who is Sam Lopez? _____*contractor*_____

   b. Who are Jack and Tom? _____

   c. What is the name of the clinic? _____

   d. How much will the wiring cost? _____

   e. How many months does the schedule give the
   workers from start to finish? _____

6. **Complete the building owner's report. Use the words in the box.**

bricklayer	budget	careful	clinic	contractor
~~dangerous~~	electrical hazard	floor plan	sick	wiring

   7/2

   I went to the construction site today. It's a _____*dangerous*_____ place! I saw some
                               a.

   _____ coming out of a box. This is a real _____.
            b.   **c.**

   Some of the workers are not very _____. One
                                          d.

   _____ fell in cement and needed to go to the _____!
           e.   **f.**

   Other workers didn't have hard hats on. Two workers called in _____
                                                               g.

   and weren't at work. Sam, the _____, said it was a bad day. Then,
                                              h.

   I showed Sam the new _____ with more offices. He looked very upset.
                                                  i.

   He's worried about the schedule. He's worried about the schedule, and I'm worried about the

   _____. Sam doesn't think three million dollars is enough!
           j.

7. **What about you? Would you like a job at the construction site in your dictionary?
   Why or why not?**

   Challenge Look in your dictionary. What safety equipment do the workers need?
             Why do they need it? Make a list. Use <u>page 179</u> in your dictionary for help.

Schools and Subjects

1. Look in your dictionary. In which school can you hear . . . ?

> Today we are going to learn about the history of the thirteen colonies.

a. _____middle school_____

> I have biology on Tuesday afternoons.

d. _____

> That's the engine.

b. _____

> Today we are going to talk about the Civil War.

e. _____

> OK, class. How much is three plus three?

c. _____

> OK, children. Let's count the ducks now.

f. _____

2. Match the student ages with the schools. Use your dictionary for help.

_2_ **a.** 20 years old

____ **b.** 3 years old

____ **c.** 7 years old

____ **d.** 16 years old

____ **e.** 12 years old

____ **f.** 30 years old

1. high school

2. college

3. preschool

4. adult school

5. elementary school

6. middle school

3. What about you? Complete the chart.

Check (✓) the schools you have attended:	Name	Location	Dates
☐ elementary school			
☐ junior high school			
☐ high school			
☐ vocational school			
☐ adult school			
☐ college / university			
☐ community college			
☐ Other: _____			

4. **Look in your dictionary. In which class can students . . . ?**

   a. learn about World War II   _history_

   b. work with numbers   _____

   c. do exercises outside   _____

   d. learn French   _____

   e. sing   _____

   f. talk about books   _____

   g. paint   _____

   h. use this workbook   _____

5. **Label the class notes. Use the words in the box.**

Math	Science	World Languages	Music	ESL / ESOL	~~History~~

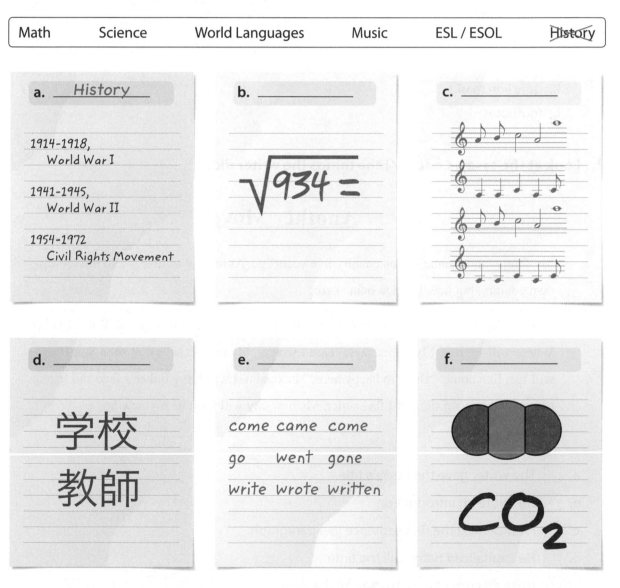

a. _History_

1914-1918,
   World War I

1941-1945,
   World War II

1954-1972
   Civil Rights Movement

b. _____

$\sqrt{934} =$

c. _____

d. _____

学校
教師

e. _____

come came come

go went gone

write wrote written

f. _____

CO_2

Challenge Go to page 255 in this book. Follow the instructions.

See page 304 for listening practice.

1. Look at the essay in your dictionary. How many . . . are there? Check (✓) the columns.

	0	1	2	3	4
a. words in the title					✓
b. paragraphs					
c. sentences in the last paragraph					
d. quotation marks					
e. commas in the first paragraph					
f. exclamation marks					
g. apostrophes					
h. parentheses					
i. colons					
j. hyphens					
k. question marks					
l. footnotes					

2. Look at the essay. Check (✓) the things the writer did.

Another Move

My family and I came to this country five years ago. At first I was lonely and missed my own country, but now I feel at home here.

Next september we're moving again—to san diego, california. I'm worried. Will I like it? Where will we live. My father says, "Don't worry." My mother says that soon San Diego will feel like home. "But I'm happy here?" I exclaim. I watch my father's face and listen to my mother's words, and I feel better. My new city will soon be my new home.

a. ✓ The writer gave the essay a title.

b. ☐ He wrote an introduction.

c. ☐ He indented the first sentence in a paragraph.

d. ☐ He capitalized names all the time.

e. ☐ He used correct punctuation all the time.

f. ☐ He wrote a conclusion.

3. **Look in your dictionary. *True* or *False*?**

    a. The writing assignment is due on September 3. ___false___

    b. The student has time to think about the assignment. _____

    c. He brainstorms ideas with other students. _____

    d. He organizes his ideas in his notebook. _____

    e. He writes a first draft on his computer. _____

    f. He edits his paper in red. _____

    g. He revises his paper before he turns it in. _____

    h. The student gets feedback from his teacher. _____

    i. He turns in his paper late. _____

    j. The composition is about his job. _____

4. **Put the words in the box into the correct columns.**

    ~~edit~~   brainstorm   get feedback   organize   rewrite

Prewriting	Writing and Revising	Sharing and Responding
_____	___edit___	_____
_____	_____	

5. **What about you? Check (✓) the columns.**

When I write a composition, I	Always	Sometimes	Never, but I would like to try this!
think about the assignment			
brainstorm ideas			
organize my ideas			
write a first draft			
edit my draft			
revise my draft			
get feedback			
write a final draft on a computer			

Challenge Write a three-paragraph essay about your life in this country. Write a first draft, edit your paper, get feedback, rewrite your essay, and turn it in to your teacher.

Mathematics

1. **Look in your dictionary. Cross out the word that doesn't belong.**

   a. **Shapes** ~~endpoint~~ rectangle circle square

   b. **Parts of a circle** radius right angle diameter circumference

   c. **Types of math** geometry algebra calculus parallelogram

   d. **Geometric solids** triangle cone sphere cylinder

   e. **Lines** straight perpendicular pyramid curved

   f. **Math operations** add subtract variable divide

   g. **Answers to math operations** base difference sum product

   h. **Types of integers** even odd positive quotient

   i. **Types of angles** acute obtuse rectangle right

2. **Complete the test. Use the words in the box.**

denominator	equation	negative	numerator
~~odd~~	product	sum	variable

   MATH 103   **TEST**

   Complete the sentences.

   1. 121 is an _____*odd*_____ number.

   2. –7 is a _____ number.

   3. The _____ in 1/2 is 2.

   4. The _____ in 1/2 is 1.

   5. The _____ of 10 + 3 is 13.

   6. The _____ of 10 x 3 is 30.

   7. An _____ has an equal (=) sign.

   8. In an equation, *x* is a _____.

3. Look in your dictionary. Circle the words to complete the sentences.

a. A triangle has three <u>curved</u> / <u>(straight)</u> lines.

b. A <u>graph</u> / <u>parallelogram</u> has a horizontal and vertical axis.

c. Perpendicular lines make <u>acute</u> / <u>right</u> angles.

d. For 18 ÷ 2 = *x*, *x* = 9 is the <u>product</u> / <u>solution</u>.

e. <u>A word problem</u> / <u>An equation</u> ends with a question.

4. Label the pictures. Use the words in the box.

| ~~circle~~ | cube | curved line | cylinder | triangle |
| cone | pyramid | sphere | square | |

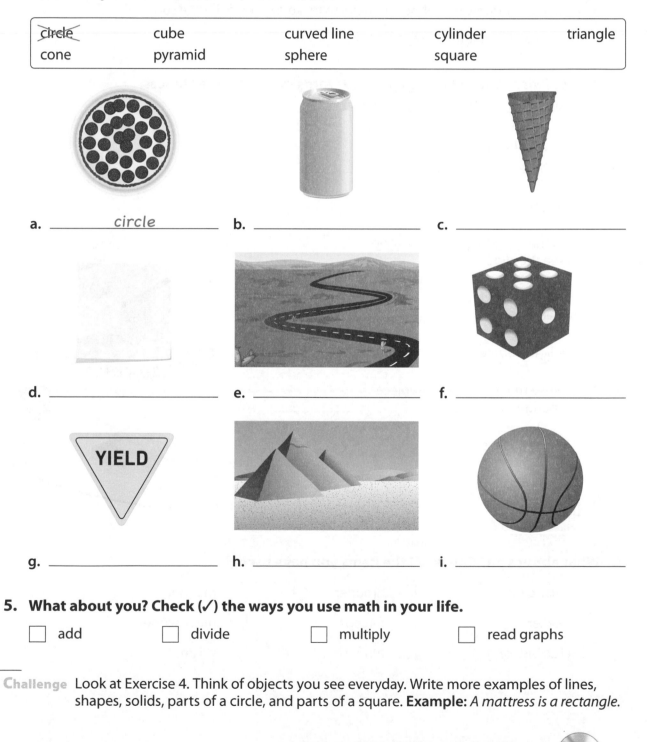

a. _____*circle*_____   b. _____   c. _____

d. _____   e. _____   f. _____

g. _____   h. _____   i. _____

5. What about you? Check (✓) the ways you use math in your life.

☐ add   ☐ divide   ☐ multiply   ☐ read graphs

Challenge Look at Exercise 4. Think of objects you see everyday. Write more examples of lines, shapes, solids, parts of a circle, and parts of a square. **Example:** *A mattress is a rectangle.*

See page 305 for listening practice.

1. Look in your dictionary. Circle the words to complete the sentences.

a. The ⟨biologist⟩/ chemist is observing something through a microscope.

b. The chemist / physicist has a formula on the board.

c. The chemist is using the periodic table / a prism.

d. An atom has chromosomes / protons.

e. Birds are vertebrates / invertebrates.

f. Plants use organisms / photosynthesis to make oxygen from the sun.

g. The ocean is a habitat / stage for fish.

2. _True_ or _False_? Correct the underlined words in the false sentences. You can use your dictionary for help.

a. You look through
the ~~fine adjustment knob.~~   *eyepiece*   ___false___

b. The slide goes on the base.   _____

c. Turn the coarse adjustment knob
to see the slide better.   _____

d. Stage clips hold the slide
in place.   _____

e. The light source is on the stage.   _____

f. You use the revolving nosepiece
to change the objective.   _____

g. The objective is connected
to the base.   _____

h. The diaphragm is under
the stage.   _____

3. What about you? Check (✓) the items you have used.

☐ balance   ☐ dropper   ☐ magnet

☐ beaker   ☐ forceps   ☐ microscope

☐ crucible tongs   ☐ funnel   ☐ prism

4. Complete the inventory. Write the number of items in the science lab.

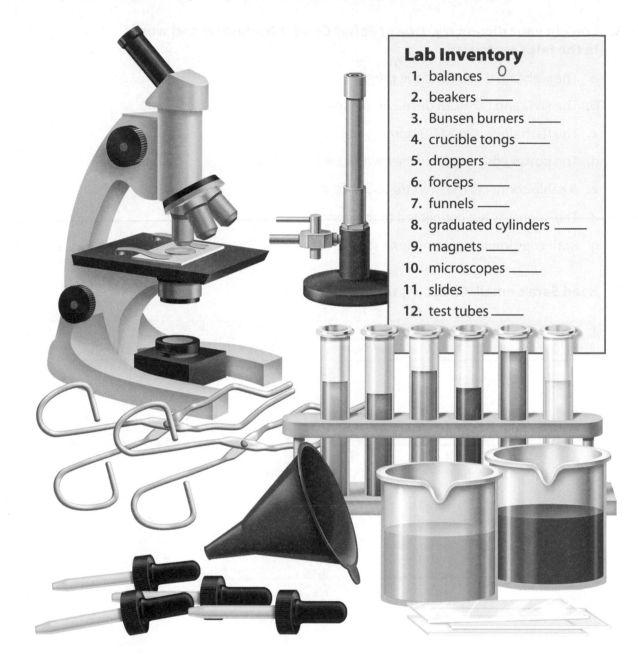

Lab Inventory
1. balances __0__
2. beakers _____
3. Bunsen burners _____
4. crucible tongs _____
5. droppers _____
6. forceps _____
7. funnels _____
8. graduated cylinders _____
9. magnets _____
10. microscopes _____
11. slides _____
12. test tubes _____

5. Number the steps of an experiment in the correct order. (1 = the first step)

____ **a.** Observe.

_1_ **b.** State a hypothesis.

____ **c.** Draw a conclusion.

____ **d.** Do an experiment.

____ **e.** Record the results.

Challenge Find out about three items in Exercise 4. What are they used for? Make a list.
Example: *crucible tongs—to hold hot items*

1. Look in your dictionary. *True* or *False*? Correct the underlined words in the false sentences.

    monitor

a. The webcam is on top of the ~~printer~~.   *false*

b. The DVD and CD-ROM drive is in the <u>tower</u>.   _____

c. The flash drive is in a <u>USB port</u>.   _____

d. The power cord connects the tower to the <u>monitor</u>.   _____

e. A <u>cable</u> connects the monitor to the keyboard.   _____

f. The mouse is not connected to the <u>printer</u>.   _____

g. Both computers have the same <u>software</u>.   _____

2. Read Sara's email. Check (✓) the things Sara did.

My Mail   — □ X

| New | Forward | Send | Delete | Junk |

To: bestpal@iol.us
Cc:
Reply to:
Subject: New computer

Hi,

I How are you?

I'm using my new computer! It's
a lap top, and I love it. See you later.

Sara

Before

My Mail   — □ X

| New | Forward | Send | Delete | Junk |

To: bestpal@iol.us
Cc:
Reply to:
Subject: New computer

Hi,

I'm using my new computer!

It's a laptop, and I really love it.

How are you?

See you later,

Sara

After

- ✓ select text
- ☐ delete a letter
- ☐ delete a word

- ☐ delete a space
- ☐ go to the next line
- ☐ type a word between *I* and *love*

Challenge   Which do you think is better: a desktop computer or a laptop? Why? Tell a classmate.

1. Look in your dictionary. Match.

1.  2. 3. 4.

__4__ **a.** back button ____ **b.** pointer ____ **c.** forward button ____ **d.** cursor

2. What do you need to . . . ? Use the words in the box.

scroll bar	~~search box~~	search engine	text box	video player

a. look for information on the Web   ____*search box*____ and _____

b. move up and down the screen   _____

c. type your password   _____

d. watch a movie on your computer   _____

3. Look at Todd's email. *True* or *False*?

a. Todd addressed the email.   __*true*__

b. He typed the subject.   _____

c. He typed the message in blue.   _____

d. He attached a picture.   _____

e. He attached a file.   _____

f. He checked the spelling.   _____

4. What about you? Check (✓) the ways you use the Internet.

☐ send email   ☐ shop   ☐ pay bills   ☐ play online games

Challenge List other ways to use the Internet. Compare your list with a classmate's.

1. **Look in your dictionary. Cross out the word that doesn't belong.**

   a. **People**   colonists   founders   ~~Bill of Rights~~

   b. **Documents**   Continental Congress   Constitution   Declaration of Independence

   c. **Soldiers**   minutemen   thirteen colonies   redcoats

   d. **Wars**   Revolutionary   Civil   Industrial Revolution

2. **Look at the headlines. Label the events. Use the words in the box.**

Civil Rights Movement	Jazz Age	Information Age
Great Depression	Space Age	~~Western Expansion~~

   a. _Western Expansion_

   b. _____

   c. _____

   d. _____

   e. _____

   f. _____

3. **What about you? Check (✓) the time periods you know about. Circle the time periods you want to learn more about.**

   ☐ Civil War   ☐ Global Age   ☐ World War II

   ☐ Cold War   ☐ Industrial Revolution   ☐ Other: _____

   ☐ Reconstruction

   Challenge Choose a time period from Exercise 3. Look online, or in an encyclopedia or history book. Write a short paragraph about that time period. When was it? What are two interesting events from that period?

1. Look in your dictionary. Match.

__4__ **a.** president

____ **b.** prime minister

____ **c.** emperor

____ **d.** dictator

1. Churchill

2. Mussolini

3. Qin Shi Huang

4. Juarez

2. What are these photos of? Use the words in the box.

ancient civilization	composition	exploration	monarch	war
modern civilization	~~invention~~	political movement	immigration	

a. _invention_

b. _____

c. _____

d. _____

e. _____

f. _____

g. _____

h. _____

i. _____

Challenge Write the name of a famous explorer, an inventor, and an immigrant. Where did they come from? What are they famous for? **Example:** *Sammy Sosa is a famous baseball player from the Dominican Republic.*

See page 307 for listening practice.

1. Look in your dictionary. Answer the questions.

a. Which states in the United States are on the Gulf of Mexico?

___Texas___ _____ _____ _____ _____

b. Which parts of Canada are on the Hudson Bay?

_____ _____ _____ _____

c. Which states in Mexico touch the United States?

_____ _____ _____ _____ _____

d. Which countries in Central America are on the Pacific Ocean?

_____ _____ _____ _____ _____

_____

e. Name four islands in the Caribbean Sea.

_____ _____ _____ _____

2. Label the parts of Canada and the United States. Use your dictionary for help.

In Canada

a. _Prince Edward Island_   b. _____   c. _____

In the United States

d. _____   e. _____   f. _____

200

3. Look in your dictionary. Circle the words to complete the sentences.

In Canada

a. Alberta is (east) / west of British Columbia.

b. Yukon is <u>east / west</u> of the Northwest Territories.

c. Nova Scotia is <u>east / west</u> of New Brunswick.

In the United States

d. California is <u>north / south</u> of Oregon.

e. Idaho is <u>north / south</u> of Utah.

f. Wisconsin is <u>east / west</u> of Minnesota.

In Central America

g. Nicaragua is <u>north / south</u> of Costa Rica.

h. Honduras is <u>northeast / northwest</u> of El Salvador.

i. Guatemala is <u>southeast / southwest</u> of Belize.

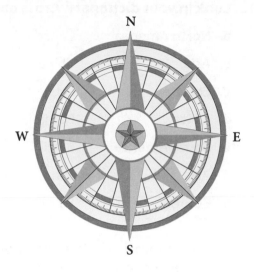

4. Match the state or province with the region and country. Write the number and a letter for each item. Use your dictionary for help.

State or Province	Region	Country
<u>5, A</u> a. Alberta	1. The Maritime Provinces	A. Canada
_____ b. Campeche	2. The Midwest	B. Mexico
_____ c. Illinois	3. New England	C. United States
_____ d. Massachusetts	4. The Southern Uplands	
_____ e. Nova Scotia	5. The Prairie Provinces	
_____ f. Jalisco	6. The Yucatan Peninsula	

5. What about you? Look at the map in your dictionary. Where have you visited? When were you there? Write sentences.

Example: *I drove to Nova Scotia in 2007.*

_____

_____

_____

_____

Challenge Imagine you are driving from Manitoba, Canada, to Durango, Mexico. List, in order, the states you drive through. Use your dictionary for help.

1. Look in your dictionary. Cross out the word that doesn't belong.

a. North America	Canada	United States	~~Chile~~	Mexico
b. Asia	China	Poland	India	Philippines
c. Europe	Latvia	Ukraine	Belarus	Kazakhstan
d. Africa	Namibia	Peru	Botswana	Sudan
e. South America	Brazil	Paraguay	Guatemala	Colombia
f. Asia	Syria	Iran	Saudi Arabia	Romania
g. Europe	Egypt	France	Germany	Sweden

2. List the countries in the box in order of population size. (1 = the most people) Use your dictionary for help.

Argentina	Belarus	Italy	Kenya
Mexico	~~Pakistan~~	Saudi Arabia	South Korea

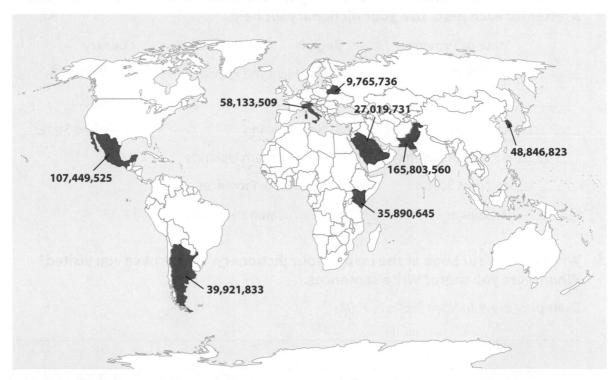

Based on information from: *The World Almanac and Book of Facts, 2007.* (New York, 2007)

1. _Pakistan_   5. _____

2. _____   6. _____

3. _____   7. _____

4. _____   8. _____

3. **Look in your dictionary. How many neighbors does . . . have? Write the number. Then write the names of the countries.**

a. **In Europe**

Romania   5   Moldova, Bulgaria, Ukraine, Serbia, Hungary

b. **In South America**

Paraguay   ____   _____

c. **In Africa**

Chad   ____   _____

d. **In Asia**

Thailand   ____   _____

e. **In North America**

Mexico   ____   _____

4. **Label the oceans. Use the words in the box.**

| Atlantic Ocean | ~~Arctic Ocean~~ | Indian Ocean | Pacific Ocean |

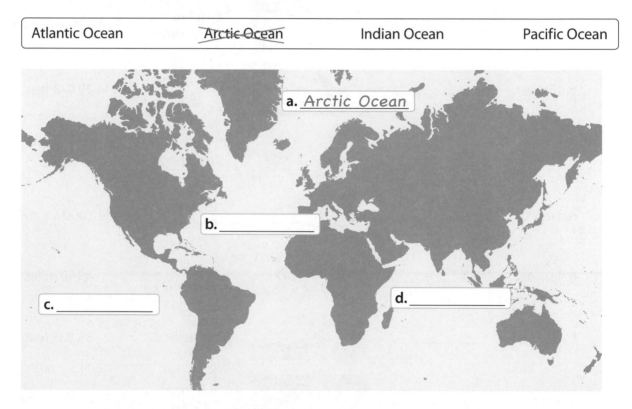

a. Arctic Ocean

b. _____

c. _____

d. _____

5. **What about you? Complete the information.**

My native country   Continent   Population

_____   _____   _____

Number of neighbors   The names of your country's neighbors

_____   _____

Challenge Choose one country. Find out information about it. Use Exercise 5 as an example.

1. **Look in your dictionary. Put the words in the correct columns.**

	Land		Water
rain forest	_____	_____	_____
_____	_____	_____	_____
_____	_____	_____	_____
_____	_____	_____	_____
_____	_____	_____	_____
			_____

2. **Complete the chart. Use words from Exercise 1.**

a. largest	_lake_		Caspian Sea (Asia/Europe)	143,244 sq. miles
b. highest	_____		Everest (Asia)	29,078 feet
c. largest	_____		Sahara (N. Africa)	3,500,000 sq. miles
d. largest	_____		Greenland (Denmark)	840,000 sq. miles
e. longest	_____		Nile (Africa)	4,160 miles
f. deepest	_____		Pacific	35,837 feet
g. largest	_____		Bengal (S. Asia)	839,000 sq. miles

3. **What about you? Check (✓) the places you've visited.**

☐ waterfall   ☐ desert   ☐ ocean

☐ canyon   ☐ bay   ☐ mountain range

Challenge Look at pages 202 and 203 in your dictionary. Write the names of two islands and two oceans. Do not use the ones from Exercise 2.

1. Look in your dictionary. *True* or *False*?

a. There are nine planets in our solar system.   _false_

b. The sun looks dark during a solar eclipse.   _____

c. The astronaut is looking through a telescope at the space station.   _____

d. The astronomer is at an observatory.   _____

e. There are six stars in the constellation.   _____

2. Complete the chart with the names of the planets. Then answer the questions.

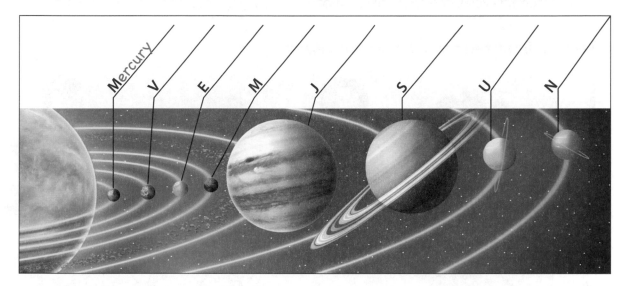

Which planet . . . ?

a. is closest to the sun   _Mercury_   e. has many rings around it   _____

b. is farthest from the sun   _____   f. is between Saturn and Neptune   _____

c. is the largest   _____   g. is our home   _____

d. is between Mercury and Earth   _____

3. What about you? Check (✓) the things you see in the sky tonight.

☐ planets   Which one(s)?   _____

☐ the moon   Which phase?   ☐ new   ☐ full   ☐ quarter   ☐ crescent

☐ stars   ☐ constellations   ☐ comets   ☐ satellites

Challenge   Find out the names of three different constellations. What do they look like? Talk about your answers with a classmate.

1. Look in your dictionary. *True* or *False*?

a. Adelia is wearing a red cap and gown.   _false_

b. The photographer is upset with the students.   _____

c. Adelia is crying in the serious photo.   _____

d. The guest speaker is taking a picture.   _____

e. The mayor is standing at the podium.   _____

f. The ceremony is funny.   _____

g. The students celebrate after the ceremony.   _____

2. Look at the pictures and the captions. Match.

_5_ a. Here's my Dad taking pictures.

____ b. Nice cap and gown!

____ c. My Mom cries when she's happy!

____ d. Hey! Where's the guest speaker?

____ e. A serious ceremony.

____ f. It's time to celebrate!

3. Look at the photos in Exercise 2. Circle the words to complete the email.

My Mail

Send To: Paljo@eol.us

Subject: Graduation

I'm attaching some photos from my graduation day.

Do you remember my father? There he is with his camera. He's the family

guest speaker / (photographer.)
a.

That's a picture of the cap / podium before the mayor spoke. She was the
b.

guest speaker this year.

The woman is my mother. She always celebrates / cries at ceremonies.
c.

The funny / serious photo of me is at the ceremony. I'm getting
d.

my diploma / gown.
e.

Finally, it was time to celebrate / take a picture! That's me with Adelia and
f.

another classmate. Don't we look happy?

I wish you had been there, too!

M

4. What about you? Answer the questions.

a. Were you ever at a graduation? ☐ Yes ☐ No

b. Who was there? ☐ a photographer ☐ a guest speaker

   ☐ Other: _____

c. Did you cry? ☐ Yes ☐ No   If *yes*, why? _____

d. Did you celebrate after the graduation? ☐ Yes ☐ No   If *yes*, how? _____

Challenge   Look in your dictionary. Read the comments on page 207. Write five more comments about the photos on Adelia's webpage.

1. Look in your dictionary. True or False?

a. You can buy flowers at the nature center. _____false_____

b. There's a bird on the roof. _____

c. Some of the plants are red. _____

d. There's a shovel near the soil. _____

e. Some children are playing on the path. _____

f. A man is painting a picture of the trees. _____

2. Look in your dictionary. How many types of . . . can you see?

a. trees ___4___   c. birds ___   e. fish ___

b. insects ___   d. mammals ___   f. flowers ___

3. Complete the signs. Use the words in the box.

| birds | sun | flowers | paths | rocks | ~~trees~~ |

a.

PLEASE DON'T CLIMB THE _____trees_____.

b.

Look and smell, but please DON'T pick the _____!

c.

Please DON'T feed the _____!

d.

Keep off the grass. Stay on the _____.

e.

Don't throw the _____!

f.

The _____ is strong. Wear a hat and drink water!

4. **Look in your dictionary. Circle the words to complete the sentences.**

   a. A man with a magnifying glass is looking at fish / (insects).

   b. There's a sign with pictures of fish / mammals.

   c. The sky / sun is blue.

   d. There are no birds in the nest / water.

5. **Look at the sign. Label the pictures. Use the words in the box.**

birds	fish	flowers	insects	mammals
paths	water	sun	~~trees~~	

LILLO Nature Center

Enjoy...

a. ___trees___   b. _____   c. _____

d. _____   e. _____   f. _____

g. _____   h. _____   i. _____

6. **What about you? Check (✓) the things you can find near your school.**

   ☐ trees   ☐ paths   ☐ plants

   ☐ birds   ☐ rocks   ☐ flowers

Challenge Look at page 255 in this book. Follow the instructions.

Trees and Plants

1. Look in your dictionary. *True* or *False*?

a. A tree has roots, limbs, branches, and twigs.   _____true_____

b. Holly is a plant.   _____

c. The birch tree has yellow leaves.   _____

d. The magnolia and dogwood trees have flowers.   _____

e. The cactus has berries.   _____

f. Poison sumac has a trunk.   _____

g. Poison ivy has three leaves.   _____

h. The willow has pinecones.   _____

i. A vine has needles.   _____

2. Look at the bar graph. Number the trees in order of height. (1 = the tallest)

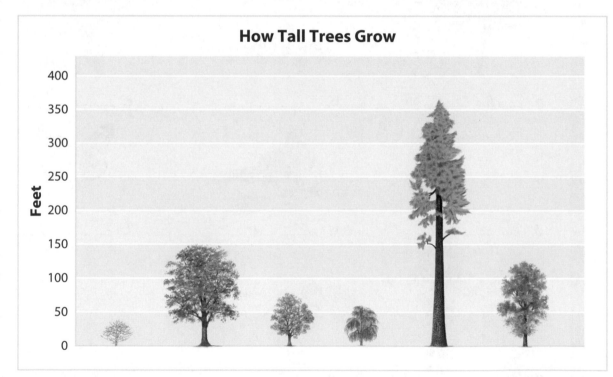

How Tall Trees Grow

Based on information from: Petrides, G.: *Peterson Field Guides. Trees and Shrubs.*
(NY: Houghton Mifflin Co., 1986)

_____ a. dogwood

_____ b. elm

_____ c. maple

_____ d. oak

__1__ e. redwood

_____ f. willow

Challenge Which trees grow near your home? Make a list.

See page 309 for listening practice.

1. Look in your dictionary. Circle the words to complete the sentences.

a. The <u>bouquet</u> / (marigold) is orange.

b. The <u>tulip / crocus</u> and the <u>gardenia / poinsettia</u> are red.

c. The <u>chrysanthemum / daffodil</u> and the <u>houseplant / lily</u> are yellow.

d. The <u>carnation / jasmine</u> and the <u>daisy / orchid</u> are white.

2. What goes below the ground? What goes above the ground? Put the words in the box in the correct part of the diagram.

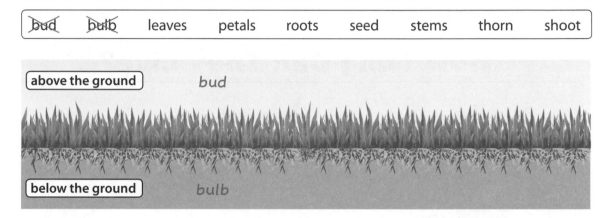

~~bud~~   ~~bulb~~   leaves   petals   roots   seed   stems   thorn   shoot

above the ground   *bud*

below the ground   *bulb*

3. Look at the pictures. Match the state name with the flower name. Use pages 200 and 201 in your dictionary for help.

<u>3</u> **a.** Kansas   **1.** iris

___ **b.** Illinois   **2.** rose

___ **c.** New York   **3.** sunflower

___ **d.** Tennessee   **4.** violet

___ **e.** Hawaii   **5.** hibiscus

4. What about you? What flowers grow in your . . . ?

home _____   neighborhood _____   country _____

Challenge Find out the names of three other state flowers. Make a list.

1. Look in your dictionary. Cross out the word that doesn't belong. Write the category.

a. _____Reptiles_____   turtle   alligator   ~~seal~~   crocodile

b. _____   fin   gills   scales   scallop

c. _____   seahorse   frog   toad   newt

d. _____   sea lion   dolphin   lizard   sea otter

e. _____   tuna   whale   bass   swordfish

2. Look at the chart. Circle the words to complete the sentences. Use your dictionary for help.

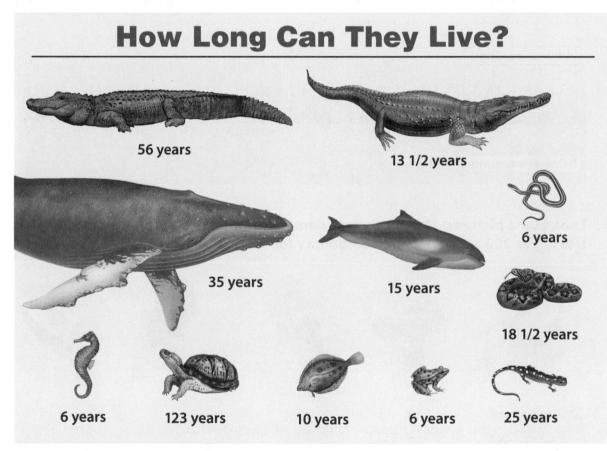

How Long Can They Live?

56 years

13 1/2 years

6 years

35 years

15 years

18 1/2 years

6 years   123 years   10 years   6 years   25 years

Based on information from: Texas Parks and Wildlife http://www.tpwd.state.tx.us/publications/ nonpwdpubs /young_naturalist/animals/animal_life_spans/

a. The (alligator) / crocodile can live fifty-six years.

b. The flounder / garter snake can live ten years.

c. The garter snake / rattlesnake can live eighteen and a half years.

d. The porpoise / seahorse can live fifteen years.

e. The frog / salamander can live twenty-five years.

f. The turtle / whale can live 123 years!

3. **Find and circle 14 more sea animal words. The words go across (→) and down (↓).**

```
J E L L Y F I S H A R
P E R B O S T Q L W A
E L S W O R M U P E D
S Y S A R M M I M A T
E O T R A P O D U S O
A C A M Y E T Y S H R
H T R E L J U D S A T
O O F L O U N D E R O
R P I M S N A I L K I
S U S X I D R B A S S
E S H R I M P O L O E
```

4. **What about you? Make two lists using the words from Exercise 3.**

Things I Eat	Things I Don't Eat

Challenge Add to your lists in Exercise 4. Use your dictionary for help.

1. **Look in your dictionary. Complete the chart.**

Name of Bird	Habitat*	Physical Appearance
a. robin	■ ■ ■ ■	brown with orange breast
b.	■ ■	blue with white on wings, head, and breast
c.	■ ■	large; brown with white head and tail; big yellow beak and claws
d.	■	large head, flat face with big eyes; brown and white feathers
e.	■ ■	blue-black feathers with purple throat
f.	■ ■	green with red throat; long, thin bill
g.	■	large; long black neck and head; white "chin" and breast
h.	■	black and white with small red spot on head; small bill
i.	■	green head and neck; white neck "ring"; brown chest and tail
j.	■ ■	small; brown, white, and gray feathers

*where the bird lives: ■ = forests   ■ = water   ■ = mountains   ■ = farms   ■ = suburban gardens   ■ = cities

2. **Look at the picture. Check (✓) the things you see.**

✓ honeybee	☐ scorpion	☐ grasshopper	☐ ladybug	☐ mosquito
☐ fly	☐ moth	☐ spider	☐ wasp	☐ tick
☐ beetle	☐ butterfly	☐ caterpillar		

Challenge Make a list of the birds and insects you can see near your home.

See page 310 for listening practice.

1. Look in your dictionary. Cross out the word that doesn't belong.

a. Pets	dog	goldfish	guinea pig	~~prairie dog~~
b. Farm animals	horse	cow	gopher	pig
c. Rodents	rat	mouse	squirrel	goat
d. Birds	parakeet	donkey	rooster	hen

2. Look at the ad. Check (✓) the animals you see.

PETE'S PET STORE
We have...
The Most Popular Pets in the United States

Visit us at 232 Parkside Avenue.

Based on information from: *The World Almanac for Kids, 2004.* (NY: World Almanac Education Group, Inc., 2003)

✓ goldfish	☐ gopher	☐ dog	☐ parakeet
☐ mouse	☐ donkey	☐ cat	☐ guinea pig
☐ pig	☐ sheep	☐ rabbit	☐ chipmunk

Challenge Survey your classmates. Find out if they had pets in their native countries. Which pets are popular?

1. Look in your dictionary. *True* or *False*?

a. The beaver lives in North America. _____true_____

b. The lion lives in South America. _____

c. The chimpanzee lives in Africa. _____

d. The orangutan lives in Asia. _____

e. The llama lives in Australia. _____

2. Look at the pictures. Circle the words to complete the sentences.

a. The antelope / (deer) has antlers / horns.

b. The platypus / porcupine has long, sharp quills / whiskers.

c. The camel / llama has a hump / trunk.

d. The lion / mountain lion has four hooves / paws.

e. The bear / monkey has a long tail / neck.

f. The hyena / kangaroo has a pouch / trunk.

g. The elephant / rhinoceros has horns / tusks.

h. The raccoon / skunk has a black and white coat / mane.

3. Look at the chart. Check (✓) the mammals that are endangered.*

SOME ENDANGERED* MAMMALS

*endangered = very few are still living; they may not continue to live.

Based on information from: World Wildlife Fund (2006) and WildFinder: Online database of species distributions, ver. Jan-06. http://www.worldwildlife.org/WildFinder

☐ anteater	✓ armadillo	☐ baboon	☐ black rhinoceros
☐ brown bear	☐ buffalo	☐ camel	☐ coyote
☐ elephant	☐ giraffe	☐ gorilla	☐ gray bat
☐ hippopotamus	☐ kangaroo	☐ koala	☐ leopard
☐ moose	☐ mountain lion	☐ opossum	☐ panda
☐ panther	☐ red wolf	☐ tiger	☐ zebra

Challenge Look online or in an encyclopedia for information about one of the mammals in your dictionary. Where does it live? What does it eat? How long does it live? Is it endangered? Write a paragraph.

See page 311 for listening practice.   **217**

1. **Look in your dictionary. Which energy sources come from . . . ?**

Atoms	The Earth	Water
nuclear energy	_____	_____
_____	_____	**The Sun**
Air	_____	_____
_____	_____	

2. **Look at the newspaper headlines. Match them with the types of pollution.**

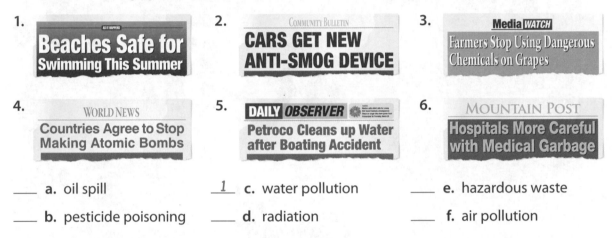

1. **Beaches Safe for** Swimming This Summer
2. COMMUNITY BULLETIN — **CARS GET NEW ANTI-SMOG DEVICE**
3. Media *WATCH* — Farmers Stop Using Dangerous Chemicals on Grapes
4. WORLD NEWS — **Countries Agree to Stop Making Atomic Bombs**
5. DAILY *OBSERVER* — **Petroco Cleans up Water after Boating Accident**
6. MOUNTAIN POST — **Hospitals More Careful with Medical Garbage**

___ **a.** oil spill   _1_ **c.** water pollution   ___ **e.** hazardous waste

___ **b.** pesticide poisoning   ___ **d.** radiation   ___ **f.** air pollution

3. **Look at the bar graph. Number the energy sources in order. (1 = used the most)**

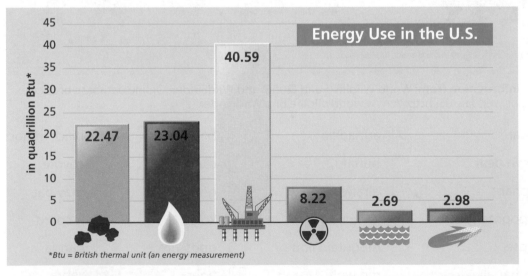

Energy Use in the U.S.

in quadrillion Btu*

22.47   23.04   40.59   8.22   2.69   2.98

Btu = British thermal unit (an energy measurement)

Based on information from: *The World Almanac and Book of Facts 2007.* (NY: World Almanac Education Group, Inc., 2007)

_1_ **a.** oil   ___ **c.** coal   ___ **e.** natural gas

___ **b.** biomass   ___ **d.** hydroelectric power   ___ **f.** nuclear energy

4. Look in your dictionary. What do these people do to conserve energy and resources?

> I never leave lights on when I leave a room.

a. _____turn off lights_____

> I always keep it at 68° in the winter.

f. _____

> I really don't need to use hot or warm water to get my shirts clean.

b. _____

> I drive to work with three people from my office.

g. _____

> I don't use paper cups for my coffee.

c. _____

> This plastic bottle goes in one of the blue containers.

h. _____

> I turn off the faucet when I brush my teeth.

d. _____

> I always bring my own bag.

i. _____

> I *never* throw things out the car window!

e. _____

> I repair our faucets so they use less water.

j. _____

5. What about you? How often do you . . . ? Check (✓) the columns.

	Always	Sometimes	Never
buy recycled products			
save water			
turn off lights			
use energy-efficient bulbs			
adjust the thermostat			
carpool			
compost food scraps			
plant trees			
Other: _____			

Challenge List three other ways to conserve water or electricity. **Example:** *I don't water my lawn.*

1. Look in your dictionary. In which pictures can you see . . . ? Check (✓) the columns.

	Yosemite	Dry Tortugas	Carlsbad Caverns
a. landmarks	✓	✓	
b. a ferry			
c. coral			
d. caves			
e. park rangers			
f. wildlife			
g. people taking a tour			

2. Look at the map symbols. Match.

1.  2. 3. 4.

5.  6.  7.

_3_ **a.** park ranger

___ **b.** ferry

___ **c.** landmark

___ **d.** path

___ **e.** tour

___ **f.** wildlife

___ **g.** coral

3. Look at the map. *True* or *False*? Use the symbols in Exercise 2 for help.

a. There are two landmarks in this park. _____ true _____

b. You can get a ferry near one of the landmarks. _____

c. There's a path to the wildlife area. _____

d. There are park rangers near the landmarks. _____

e. You can find coral near the ferry. _____

f. You can take a tour of this park. _____

4. Complete the postcard. Use the words in the box.

| caves |
| coral |
| park ranger |
| ~~tour~~ |
| paths |
| wildlife |

Carlsbad Caverns is great! Today we took a
___ tour ___ of the _____. They are DARK!
   a.   b.
A _____ held a big flashlight so we could
    c.
see. Tania was afraid of the bats. I prefer bats to
other _____. (Last year we saw bears at
       d.
Yosemite!) She also says she likes to hike on
_____ above ground—not 830 feet below
  e.
the desert. And, of course, she loved the pretty
pink _____ we saw in Florida two years
    f.
ago. But for me, Carlsbad is the best park in
the world! Vlad

ADDRESS

5. What about you? Look in your dictionary. Which national park would you like to visit? Why? Tell a classmate.

Challenge Imagine you visited Yosemite or Dry Tortugas National Park. What did you do there? What did you see? Write a postcard about the experience.

1. **Look at page 222 in your dictionary. Put the words in the correct columns.**

Inside Events	Outside Events
_____	_____zoo_____
_____	_____
_____	_____
_____	

2. **Look at the events in Exercise 1. Where can you go to . . . ?**

    a. listen to music   _____rock concert_____

    b. see animals   _____

    c. see fish   _____

    d. buy clothes   _____

    e. watch a film   _____

    f. see flowers and plants   _____

    g. play a game   _____

3. **Circle the words to complete the sentences.**

    a. It's nice to walk through the ~~botanical gardens~~ / movies.

    b. Elissa bought a used T-shirt at the bowling alley / swap meet.

    c. There's a new baby elephant at the aquarium / zoo.

    d. The music was very loud at the botanical gardens / rock concert.

4. **What about you? How often do you go to . . . ? Complete the chart.**

	Often	Sometimes	Never	Never, but I'd like to go
a zoo				
the movies				
a botanical garden				
a bowling alley				
a swap meet				
a rock concert				
an aquarium				

5. Look at page 223 in your dictionary. Complete the event listings below.

WHAT'S HAPPENING

ART

NEWPORT _Art Museum_
a.
Special exhibit of sculpture and paintings by local artists. Through August 25. **$5.00**.

MUSIC

CITY CENTER

Adriana Domingo sings the leading role in Antonio Rivera's new _____,
b.
Starry Night. 8:00 P.M., August 14 and 15.

Tickets $10–$30.

PLUM HALL

Oakland Chamber Orchestra, with Lily Marksen at the piano, performs a _____
c.
featuring works by Beethoven, Bach, and Brahms. 8:00 P.M., August 15.

Tickets $20–$30.

THEATER

CURTAINS UP

The Downtown Players perform *The Argument*, a new _____ by J.L. Mason, starring
d.
Vanessa Thompson and Tyrone Williams as a married couple. Through August 20. **Tickets $20**.

CHILDREN

CROWN_____
e.
Roller coaster, merry-go-round, and other rides provide fun for kids and adults. Great popcorn, too! **Open daily**.

10:00 A.M. TO 5:00 P.M. **Free admission**.

GENERAL INTEREST

Newport _____
f.
Food, exhibitions, and prizes for best cow, quilt, and more.

August 14–15, 10:00 A.M. TO SUNSET. **Free**.

Sal's_____
g.
Dance to the music of the rock band, Jumpin' Lizzards. 8:00 P.M. TO MIDNIGHT. Must be 18 or older (ID required). **$10.00** (includes 1 beverage).

---

6. Look at the events in Exercise 5. *True* or *False*?

a. The play is free. _____false_____

b. You can see an opera at City Center. _____

c. The county fair is open nights. _____

d. A seventeen-year-old can go to Sal's. _____

e. There's an afternoon concert at Plum Hall on August 15. _____

f. Tickets to the amusement park are expensive. _____

g. You can see the special art exhibit for $5.00. _____

Challenge Look at the listings in Exercise 5. Talk to two classmates and agree on a place to go. Write your decision and give a reason.

1. **Look in your dictionary. Where can you . . . ?**

a. have a picnic _picnic table_

b. play baseball _____

c. see a cyclist _____

d. get a drink _____

e. push a swing _____

f. sit and read _____

2. **Look at the map. Complete the legend. Use the words in the box.**

| ball field   bike path   fountain   picnic table   playground   ~~tennis court~~   water fountain |

a. _tennis court_

b. _____

c. _____

d. _____

e. _____

f. _____

g. _____

3. **Look at the map in Exercise 2. _True_ or _False_?**

a. There's a water fountain in the playground. _____true_____

b. The tennis court is to the left of the ball field. _____

c. There's a seesaw in the playground. _____

d. There are benches near the swings. _____

e. The bike path goes around the fountain. _____

4. **What about you? Check (✓) the activities you did as a child.**

☐ ride a tricycle   ☐ go down a slide   ☐ use a jump rope

☐ climb the bars   ☐ pull a wagon   ☐ picnic in the park

☐ play in the sandbox   ☐ ride a skateboard   ☐ Other: _____

Challenge Look at the park in your dictionary. What are people doing? Write eight sentences.
Example: _A little boy is riding a tricycle._

1. Look in your dictionary. What are people using to . . . ?

    a. play in the sand   _____pail_____

    b. sit on the sand   _____ and _____

    c. keep drinks and food cold   _____

    d. protect their skin from the sun   _____ and _____

    e. stay warm in the ocean   _____

    f. breathe underwater   _____

    g. see underwater   _____

2. Look at the chart. *True* or *False*?

Charles Beach	•		•		•	•	•
Moonstone Beach				•	•		•
Town Beach	•	•	•			•	

    a. You can swim at Charles Beach.   _____true_____

    b. Surfers can use their surfboards only at Moonstone Beach.   _____

    c. You can go out in your sailboat at Town Beach.   _____

    d. You can use a scuba tank at Charles Beach.   _____

    e. You can rent a beach umbrella at Moonstone Beach.   _____

    f. There's a lifeguard at all three beaches.   _____

    g. There's a pier at Town Beach.   _____

3. What about you? How important are these things to you? Circle the number.

	Very Important				Not Important
clean sand	4	3	2	1	0
big waves	4	3	2	1	0
seashells	4	3	2	1	0
lifeguard station	4	3	2	1	0

Challenge Look at the chart in Exercise 2. Which beach would you like to go to? Why?

1. Look in your dictionary. How many people are . . . ?

a. backpacking __1__   b. rafting ____   c. camping ____   d. canoeing ____

2. Look at the bar graph. *True* or *False*?

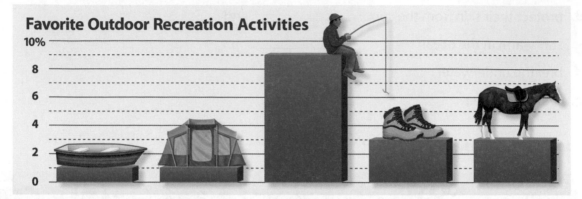

Favorite Outdoor Recreation Activities

Based on information from: 2003 Harris interactive poll survey.
http://www.harrisinteractive.com/harris_poll Harris Interactive Inc, 2004.

a. Only one percent of people said boating is their favorite activity. ____*true*____

b. Nine percent said fishing is their favorite. _____

c. Three percent said camping is their favorite. _____

d. Three percent said hiking is their favorite. _____

e. Two percent said horseback riding is their favorite. _____

3. Read the sentences. What do the people need? Match.

__5__ a. It's too dark in this tent. I can't read.   1. camping stove

____ b. It's cold. Let's build a campfire.   2. canteen

____ c. Where's my backpack? I'm thirsty.   3. fishing pole

____ d. Ouch! These mosquitoes keep biting me!   4. insect repellent

____ e. Brian's afraid of the water. He can't swim.   5. lantern

____ f. Everyone's hungry. I'll start the hamburgers.   6. life vest

____ g. I'm tired. Good night.   7. matches

____ h. I'd like to catch some of those trout in the lake.   8. sleeping bag

4. What about you? Check (✓) the activities you like.

☐ camping   ☐ mountain biking   ☐ fishing   ☐ canoeing

Challenge Choose your favorite outdoor activity. What do you need to do it? Make a list.

See page 313 for listening practice.

1. Look in your dictionary. Circle the words to complete the sentences.

    a. The man in the red vest is <u>cross-country skiing /</u> (<u>downhill skiing</u>)

    b. Two people are <u>snowboarding / sledding</u>.

    c. The skater with the white skates is <u>figure skating / ice skating</u>.

    d. A woman and man are <u>scuba diving / snorkeling</u>.

2. Look at the hotel information. Where should people stay? Write the letter(s).

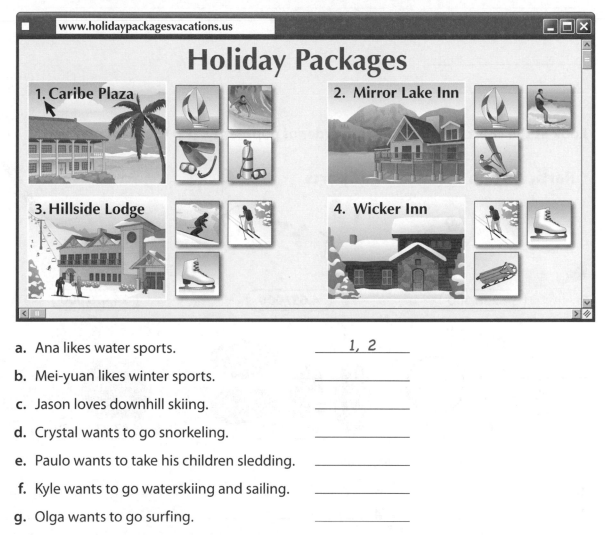

    a. Ana likes water sports.   <u> 1, 2 </u>

    b. Mei-yuan likes winter sports.   <u>   </u>

    c. Jason loves downhill skiing.   <u>   </u>

    d. Crystal wants to go snorkeling.   <u>   </u>

    e. Paulo wants to take his children sledding. <u>   </u>

    f. Kyle wants to go waterskiing and sailing. <u>   </u>

    g. Olga wants to go surfing.   <u>   </u>

    h. Taro loves sailing and windsurfing.   <u>   </u>

3. What about you? Look at Exercise 2. Where would you like to stay? Why?

    Example: *I want to stay at the Wicker Inn or Hillside Lodge. I like ice skating.*

    Challenge   Interview two people. Which winter or water sports do they like? Recommend a hotel from Exercise 2.

1. Look in your dictionary. Put the words in the correct columns.

Outdoor Sports	Indoor Sports	
archery		

2. Look at the chart. List the sports in order of popularity. (1 = the most popular)

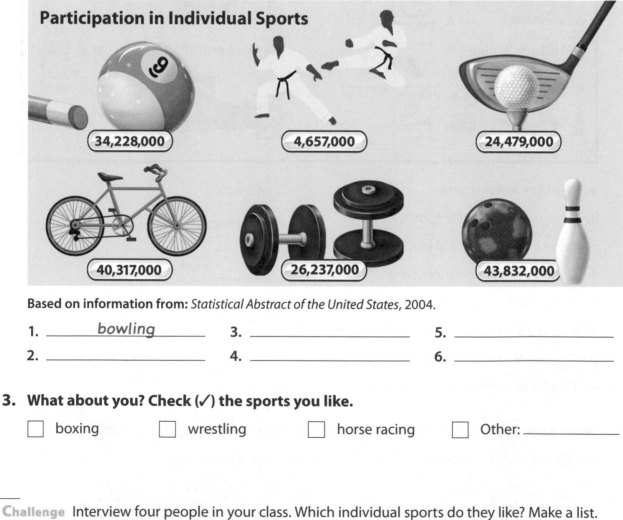

Participation in Individual Sports

34,228,000   4,657,000   24,479,000

40,317,000   26,237,000   43,832,000

Based on information from: *Statistical Abstract of the United States*, 2004.

1. ____*bowling*____   3. _____   5. _____

2. _____   4. _____   6. _____

3. What about you? Check (✓) the sports you like.

☐ boxing   ☐ wrestling   ☐ horse racing   ☐ Other: _____

Challenge Interview four people in your class. Which individual sports do they like? Make a list.
Example: *Two students like weightlifting.*

See page 314 for listening practice.

1. Look at the basketball court at the top of your dictionary page. Write the numbers.

a. How many teams are there?   <u>2</u>

b. How many fans are holding a sign?   ___

c. How many players can you see?   ___

d. How many coaches can you see?   ___

e. How many referees can you see?   ___

f. What's the score for the home team?   ___

2. Look at the bar graph. *True* or *False*? Correct the <u>underlined</u> words in the false sentences.

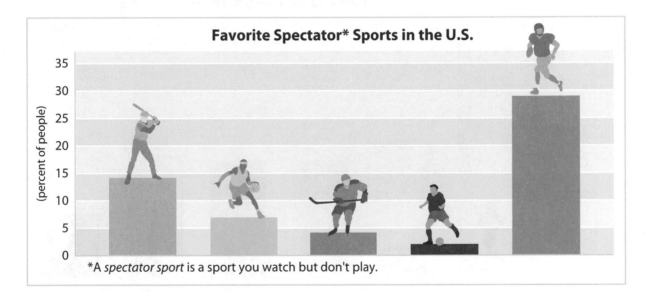

Favorite Spectator* Sports in the U.S.

(percent of people)

*A *spectator sport* is a sport you watch but don't play.

Based on information from: Harris Poll, January 9, 2007. http://www.harrisinteractive.com/harris_poll

a. Almost 15% said ~~ice hockey~~ *baseball* is their favorite sport.   <u>*false*</u>

b. Only 2% said <u>soccer</u> is their favorite.   _____

c. Almost 5% said <u>baseball</u> is their favorite.   _____

d. About 7% said <u>basketball</u> is their favorite.   _____

e. For almost 30%, <u>football</u> is their favorite sport.   _____

3. What about you? Circle the sports you play. <u>Underline</u> the sports you watch.

softball   football   basketball   baseball

volleyball   ice hockey   water polo   soccer

Challenge Go to page 256 in this book. Follow the instructions.

See page 314 for listening practice.   **229**

1. Look in your dictionary. Circle the words to complete the sentences.

a. One man is (kicking) / passing / throwing a football.

b. A woman is <u>bending / swimming / racing</u> at the gym.

c. The woman at the gym is <u>jumping / tackling / exercising</u>.

d. The man on the tennis court is <u>pitching / serving / swinging</u>.

e. A man in orange shorts at the track is <u>finishing / dribbling / stretching</u>.

f. A man on the baseball field is <u>catching / hitting / swinging</u> with his glove.

2. Look at the bar graph. Complete the sentences.

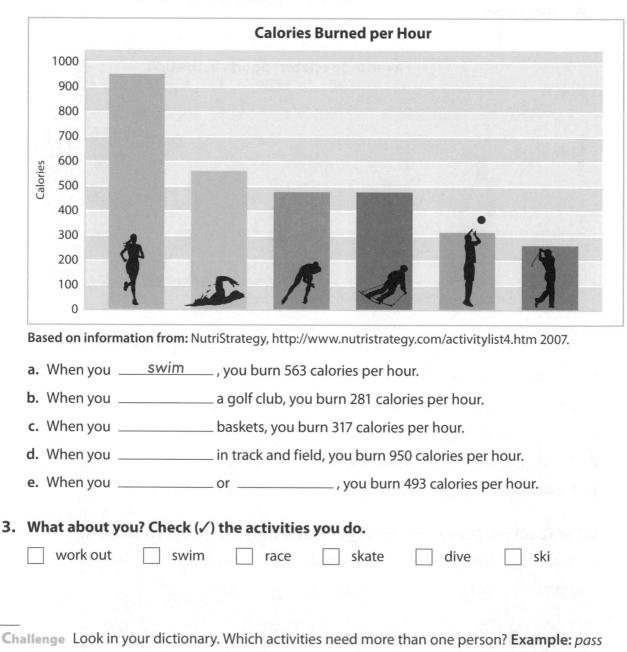

Calories Burned per Hour

Based on information from: NutriStrategy, http://www.nutristrategy.com/activitylist4.htm 2007.

a. When you _____*swim*_____ , you burn 563 calories per hour.

b. When you _____ a golf club, you burn 281 calories per hour.

c. When you _____ baskets, you burn 317 calories per hour.

d. When you _____ in track and field, you burn 950 calories per hour.

e. When you _____ or _____ , you burn 493 calories per hour.

3. What about you? Check (✓) the activities you do.

☐ work out ☐ swim ☐ race ☐ skate ☐ dive ☐ ski

Challenge Look in your dictionary. Which activities need more than one person? **Example:** *pass*

See page 315 for listening practice.

1. Look in your dictionary. What do you see? Put the words in the correct categories.

arrow	bat	boots	bow	catcher's mask
club	glove	helmet	poles	racket
inline skates	~~uniform~~	shoulder pads	target	shin guards

Baseball   **Skiing**   **Golf**   **Skating**

uniform _____   _____   _____   _____

_____   _____   **Tennis**   **Archery**

_____   _____   _____   _____

_____   **Football**   _____   _____

_____   _____   **Soccer**

          _____   _____   _____

2. Look at the chart. Number the items in order of size. (1 = the biggest)

How Big* Are They?

26"

29.5"

9"

28"

27"

* regulation circumference size

a. ___ baseball   c. ___ soccer ball   e. ___ volleyball

b. _1_ basketball   d. ___ bowling ball

3. What about you? Check (✓) the sports equipment you have used.

☐ bowling ball   ☐ ice skates   ☐ flying disc   ☐ snowboard

☐ weights   ☐ football   ☐ skis   ☐ Other: _____

☐ volleyball   ☐ hockey stick

Challenge Look at <u>pages 228 and 229</u> in your dictionary. What kinds of sports equipment do you see? Make a list. You have only three minutes!

See page 315 for listening practice.

1. **Look in your dictionary. Cross out the word that doesn't belong.**

   a. Types of paint   acrylic   ~~glue stick~~   oil   watercolor

   b. Things to collect   action figures   baseball cards   clubs   figurines

   c. Games   cards   checkers   chess   crochetting

   d. Cards   hearts   diamonds   paper dolls spades

   e. Painting   canvas   easel   paintbrush   dice

2. **Look at the chart. Circle the words to complete the sentences.**

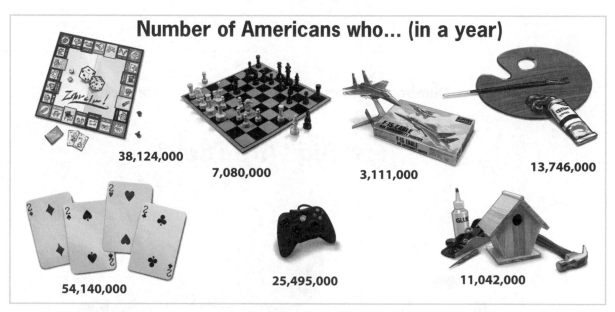

Number of Americans who... (in a year)

38,124,000

7,080,000

3,111,000

13,746,000

54,140,000

25,495,000

11,042,000

Based on information from: *Statistical Abstract of the United States, 2007.*

   a. 38,124,000 people play (board games)/ chess.

   b. 25,495,000 people play <u>cards / video games</u>.

   c. 13,746,000 people draw or <u>paint /quilt</u>.

   d. 11,042,000 people use <u>model / woodworking</u> kits.

   e. 7,080,000 play <u>checkers / chess</u>.

   f. 3,111,000 people use <u>doll making / model</u> kits.

3. **What about you? Look at the hobbies in Exercise 2. Write them in the correct column.**

Hobbies I Do	Hobbies I Don't Do	Hobbies I Would Like to Do
_____	_____	_____
_____	_____	_____
_____	_____	_____

4. **Unscramble these hobby and game words. You can use your dictionary for help.**

   a. DEMLO STRIAN   M O D (E) L   T R A I N S

   b. DIVOE MAGE   __ __ ◯ __ __   __ __ ◯ __

   c. RANY   ◯ __ __ __

   d. TUILQ CLOBK   __ __ ◯ __ __ ◯ __ __ __ __

   e. TROARY TRUTEC   __ ◯ __ __ __ __   __ __ __ __ __ __ ◯

   f. TREASH   __ ◯ __ ◯ __ __

   Put the letters into the circles.

   ◯ ◯ ◯ ◯ ◯ ◯ ◯ ◯ ◯ ◯

   Unscramble the letters in the circles.

   A hobby: __ __ __ __ __ __ __ __ __ __

5. **What is it? Use unscrambled words from Exercise 4 to write what people are talking about.**

   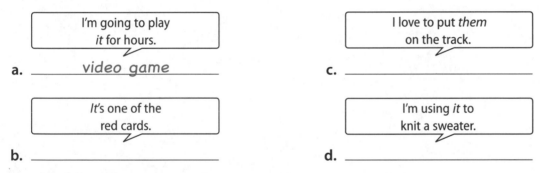

   I'm going to play *it* for hours.

   a. ___video game___

   It's one of the red cards.

   b. _____

   I love to put *them* on the track.

   c. _____

   I'm using *it* to knit a sweater.

   d. _____

6. **What about you? How much do you like to . . . ? Check (✓) the columns.**

	I love it.	I like it.	It's OK.	I don't like it.	I don't know.
paint					
do crafts					
play cards					
collect things					
play games					
pretend					

Challenge   What can you do with construction paper? **Example:** *You can make posters.*

See page 315 for listening practice.

1. Look in your dictionary. Cross out the word that doesn't belong.

a. **Things you carry**   CD boombox   ~~DVD player~~   portable cassette player

b. **Things you watch**   flat screen TV   portable DVD player   microphone

c. **Things that are small**   MP3 player   portable TV   tuner

d. **Things for music**   adapter   speakers   turntable

e. **Things that take pictures**   digital camera   LCD projector   film camera

f. **Things for a camera**   dock   tripod   zoom lens

2. Look at the ad. How much money can you save?

a. speakers   _$25.00_   e. CD boombox   _____

b. portable cassette player   _____   f. MP3 player   _____

c. personal CD player   _____   g. 35 mm camera   _____

d. camcorder   _____   h. digital camera   _____

3. **Look at the universal remote buttons. Write the function. Use the words in the box.**

fast forward	pause	play	~~rewind~~

a. ___rewind___   b. _____   c. _____   d. _____

4. **Look at the pictures. Which one is . . . ? Write the number.**

1.   2.   3.

4.   5.

a. overexposed   _3_   d. from black and white film ___

b. good for a photo album ___   e. underexposed   ___

c. out of focus   ___

5. **What about you? Check (✓) the items you have. Circle the items you want.**

☐ CD boombox   ☐ portable DVD palyer   ☐ tripod

☐ MP3 player   ☐ digital camera   ☐ camera case

☐ personal CD player   ☐ film camera   ☐ LCD projector

☐ flat screen TV   ☐ camcorder   ☐ photo album

Challenge Look in the newspaper or online. Find out today's prices for three of the items in Exercise 2. Compare the prices with the prices in the ad.

1. Look in your dictionary. Circle all the dictionary words in the TV schedule.

Saturday Evening ◁▷ ▽△

	8:00	8:30	9:00	9:30	10:00	10:30	11:00
2	**It's Family!!** Eddie goes to the office in the last show of this popular sitcom.	**Lisa!** Talk show host interviews a soap opera star.	**Movie: There He Goes!** (2001 comedy) Karl Chaps looks for a job in the big city, but finds many problems along the way–including a banana peel! Lots of laughs. **				News
4	**Italy v. France** Final game of the World Cup				**Movie: Jersey Jim** (2006 action-adventure) Snakes, rocks, waterfalls, and much more. With Johnny Diamond.****		
5	**Wild World** Nature program looks at the endangered panda.		**Mystery!** Holmes investigates a murder in a small town. Filled with suspense.		**The Truth is Out There** Visitors from Mars.		News
6	**Movie: Marta** (2008) Two lonely people find romance in this sweet movie by director Emanuel Soto.****				**Home** The camera follows 16 real people as they do their daily activities, such as brushing their teeth. But do they floss, too?		
7	**Time's Up!** New game show	**Max and Minnie** Cartoon	**Movie: The Shadow** (2008) A mysterious stranger terrorizes a town. Directed by Hideaki Tanaka.**				

2. Look at Exercise 1. Write the time and channel to watch these types of shows. You can use your dictionary for help.

a. watch a funny program   _8:00, Channel 2_

b. watch a sports program   _____

c. see a program about animals   _____

d. watch a funny movie   _____

e. see a reality show   _____

f. watch a science fiction story _____

g. see a love story   _____

h. learn what's happening in the world _____ or _____

i. be scared by a movie   _____

3. What about you? Work with a partner. Look at the TV schedule in Exercise 1. Try to find a program you both want to watch.

4. What kind of entertainment is it? Match.

__4__ **a.** "Romeo and Juliet are dead!" **1.** children's program

____ **b.** "And the score is: Alicia 25, Todd 12." **2.** shopping program

____ **c.** "You can buy this for just $29.99 plus shipping." **3.** game show

____ **d.** "Good-bye boys and girls. See you tomorrow." **4.** tragedy

____ **e.** "Get off your horses, cowboys!" **5.** western

5. Look at the chart. Circle the words to complete the sentences. Use your dictionary for help.

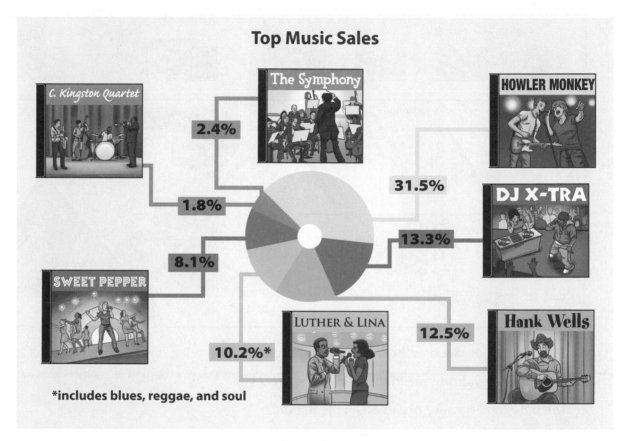

Top Music Sales

C. Kingston Quartet

The Symphony

HOWLER MONKEY

2.4%

31.5%

DJ X-TRA

1.8%

13.3%

8.1%

SWEET PEPPER

LUTHER & LINA

12.5%

Hank Wells

10.2%*

*includes blues, reggae, and soul

Based on information from: *The World Almanac and Book of Facts 2007.* (NY: World Almanac Education Group, Inc, 2007)

a. (Rock)/ Hip hop was 31.5% of the total sales. **d.** The most popular music was rock / pop.

b. Classical / Country was 12.5%. **e.** Blues / Hip hop was 13.3% of total sales.

c. Pop / Jazz was 1.8%.

6. What about you? What kind of music do you listen to? When do you listen to it?

Challenge Take a survey. Find out your classmates' favorite kind of music.
Example: *Five students prefer reggae.*

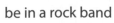
1. Look in your dictionary. Which instruments have . . . ?

   a. strings   _violin_ _____ _____ _____ _____

   b. a keyboard   _piano_ _____ _____ _____

2. Look at the orchestra seating plan. Circle the words to complete the sentences. Use your dictionary for help.

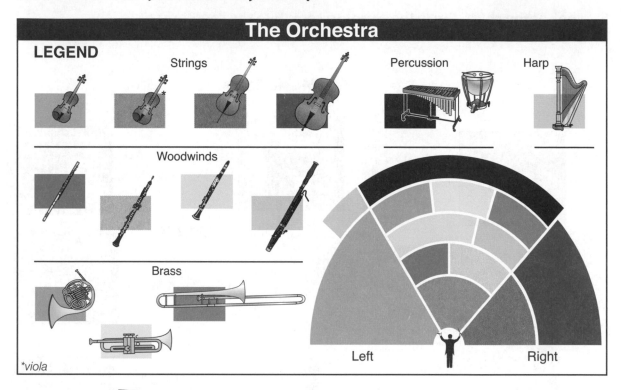

The Orchestra

LEGEND

Strings · Percussion · Harp

Woodwinds

Brass

*viola

Left   Right

   a. The cellos / (violins) are to the left of the conductor.

   b. The bassoons / drums are in the back of the orchestra.

   c. The flutes and basses / oboes are in the middle.

   d. The trumpets / trombones are also in the middle.

   e. The trumpets are between the French horns and the tambourines / trombones.

   f. The cellos / clarinets are to the right of the conductor.

   g. There are no harmonicas / xylophones in this orchestra.

3. What about you? What would you like to do? Check (✓) the items.

   ☐ sing a song   ☐ conduct an orchestra

   ☐ be in a rock band   ☐ play an instrument (Which one?) _____

Challenge Find out about these instruments: viola, harmonica, harp, and bugle. What kinds of instruments are they? Look at the categories in your dictionary for help.

1. Look in your dictionary. *True* or *False*?

a. There's a parade on New Year's Day. _____true_____

b. Children get candy canes on Halloween. _____

c. Couples use string lights on Valentine's Day. _____

2. Write the names of the holidays on the cards. Then circle the words to complete the sentences.

Happy _____New Year's Day_____ !

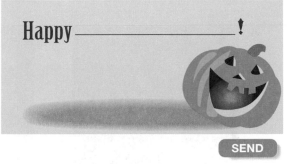

Happy _____ !

a. The card shows (confetti) / fireworks.

b. There's a float / jack-o'-lantern on the card.

Happy _____ !

Happy _____ !

c. There's candy / turkey on the plate. It's part of a holiday costume / feast.

d. There's a red heart / mask on the card.

Merry _____ !

Happy _____ !

e. There's a flag / tree with confetti / ornaments on the card.

f. The card shows fireworks / string lights.

Challenge Make a holiday card.

1. **Look in your dictionary. Who is. . . ? Match.**

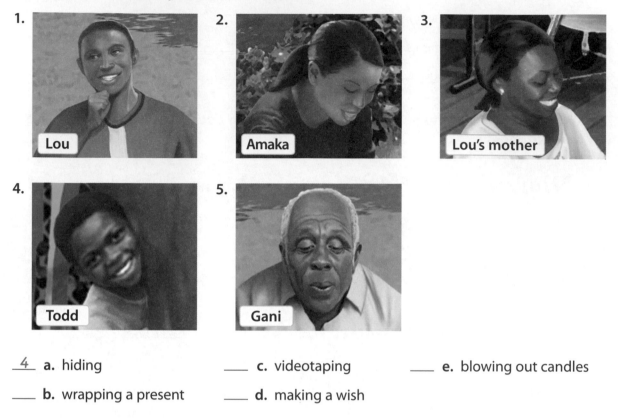

1. Lou
2. Amaka
3. Lou's mother
4. Todd
5. Gani

_4_ **a.** hiding

___ **b.** wrapping a present

___ **c.** videotaping

___ **d.** making a wish

___ **e.** blowing out candles

2. **Melissa is planning a party. Look at her list and the picture. Check (✓) the things Melissa did.**

For The Party

- ☑ buy decorations
- ☐ hang decorations
- ☐ buy a present
- ☐ wrap the present
- ☐ buy candles
- ☐ sweep the deck
- ☐ bake a cake

3. Look in your dictionary. Where are they? Check (✓) the columns.

	Backyard	Deck
a. decorations	✓	✓
b. presents		
c. cakes		
d. lemonade		
e. tables		
f. candles		
g. the woman videotaping		
h. the boy hiding		
i. the girl wrapping		

4. Complete Lou's sister's diary entry. Use the words in the box.

blow out	brought	~~deck~~	hid
make	presents	videotaped	wrapped

March 3
_____

Today was Lou and Grandpa Gani's birthday party! It was great. Mom made hamburgers

on the ____deck____, and we all ate at a big table in the backyard. Lou got a lot of cool
    a.

_____. One man _____ two boxes—one for Lou and one for
  b.   **c.**

Grandpa. He _____ them with pretty blue paper. Best of all, there were two
    d.

cakes! I wanted Lou and Grandpa to hurry up and _____ a wish and
      e.

_____ the candles so we could eat them! Mom _____ the whole
  f.   **g.**

party. Poor Todd. He _____ because he doesn't like to sing. This year Lou is
    h.

18 and Grandpa is 80. Next year, I'll be 14! I hope I get two cakes, too.

5. What about you? Think about a party you went to. Check (✓) the things that happened. Did people . . . ?

☐ bring presents   ☐ videotape the party   ☐ blow out candles   ☐ make a wish

Challenge Look in your dictionary. Imagine you were at Lou and Gani's birthday party. Write a paragraph about it. Who was there? What did they do?

"C" Search

Look at the picture. There are more than 20 items that begin with the letter **c**. Find and circle them. Make a list of the items that you circled.

Example: *coins*

Picture Crossword Puzzle

Complete the puzzle.

		¹				
²S	C	I	S	S	O	R	³S
			⁴			
	⁵					
				⁶		⁷
⁸						
⁹						

Across →

Down ↓

Picture Word Search

There are 15 housing words in the word search. They go across (→) and down (↓). Find and circle 13 more.

```
M  A  I  L  B  O  X  A  K  Y
I  B  L  O  L  G  A  T  E  N
R  E  U  V  E  G  N  O  Y  G
R  L  P  A  N  M  O  I  T  A
O  M  O  S  D  O  L  L  V  R
R  A  T  O  E  R  T  E  M  A
Y  S  E  C  R  I  B  T  O  G
L  N  R  X  S  P  O  N  G  E
E  W  I  N  D  O  W  T  U  L
V  M  D  E  I  U  L  M  P  I
```

"C" Search

Look at the picture. There are more than 25 items that begin with the letter *c.* Find and circle them. Make a list of the items that you circled.

Example: *coconut*

Picture Word Search

There are 17 clothing words in the word search. They go across (→) and down (↓). Find and circle 15 more.

S	W	E	A	T	S	H	I	R	T
O	A	T	S	I	O	A	B	I	U
C	L	A	V	E	S	T	E	N	R
K	L	O	A	F	E	R	S	G	T
S	E	T	E	N	N	O	R	O	L
S	T	H	R	E	A	D	O	B	E
B	R	A	O	E	N	I	R	O	N
E	L	M	E	D	I	U	M	O	E
L	O	R	A	L	R	P	A	T	C
T	E	N	J	E	A	N	S	S	K

Picture Crossword Puzzle

Complete the puzzle.

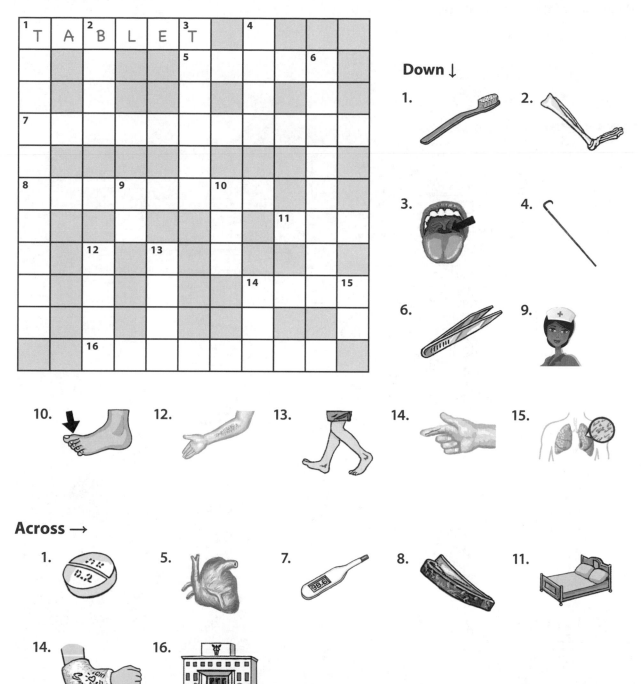

Down ↓

1.

2.

3.

4.

6.

9.

10.

12.

13.

14.

15.

Across →

1.

5.

7.

8.

11.

14.

16.

"C" Search

Look at the picture. There are more than 10 items that begin with the letter **c.** Find and circle them. Make a list of the items that you circled.

Example: *coffee shop*

Where Have All the Flowers Gone?

Look at the picture. Circle all the flowers. Write the locations of the flowers.

Example: *on the bus*

Picture Word Search

There are 18 work words in the word search. They go across (→) and down (↓). Find and circle 16 more.

N	N	U	T	T	**P**	**O**	**O**	**L**	A	X	S
U	U	X	R	I	D	B	A	R	N	E	E
R	R	E	S	P	I	R	A	T	O	R	R
S	S	E	W	E	X	T	S	I	L	V	V
E	E	S	E	R	A	V	M	S	A	E	E
	M	F	L	O	R	I	S	T	F	R	R
	L	A	D	D	E	R	E	O	D	A	A
	E	Z	E	S	T	A	P	L	E	K	K
	F	O	R	K	L	I	F	T	S	E	E
	M	P	A	Y	C	H	E	C	K	X	X

Scrambled Notes

Unscramble the words for these school subjects.

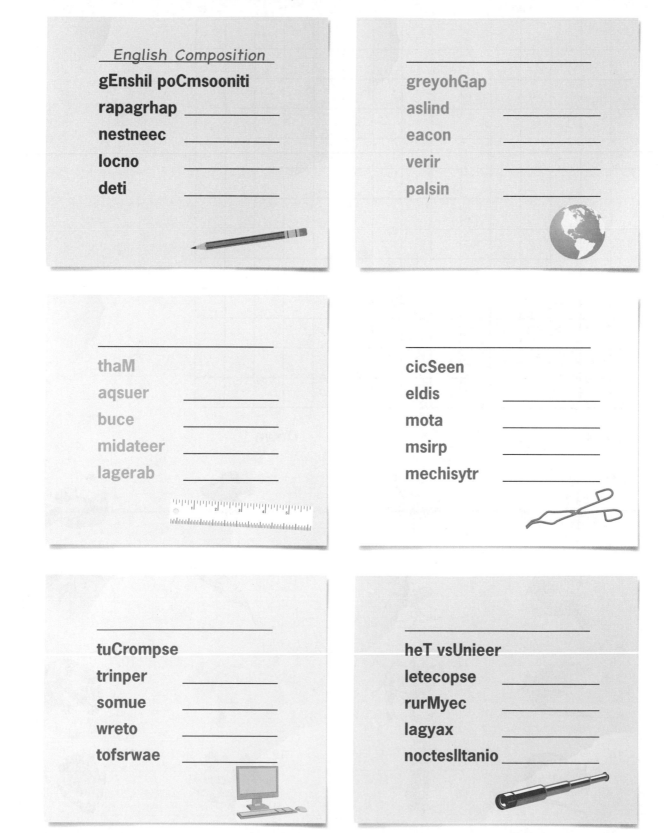

English Composition

gEnshil poCmsooniti

rapagrhap _____

nestneec _____

locno _____

deti _____

_____

greyohGap

aslind _____

eacon _____

verir _____

palsin _____

_____

thaM

aqsuer _____

buce _____

midateer _____

lagerab _____

_____

cicSeen

eldis _____

mota _____

msirp _____

mechisytr _____

_____

tuCrompse

trinper _____

somue _____

wreto _____

tofsrwae _____

_____

heT vsUnieer

letecopse _____

rurMyec _____

lagyax _____

nocteslltanio _____

Picture Crossword Puzzle

Complete the puzzle.

			¹S										
²			T						³				
			A		⁴			⁵					
	⁶		R										
			F			⁷	⁸						
⁹			I		¹⁰								
			S										
			H		¹¹		¹²						
		¹³											
					¹⁴								
	¹⁵												

Across →

2.
4.
5.
7.
9.
11.
14.
15.

Down ↓

1.
3.
4.
6.
8.
10.
12.
13.

"C" Search

Look at the picture. There are more than 25 items and activities that begin with the letter **c**. Find and circle them. Make a list of the items and activities that you circled.

Example: *cooler*

Challenge for page 27

Complete the receipt.

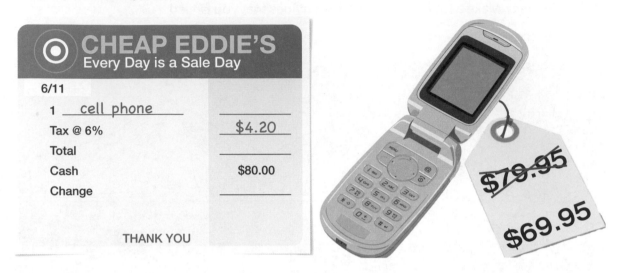

Challenge for page 75

Look at Exercise 2 on page 75 in this book. Convert the U.S. measures to metric measures. Use the charts in your dictionary for help.

a. _____1 1/2 pounds_____ = _____about 680.4 grams_____

b. _____ = _____

c. _____ = _____

e. _____ = _____

Challenge for page 165

Complete Enrique Gutierrez's paycheck from page 165. Use the information in Exercise 4 and your dictionary for help.

IRINA'S COMPUTER SERVICE

Check number:
123456789 999999999 124

7000 Main Street
Houston, TX 77031

Pay to the order of _Enrique Gutierrez_ $ _____

Six hundred _____ and _____/100 dollars

Town Bank

Irina Gorkov

Challenge for page 167

Ask four people about their jobs. What do they do? How many hours a week do they work? Fill in the chart below. Then, write sentences about them. Follow the example below.

What is your name?	What do you do?	How many hours a week do you work?
Meng	cashier	25
1.		
2.		
3.		
4.		

Example: *Meng is a cashier. She works twenty-five hours a week.*

Challenge for page 189

Think of different types of schools in another country. List in order the schools and students' ages. Follow the example below.

Country	School	Ages
Peru	preschool	2 to 5 years old
	primary school	6 to 11 years old
	secondary school	12 to 17 years old

Country	School	Ages

Challenge for page 209

Work with a partner. Look at <u>pages 208 and 209</u> in your dictionary. Write at least two examples for each category. Use <u>pages 211, 212, 214, and 216</u> in your dictionary for help.

In the Lillo Nature Center	
Trees	oak,
Flowers	
Insects	
Mammals	

How many players are there on a . . . team? If you don't know, try to find out.

basketball _____

soccer _____

baseball _____

ice hockey _____

football _____

volleyball _____

Listening Exercises

Meeting and Greeting pages 2 and 3, CD 1, Track 2

Listen. What are the people doing? Check (✓) the answers.

1. ✓ **a.** saying, "Hello."   ☐ **b.** saying, "Goodbye."
2. ☐ **a.** introducing himself   ☐ **b.** introducing a friend
3. ☐ **a.** greeting people   ☐ **b.** saying, "Goodbye."
4. ☐ **a.** bowing   ☐ **b.** kissing
5. ☐ **a.** asking, "How are you?"   ☐ **b.** hugging
6. ☐ **a.** greeting people   ☐ **b.** introducing herself

Personal Information page 4, CD 1, Track 3

Listen. Check (✓) the answers.

1. ☐ **a.** Ana   ✓ **b.** Garcia
2. ☐ **a.** 212   ☐ **b.** 10003-1100
3. ☐ **a.** Mexico City   ☐ **b.** 4/6/90
4. ☐ **a.** 10   ☐ **b.** 401-555-0323
5. ☐ **a.** 534-12-0000   ☐ **b.** 1-(917)-555-0747
6. ☐ **a.** Ana Garcia   ☐ **b.** *Ana Garcia*

Ana Garcia

School page 5, CD 1, Track 4

Listen. Write the number of the conversation.

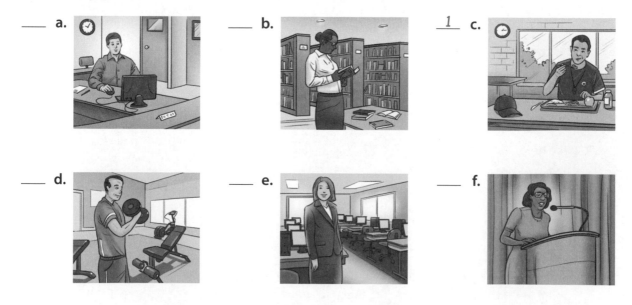

___ **a.**   ___ **b.**   _1_ **c.**

___ **d.**   ___ **e.**   ___ **f.**

A Classroom pages 6 and 7, CD 1, Track 5

Listen. Circle the words you hear.

1. Do you have a pen / pencil?
2. It's my workbook / textbook.
3. I love the dictionary / picture dictionary.
4. Can I have the eraser / dry erase marker?
5. Is this your spiral notebook / notebook?
6. I need notebook paper / a notebook.
7. Can I use your pencil eraser / pencil sharpener?

Studying pages 8 and 9, CD 1, Track 6

Listen. Follow the directions.

1. ☑
2. This is my pencil.
3. pencil   pen   desk   marker
4. This is a good book.
5. _____
6. book _____
7.
8. _____
9. _____

Succeeding in School page 10, CD 1, Track 7

Listen. Write the numbers.

_____ **a.** Ask for help.

_1_ **b.** Clear off your desks.

_____ **c.** Give the test booklets.

_____ **d.** Bubble in the answer.

_____ **e.** Check your work.

_____ **f.** Hand in your test.

_____ **g.** Give the answer sheets.

_____ **h.** Erase the mistake.

_____ **i.** Work on your own.

A Day at School   page 11, CD 1, Track 8

Listen. Circle the words you hear.

1. Please <u>turn off</u> / (turn on) the lights.

2. Don't <u>enter</u> / <u>leave</u> the room now.

3. It's 3:00. I have to <u>run</u> / <u>walk</u> to class now.

4. Can you help me <u>carry</u> / <u>deliver</u> these books?

5. What do you want to <u>eat</u> / <u>drink</u>?

6. It's 4:00. Let's <u>go back</u> / <u>walk</u> to class.

7. I'll <u>carry</u> / <u>throw away</u> the trash over there.

Everyday Conversation   page 12, CD 1, Track 9

Listen. *True* or *False*? Check (✓) the answers.

		True	False
1.	He's explaining something.	✓	☐
2.	They disagree.	☐	☐
3.	She's complimenting someone.	☐	☐
4.	She's accepting an invitation.	☐	☐
5.	He's offering something.	☐	☐
6.	They're checking their understanding.	☐	☐
7.	He's apologizing.	☐	☐
8.	He's thanking someone.	☐	☐

Weather   page 13, CD 1, Track 10

Listen. Write the number of the weather report.

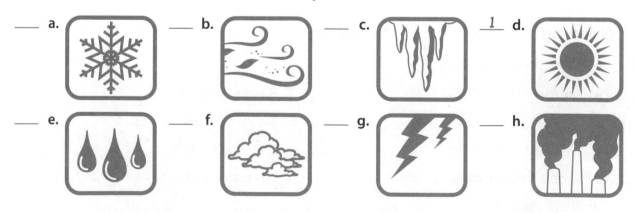

___ a.   ___ b.   ___ c.   _1_ d.

___ e.   ___ f.   ___ g.   ___ h.

The Telephone pages 14 and 15, CD 1, Track 11

Listen. Circle the answers.

1. a. ✳   (b.) #

2. a. SEND   b. END

3. **a.** 411   **b.** 911

4. **a.** Ricardo Fuentes   **b.** 413-555-0102

5. **a.** California.   **b.** There's a fire!

6. a. 0   b. ✳

7. **a.** 212   **b.** 411

8. **a.** 1   **b.** 57

9. **a.** "For store hours, please press 2."   **b.** "Hi, it's me. Please call me!"

Numbers page 16, CD 1, Track 12

Listen. Check (✓) the numbers you hear.

1. ✓ **a.** 24   ☐ **b.** 42

2. ☐ **a.** 13th   ☐ **b.** 30th

3. ☐ **a.** 18   ☐ **b.** 80

4. ☐ **a.** 100   ☐ **b.** 1,000

5. ☐ **a.** 50   ☐ **b.** 50th

6. ☐ **a.** 101   ☐ **b.** 111

7. ☐ **a.** 1,000   ☐ **b.** 10,000

8. ☐ **a.** 5th   ☐ **b.** 6th

9. ☐ **a.** 1,000,000   ☐ **b.** 1,000,000,000

Measurements   page 17, CD 1, Track 13

Listen. Write the dimensions.

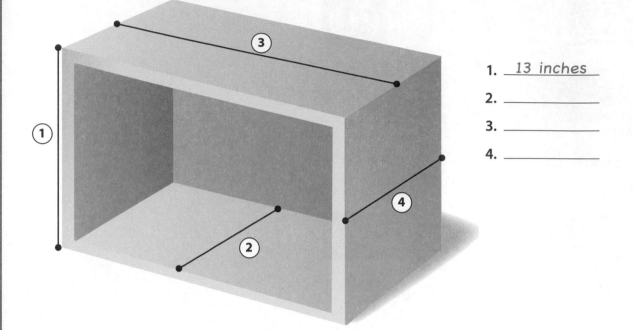

1. _13 inches_
2. _____
3. _____
4. _____

Time   pages 18 and 19, CD 1, Track 14

Listen. Write the times. Circle *a.m.* or *p.m.*

1. [8:00] (a.m.) p.m.

2. [:] a.m. p.m.

3. [:] a.m. p.m.

4. [:] a.m. p.m.

5. [:] a.m. p.m.

6. [:] a.m. p.m.

7. [:] a.m. p.m.

The Calendar   pages 20 and 21, CD 1, Track 15

Listen. Circle the words you hear.

1. What's the (date) / day?

2. Do you work weekdays / weekends?

3. Is today Tuesday / Thursday?

4. School begins this week / next week.

5. I have English twice / three times a week.

6. I play soccer every Monday / Sunday.

7. Ana's birthday is in June / July.

Calendar Events page 22, CD 1, Track 16

Listen. Write the number of the conversation.

___ a.

___ b.

___ c.

___ d.

___ e.

_1_ f.

Describing Things page 23, CD 1, Track 17

Listen. Circle the words you hear.

1. (little)   cheap   (expensive)   thick
2. empty   big   heavy   soft
3. bad   good   thick   thin
4. easy   slow   soft   ugly
5. empty   full   loud   quiet
6. bad   fast   good   slow

Colors page 24, CD 1, Track 18

Listen. *True* **or** *False*? **Check (✓) the answers.**

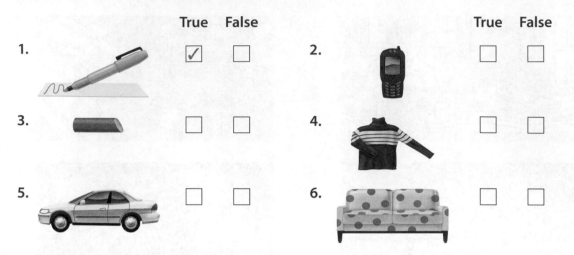

		True	False			True	False
1.		✓	☐	2.		☐	☐
3.		☐	☐	4.		☐	☐
5.		☐	☐	6.		☐	☐

Prepositions page 25, CD 1, Track 19

Listen. Circle the words to complete the sentences.

1. The red sweaters are on the left / right.

2. The blue sweaters are below / behind the white sweaters.

3. The green sweaters are above / under the black sweaters.

4. The white sweaters are behind / between the pink sweaters and the orange sweaters.

5. The gray sweaters are in / on the box over there.

6. The purple sweaters are on the left / right.

7. The yellow sweaters are in front of / next to the orange sweaters.

Money page 26, CD 1, Track 20

Listen. Circle the correct amount.

1. **a.** $15.00   **b.** $50.00

2. **a.** four quarters   **b.** four nickels

3. **a.** $.20   **b.** $20.00

4. **a.** $.50   **b.** $1.00

5. **a.** $5.00   **b.** $50.00

6. **a.** 10 dimes   **b.** 10 pennies

7. **a.** $20.00   **b.** $21.00

Shopping page 27, CD 1, Track 21

Listen. *True* or *False*? Check (✓) the answers.

		True	False
1.	She wants to buy the lamp.		✓
2.	She wants to exchange it.		
3.	She used a debit card.		
4.	She has the receipt.		
5.	He wants to return a lamp.		
6.	The sale price is $20.00		
7.	There's sales tax.		
8.	He's going to write a check.		

Same and Different pages 28 and 29, CD 1, Track 22

Look in your dictionary. Listen. Who said . . . ? Check (✓) the columns.

	Anya	Manda	Mrs. Kumar	Sales Assistant
1.		✓		
2.				
3.				
4.				
5.				
6.				
7.				

Adults and Children pages 30 and 31, CD 1, Track 23

Listen. Who's talking? Check (✓) the answers.

1. ✓ **a.** a man and a woman — ☐ **b.** two men
2. ☐ **a.** a boy and a man — ☐ **b.** a baby and a man
3. ☐ **a.** a senior citizen — ☐ **b.** a teenager
4. ☐ **a.** a woman and an infant — ☐ **b.** a woman and a little girl
5. ☐ **a.** two teens — ☐ **b.** two toddlers
6. ☐ **a.** a boy and a man — ☐ **b.** a girl and a man

Describing People page 32, CD 1, Track 24

Listen. Circle the words you hear. Then, label the pictures with the correct names.

1. **Jake:** short — mole — (tall) — (thin)
2. **Joelle:** middle-aged — average height — average weight — attractive
3. **Bob:** elderly — hearing impaired — sight impaired — young
4. **Pam:** cute — fat — pierced ears — pregnant
5. **Brian:** mole — short — young — tattoo
6. **Elissa:** short — slender — pregnant — elderly

a.

Joelle

b.

c.

d.

Describing Hair page 33, CD 1, Track 25

Listen. What do the people want? Check (✓) the answers.

1. ☐ **a.** color ☑ **b.** cut
2. ☐ **a.** bangs ☐ **b.** part
3. ☐ **a.** black ☐ **b.** brown
4. ☐ **a.** blond ☐ **b.** red
5. ☐ **a.** straight hair ☐ **b.** wavy hair
6. ☐ **a.** shoulder-length hair ☐ **b.** short hair
7. ☐ **a.** color his beard ☐ **b.** color his mustache
8. ☐ **a.** perm ☐ **b.** set

Families pages 34 and 35, CD 1, Track 26

Listen. Who are they talking about? Check (✓) the answers.

1. ✓ **a.** brother   ☐ **b.** brother-in-law
2. ☐ **a.** mother   ☐ **b.** grandmother
3. ☐ **a.** son   ☐ **b.** son-in-law
4. ☐ **a.** half sister   ☐ **b.** stepsister
5. ☐ **a.** divorced couple   ☐ **b.** married couple
6. ☐ **a.** mother   ☐ **b.** stepmother
7. ☐ **a.** cousin   ☐ **b.** niece
8. ☐ **a.** aunt   ☐ **b.** uncle

Childcare and Parenting pages 36 and 37, CD 1, Track 27

Listen. *True* or *False*? Check (✓) the answers.

	True	False
1. She's feeding the baby.	✓	☐
2. He's reading to his child.	☐	☐
3. She's kissing her child goodnight.	☐	☐
4. She's comforting her child.	☐	☐
5. He's singing a lullaby.	☐	☐
6. She's disciplining her child.	☐	☐
7. She's dressing the baby.	☐	☐
8. He's playing with his child.	☐	☐

Daily Routines pages 38 and 39, CD 1, Track 28

Listen. Match. Write the number of the conversation.

____ **a.** do homework

____ **b.** exercise

____ **c.** go to bed

____ **d.** go to work

____ **e.** eat lunch

_1_ **f.** get up

____ **g.** go to school

____ **h.** make lunch

Life Events and Documents pages 40 and 41, CD 1, Track 29

Look at the documents. Listen. Write the number of the conversation.

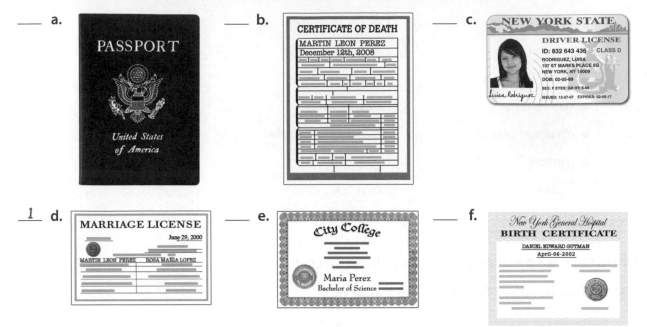

___ a.

PASSPORT
United States of America

___ b.

CERTIFICATE OF DEATH
MARTIN LEON PEREZ
December 12th, 2008

___ c.

NEW YORK STATE
DRIVER LICENSE
ID: 832 643 436   CLASS D
RODRIGUEZ, LUISA
107 ST MARKS PLACE 5G
NEW YORK, NY 10009
DOB: 02-05-89
SEX: F EYES: GR HT: 5-05
ISSUED: 12-27-07   EXPIRES: 02-05-17

1 d.

MARRIAGE LICENSE
June 29, 2000
MARTIN LEON PEREZ   ROSA MARIA LOPEZ

___ e.

City College
Maria Perez
Bachelor of Science

___ f.

New York General Hospital
BIRTH CERTIFICATE
DANIEL EDWARD GUTMAN
April-06-2002

Feelings pages 42 and 43, CD 1, Track 30

Listen. *True* or *False*? Check (✓) the answers.

	True	False			True	False
1. She's nervous.	✓	☐	5. She's angry.		☐	☐
2. He's sick.	☐	☐	6. He's disgusted.		☐	☐
3. She's bored.	☐	☐	7. He's homesick.		☐	☐
4. He's tired.	☐	☐				

A Family Reunion pages 44 and 45, CD 1, Track 31

Listen. Circle the words to complete the sentences.

1. They're talking about the balloons / banner.

2. They're laughing / misbehaving.

3. They're talking about Ben's opinion / family.

4. They're talking about the balloons / banner.

5. The man and the woman have the same / different opinions.

6. Tommy is laughing / misbehaving.

7. The man is talking about a baseball game / his relatives.

The Home pages 46 and 47, CD 1, Track 32

Listen. Where are they? Match.

1. _g_   **a.** attic

2. ___   **b.** baby's room

3. ___   **c.** bathroom

4. ___   **d.** basement

5. ___   **e.** dining area

6. ___   **f.** garage

7. ___   **g.** kitchen

8. ___   **h.** living room

Finding a Home pages 48 and 49, CD 1, Track 33

Listen. What are they doing? Circle the words to complete the sentences.

1. She's calling the manager / submitting an application.

2. They're making an offer / moving in.

3. He's meeting the neighbors / meeting with a realtor.

4. She's asking about features / putting the utilities in her name.

5. They're arranging furniture / packing.

6. She's looking at houses / signing a rental agreement.

7. He's making a mortgage payment / taking ownership.

Apartments pages 50 and 51, CD 1, Track 34

Listen. Check (✓) the building features.

Parkview Apartments
Post Oak Drive, Hammond, NM 60863

F E A T U R E S:

☑ *washers and dryers*	☐ *security cameras*
☐ *swimming pool*	☐ *playground*
☐ *recreation room*	☐ *roof garden*
☐ *pool table*	☐ *parking spaces*
☐ *big-screen TV*	☐ *storage lockers*
☐ *security gates*	

505-555-9998

Different Places to Live page 52, CD 1, Track 35

Listen. Where do the people live? Check (✓) the columns.

	Condo	Dorm	Farm	Nursing Home	Ranch	Senior Housing	Townhouse
1.			✓				
2.							
3.							
4.							
5.							
6.							
7.							

A House and Yard page 53, CD 1, Track 36

Listen. What are the people using? Check (✓) the answers.

1. ☑ **a.** doorbell   ☐ **b.** mailbox

2. ☐ **a.** flower bed   ☐ **b.** hammock

3. ☐ **a.** gate   ☐ **b.** grill

4. ☐ **a.** patio furniture   ☐ **b.** satellite dish

5. ☐ **a.** mailbox   ☐ **b.** chimney

6. ☐ **a.** front door   ☐ **b.** gate

A Kitchen   page 54, CD 1, Track 37

Look at the picture. Listen. *True* or *False*? Check (✓) the answers.

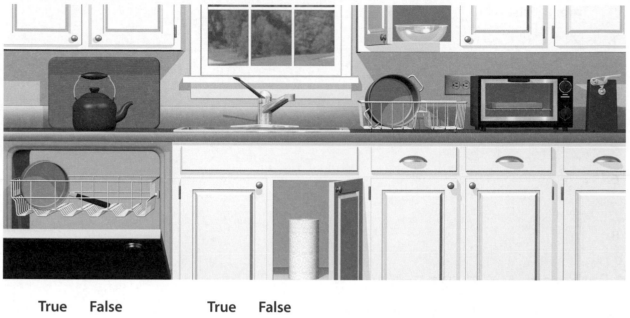

	True	False		True	False
1.	☐	✓	**5.**	☐	☐
2.	☐	☐	**6.**	☐	☐
3.	☐	☐	**7.**	☐	☐
4.	☐	☐			

A Dining Area   page 55, CD 1, Track 38

Listen. Complete the drawing.

A Living Room page 56, CD 1, Track 39

Look in your dictionary. Listen. *True* or *False*? Check (✓) the answers.

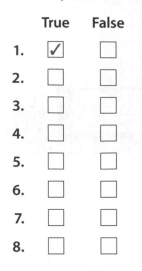

	True	False
1.	✓	☐
2.	☐	☐
3.	☐	☐
4.	☐	☐
5.	☐	☐
6.	☐	☐
7.	☐	☐
8.	☐	☐

A Bathroom page 57, CD 1, Track 40

Listen. Where are they? Circle the answers.

1. Danny is on the <u>bath mat</u> / <u>scale</u>.

2. The washcloth is on the <u>grab bar</u> / <u>towel rack</u>.

3. The soap is in the <u>bathtub</u> / <u>soap dish</u>.

4. The hand towel is in the <u>wastebasket</u> / <u>hamper</u>.

5. The toothbrush is in the <u>toothbrush holder</u> / <u>medicine cabinet</u>.

6. The man is waiting for a <u>hand towel</u> / <u>bath towel</u>.

7. The woman is turning on more <u>hot water</u> / <u>cold water</u>.

A Bedroom page 58, CD 1, Track 41

Look at the ad. Listen. Circle the things they are going to buy.

THE **bed**STORE
Spring Sale
Our prices are a dream!

$399.99 $59.99 $19.99 $699.99 $29.99 $59.99 $24.99

The Kids' Bedroom page 59, CD 1, Track 42

Look in your dictionary. Listen. *True* or *False*? Check (✓) the answers.

	True	False
1.	✓	☐
2.	☐	☐
3.	☐	☐
4.	☐	☐
5.	☐	☐
6.	☐	☐
7.	☐	☐

Housework page 60, CD 1, Track 43

Listen. What are the people doing? Check (✓) the answers.

1. ☐ **a.** drying the dishes   ✓ **b.** changing the sheets
2. ☐ **a.** putting away toys   ☐ **b.** recycling the newspapers
3. ☐ **a.** mopping the floor   ☐ **b.** vacuuming the carpet
4. ☐ **a.** washing the dishes   ☐ **b.** washing the windows
5. ☐ **a.** polishing the furniture ☐ **b.** wiping the counter
6. ☐ **a.** putting away the toys ☐ **b.** taking out the garbage
7. ☐ **a.** dusting the furniture ☐ **b.** making the bed

Cleaning Supplies page 61, CD 1, Track 44

Listen. Look at the list. Check (✓) the things they need.

To Buy

☑ glass cleaner   ☐ furniture polish
☐ cleanser   ☐ oven cleaner
☐ sponges   ☐ steel-wool soap pads
☐ scrub brush   ☐ trash bags
☐ dishwashing liquid ☐ bucket

Household Problems and Repairs   pages 62 and 63, CD 1, Track 45

Listen. Write the number of the ad.

____ **a.** carpenter

____ **b.** electrician

____ **c.** exterminator

____ **d.** locksmith

____ **e.** plumber

_1_ **f.** repair person

____ **g.** roofer

The Tenant Meeting   pages 64 and 65, CD 1, Track 46

Look in your dictionary. Listen. Who said . . . ? Check (✓) the columns.

	The DJ	A Roommate	The Manager	A Neighbor
1.		✓		
2.				
3.				
4.				
5.				
6.				

Back from the Market   pages 66 and 67, CD 2, Track 2

Listen. Complete the shopping list.

Shopping List

chicken

Fruit page 68, CD 2, Track 3

Listen. Match.

__f__ **1.** $2.50/box   **a.** coconut

___ **2.** $.59/each   **b.** bananas

___ **3.** $1.29/each   **c.** kiwis

___ **4.** $.49/each   **d.** apples

___ **5.** $1.00/2 bunches   **e.** pineapples

___ **6.** $4.00/each   **f.** raspberries

___ **7.** $.99/pound   **g.** tangerines

Vegetables page 69, CD 2, Track 4

Look in your dictionary. Listen. *True* or *False*? Check (✓) the answers.

	True	False			True	False
1.	✓	☐		**5.**	☐	☐
2.	☐	☐		**6.**	☐	☐
3.	☐	☐		**7.**	☐	☐
4.	☐	☐		**8.**	☐	☐

Meat and Poultry page 70, CD 2, Track 5

Listen. Check (✓) the items the man is going to buy.

☐ stewing beef   ✓ ground beef   ☐ beef ribs

☐ pork chops   ☐ lamb chops   ☐ lamb shanks

☐ liver   ☐ turkey   ☐ chicken wings

☐ chicken breasts   ☐ chicken legs   ☐ tripe

Seafood and Deli   page 71, CD 2, Track 6

Listen. Complete the orders. Check (✓) the food the people order.

1.

Dan's
DELI SANDWICHES   ORDER FORM

Meat/Poultry   *Cheese*
✓ roast beef   ☐ American
☐ corned beef   ☐ Swiss
☐ salami   ☐ cheddar
☐ pastrami   ☐ mozzarella
☐ smoked turkey
                        Bread
                        ☐ rye
                        ☐ white
                        ☐ wheat

2.

Dan's
DELI SANDWICHES   ORDER FORM

Meat/Poultry   *Cheese*
☐ roast beef   ☐ American
☐ corned beef   ☐ Swiss
☐ salami   ☐ cheddar
☐ pastrami   ☐ mozzarella
☐ smoked turkey
                        Bread
                        ☐ rye
                        ☐ white
                        ☐ wheat

3.

Dan's
DELI SANDWICHES   ORDER FORM

Meat/Poultry   *Cheese*
☐ roast beef   ☐ American
☐ corned beef   ☐ Swiss
☐ salami   ☐ cheddar
☐ pastrami   ☐ mozzarella
☐ smoked turkey
                        Bread
                        ☐ rye
                        ☐ white
                        ☐ wheat

4.

Dan's
DELI SANDWICHES   ORDER FORM

Meat/Poultry   *Cheese*
☐ roast beef   ☐ American
☐ corned beef   ☐ Swiss
☐ salami   ☐ cheddar
☐ pastrami   ☐ mozzarella
☐ smoked turkey
                        Bread
                        ☐ rye
                        ☐ white
                        ☐ wheat

A Grocery Store   pages 72 and 73, CD 2, Track 7

Listen. Write the aisle numbers.

	Aisle
aluminum foil	____
apple juice	____
bagels	____
canned beans	6
coffee	____
ice cream	____
yogurt	____

Containers and Packaging page 74, CD 2, Track 8

Listen. Match.

_f_ **1.** bag   **a.** juice

___ **2.** bottle   **b.** soda

___ **3.** container   **c.** pasta

___ **4.** box   **d.** water

___ **5.** can   **e.** cookies

___ **6.** six-pack   **f.** nuts

___ **7.** package   **g.** yogurt

Weights and Measurements page 75, CD 2, Track 9

Listen. Circle the words you hear.

1. a pint / (a quart)

2. a teaspoon / a tablespoon

3. a cup / a quart

4. a pint / a gallon

5. two teaspoons / two tablespoons

6. two ounces / three ounces

Food Preparation and Safety pages 76 and 77, CD 2, Track 10

**Look at the pictures. Listen to the recipe. Number the pictures in order.
(1 = the first step)**

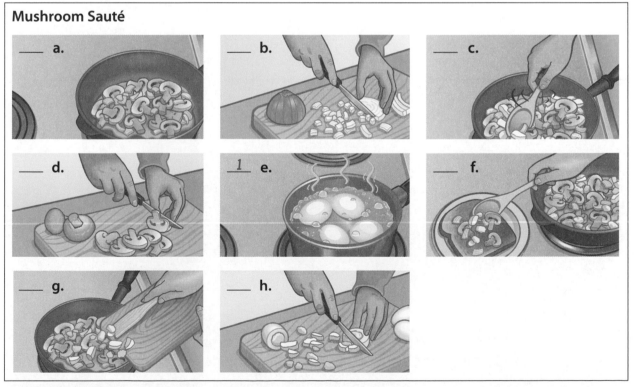

Mushroom Sauté

___ **a.**   ___ **b.**   ___ **c.**

___ **d.**   _1_ **e.**   ___ **f.**

___ **g.**   ___ **h.**

Based on a recipe from: Richmond, S. *International Vegetarian Cooking.* (NY: Arco Publishing Co., 1970)

Kitchen Utensils page 78, CD 2, Track 11

Look in your dictionary. Listen. *True* **or** *False* **? Check (✓) the answers.**

	True	False
1.	✓	
2.		
3.		
4.		
5.		
6.		
7.		

Fast Food Restaurant page 79, CD 2, Track 12

Look in your dictionary. Listen. Who said . . . ? Check (✓) the columns.

	Counterperson	Customers at the Counter	Cook	Customers at the Table
1.		✓		
2.				
3.				
4.				
5.				
6.				
7.				

A Coffee Shop Menu   pages 80 and 81, CD 2, Track 13

Listen. Complete the orders.

1.

Coffee Shop
ORDER FORM

pancakes

2.

Coffee Shop
ORDER FORM

3.

Coffee Shop
ORDER FORM

4.

Coffee Shop
ORDER FORM

A Restaurant   pages 82 and 83, CD 2, Track 14

Listen. Who said . . . ? Circle the answers.

1. the busser / the hostess

2. the chef / a server

3. the busser / a patron

4. the dishwasher / the hostess

5. the busser / the chef

6. a waiter / a waitress

7. a diner / a server

8. the busser / the hostess

The Farmers' Market pages 84 and 85, CD 2, Track 15

Look in your dictionary. Listen. What are the people doing? Check (✓) the answers.

1. ☑ **a.** eating free samples   ☐ **b.** eating organic strawberries
2. ☐ **a.** eating fruit   ☐ **b.** drinking lemonade
3. ☐ **a.** listening to live music   ☐ **b.** talking to vendors
4. ☐ **a.** counting avocados   ☐ **b.** counting tomatoes
5. ☐ **a.** eating a cookie   ☐ **b.** eating a taco
6. ☐ **a.** buying herbs   ☐ **b.** eating lunch

Everyday Clothes pages 86 and 87, CD 2, Track 16

Look in your dictionary. Who said . . . ? Circle the answers.

1. the man in jeans / (the suit)
2. the woman with the handbag / sweater
3. the person in the baseball cap / tan slacks
4. the man in the blue shirt / suit
5. the woman wearing a skirt / yellow dress
6. the man wearing a T-shirt / jeans
7. the man in the blue / green shirt

Casual, Work, and Formal Clothes pages 88 and 89, CD 2, Track 17

Listen. *True* or *False*? Check (✓) the answers.

	True	False
1. She wears a uniform to work.	☑	☐
2. He wears sweatpants and a tank top at the gym.	☐	☐
3. She's going to wear a cocktail dress.	☐	☐
4. She's going to wear capris and sandals.	☐	☐
5. He's going to wear a tuxedo.	☐	☐
6. He's going to wear a sports jacket.	☐	☐
7. She's going to take a cardigan sweater.	☐	☐

Seasonal Clothing page 90, CD 2, Track 18

Listen. Write the floor number.

DIRECTORY	FLOOR	DIRECTORY	FLOOR
coats	_____	rain boots	_____
gloves	_____	sunglasses	_____
hats	_____	swimsuits	_5_
leggings	_____	umbrellas	_____

Underwear and Sleepwear page 91, CD 2, Track 19

Listen. Check (✓) the items that are on sale.

☐ undershirts   ✓ bras   ☐ slippers   ☐ thermal undershirts

☐ panties   ☐ long underwear   ☐ panty hose   ☐ nightgowns

☐ slips   ☐ pajamas

Workplace Clothing pages 92 and 93, CD 2, Track 20

Listen. Check (✓) the items the people want to buy.

1. ✓ safety glasses
   ✓ apron
   ☐ chef's hat
   ☐ waist apron
   ✓ bump cap

2. ☐ work shirt
   ☐ work gloves
   ☐ work pants
   ☐ bandana
   ☐ latex gloves

3. ☐ safety glasses
   ☐ security pants
   ☐ security shirt
   ☐ work pants
   ☐ polo shirt

4. ☐ cowboy hat
   ☐ ventilation mask
   ☐ hard hat
   ☐ blazer
   ☐ steel toe boots

5. ☐ helmet
   ☐ latex gloves
   ☐ hairnets
   ☐ disposable gloves
   ☐ smock

6. ☐ face mask
   ☐ scrubs
   ☐ ventilation mask
   ☐ lab coat
   ☐ surgical mask

7. ☐ coveralls
   ☐ lab coat
   ☐ scrubs
   ☐ latex gloves
   ☐ jumpsuit

Shoes and Accessories   pages 94 and 95, CD 2, Track 21

Look at the top picture in your dictionary. Listen. Who said . . . ? Circle the answers.

1. the salesclerk <u>in the jewelry department</u> / <u>(near the belts)</u>

2. the woman with the <u>backpack</u> / <u>shoulder bag</u>

3. the customer in the <u>jewelry</u> / <u>shoe</u> department

4. the salesclerk <u>near the wallet display case</u> / <u>in the jewelry department</u>

5. the man <u>looking at rings</u> / <u>waiting in line</u>

6. the man purchasing <u>a shirt</u> / <u>shoes</u>

7. the woman <u>assisting a customer</u> / <u>purchasing shoes</u>

Describing Clothes   pages 96 and 97, CD 2, Track 22

Listen. What is the problem? Check (✓) the answers.

1. ☐ **a.** A button is missing.   ✓ **b.** The zipper is broken.

2. ☐ **a.** They're too light.   ☐ **b.** They're too tight.

3. ☐ **a.** They're too wide.   ☐ **b.** They're too high.

4. ☐ **a.** It's stained.   ☐ **b.** It's torn.

5. ☐ **a.** It's too heavy.   ☐ **b.** It's too fancy.

6. ☐ **a.** It's too small.   ☐ **b.** It's too big.

7. ☐ **a.** They're too low.   ☐ **b.** They're too loose.

Making Clothes   pages 98 and 99, CD 2, Track 23

Listen. Circle the words to complete the sentences.

1. It's a <u>cotton</u> / <u>(wool)</u> sweater.

2. The man wants <u>leather</u> / <u>suede</u> shoes.

3. The woman wants a <u>lace</u> / <u>silk</u> camisole.

4. The woman loves <u>cashmere</u> / <u>velvet</u>.

5. It's a <u>linen</u> / <u>nylon</u> jacket.

6. The dress closes with a <u>snap</u> / <u>zipper</u>.

7. The woman likes the <u>beads</u> / <u>fringe</u>.

Making Alterations page 100, CD 2, Track 24

Listen. Check (✓) the things the tailor will do.

1. Tailor Made
Quality Tailoring Repairs and Alterations

CLOTHING	ALTERATIONS	REPAIR
✓ pants	☐ lengthen	☐ collar
☐ shirt (sleeves)	✓ shorten	☐ waistband
	☐ let out	☐ sleeve
☐ skirt	✓ take in	✓ pocket

2. Tailor Made
Quality Tailoring Repairs and Alterations

CLOTHING	ALTERATIONS	REPAIR
☐ pants	☐ lengthen	☐ collar
☐ shirt (sleeves)	☐ shorten	☐ waistband
	☐ let out	☐ sleeve
☐ skirt	☐ take in	☐ pocket

3. Tailor Made
Quality Tailoring Repairs and Alterations

CLOTHING	ALTERATIONS	REPAIR
☐ pants	☐ lengthen	☐ collar
☐ shirt (sleeves)	☐ shorten	☐ waistband
	☐ let out	☐ sleeve
☐ skirt	☐ take in	☐ pocket

4. Tailor Made
Quality Tailoring Repairs and Alterations

CLOTHING	ALTERATIONS	REPAIR
☐ pants	☐ lengthen	☐ collar
☐ shirt (sleeves)	☐ shorten	☐ waistband
	☐ let out	☐ sleeve
☐ skirt	☐ take in	☐ pocket

Doing the Laundry page 101, CD 2, Track 25

Listen. *True* or *False*? Check (✓) the answers.

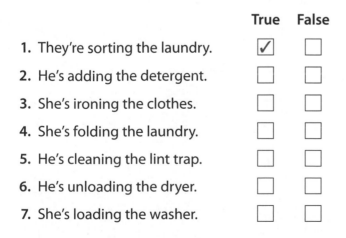

	True	False
1. They're sorting the laundry.	✓	☐
2. He's adding the detergent.	☐	☐
3. She's ironing the clothes.	☐	☐
4. She's folding the laundry.	☐	☐
5. He's cleaning the lint trap.	☐	☐
6. He's unloading the dryer.	☐	☐
7. She's loading the washer.	☐	☐

A Garage Sale pages 102 and 103, CD 2, Track 26

Listen. Circle the words to complete the sentences.

1. They're talking about a green sticker / sweatshirt.
2. They're bargaining / browsing.
3. She wants to buy a VCR / clock radio.
4. He's bargaining / browsing.
5. She's looking at a flyer / sticker.
6. They're talking about used clothing / VCRs.

The Body pages 104 and 105, CD 2, Track 27

Listen. Circle the words to complete the sentences.

1. His finger / shoulder hurts.
2. She's having a problem with her ears / eyes.
3. He has a pain in his nose / toes.
4. Her head / hand hurts.
5. Her back / neck hurts.
6. His mouth / foot hurts.

Inside and Outside the Body pages 106 and 107, CD 2, Track 28

Listen. What is the teacher talking about? Check (✓) the answers.

1. ☑ **a.** skin   ☐ **b.** shin
2. ☐ **a.** gums   ☐ **b.** lungs
3. ☐ **a.** brain   ☐ **b.** bone
4. ☐ **a.** skeleton   ☐ **b.** skull
5. ☐ **a.** thumb   ☐ **b.** tongue
6. ☐ **a.** bladder   ☐ **b.** gallbladder
7. ☐ **a.** knees   ☐ **b.** kidneys

Personal Hygiene pages 108 and 109, CD 2, Track 29

Listen. What are they doing? Circle the words to complete the sentences.

1. She's <u>combing</u> / <u>washing</u> her hair.

2. She's <u>polishing</u> / <u>cutting</u> her nails.

3. He's brushing his <u>hair</u> / <u>teeth</u>.

4. He's <u>shaving</u> / <u>using deodorant</u>.

5. She's <u>drying</u> / <u>rinsing</u> her hair.

6. He's <u>gargling</u> / <u>taking a bath</u>.

7. She's <u>putting on</u> / <u>taking off</u> mascara.

Symptoms and Injuries page 110, CD 2, Track 30

Listen. Complete the medical chart. Check (✓) the symptoms.

⊕ MEDICAL CENTER

Dr. Eng

10 Oak Drive, Richmond, CA

DATE: 3/5

PATIENT'S NAME: *Enrique Rivera*

✓ sore throat	☐ stomachache	☐ cough
☐ nasal congestion	☐ toothache	☐ sneeze
☐ fever	☐ earache	☐ feel dizzy
☐ chills	☐ headache	☐ feel nauseous
☐ rash	☐ backache	☐ throw up

Illnesses and Medical Conditions page 111, CD 2, Track 31

Listen. Check (✓) the illness or medical condition.

1. ✓ **a.** flu   ☐ **b.** cold

2. ☐ **a.** ear infection   ☐ **b.** strep throat

3. ☐ **a.** allergies   ☐ **b.** asthma

4. ☐ **a.** measles   ☐ **b.** mumps

5. ☐ **a.** HIV   ☐ **b.** TB

6. ☐ **a.** diabetes   ☐ **b.** dementia

7. ☐ **a.** heart disease   ☐ **b.** hypertension

A Pharmacy pages 112 and 113, CD 2, Track 32

Listen. Write the number of the conversation.

___ a. DO NOT TAKE WITH DAIRY PRODUCTS

___ b. DO NOT DRIVE OR OPERATE HEAVY MACHINERY

___ c. DO NOT DRINK ALCOHOL

_1_ d. IMPORTANT FINISH ALL MEDICATION

___ e. TAKE WITH FOOD OR MILK

Taking Care of Your Health pages 114 and 115, CD 2, Track 33

Listen. Circle the words to complete the sentences.

1. He's <u>following medical advice</u> / <u>seeking medical attention</u>.

2. She's <u>eating a healthy diet</u> / <u>taking medicine</u>.

3. He's <u>drinking fluids</u> / <u>getting bed rest</u>.

4. She's <u>having regular checkups</u> / <u>staying fit</u>.

5. He's having <u>physical</u> / <u>talk</u> therapy.

6. She's seeing an <u>audiologist</u> / <u>optometrist</u>.

7. He has <u>hearing loss</u> / <u>vision problems</u>.

Medical Emergencies page 116, CD 2, Track 34

Listen. *True* or *False*? Check (✓) the answers.

	True	False			True	False
1. He burned himself.	✓	☐	5. Susan is unconscious.		☐	☐
2. She got frostbite.	☐	☐	6. He swallowed poison.		☐	☐
3. He's bleeding.	☐	☐	7. She got an electric shock.		☐	☐
4. She's choking.	☐	☐				

First Aid page 117, CD 2, Track 35

Listen. Check (✓) the items inside the first aid kit.

🩺 FIRST AID KIT

- ☐ tweezers
- ☑ adhesive bandages
- ☐ sterile pads
- ☐ sterile tape
- ☐ gauze
- ☐ hydrogen peroxide
- ☐ antibacterial ointment
- ☐ antihistamine cream
- ☐ elastic bandages
- ☐ ice pack

Medical Care page 118, CD 2, Track 36

Look in your dictionary. Listen. Who said . . . ? Check (✓) the columns.

	Patient	Doctor	Nurse	Receptionist
1.			✓	
2.				
3.				
4.				
5.				
6.				
7.				

Dental Care page 119, CD 2, Track 37

Listen. What is the dentist or dental hygienist doing? Write the numbers.

____ **a.** taking x-rays

____ **b.** numbing the mouth

____ **c.** filling a cavity

____ **d.** pulling a tooth

____ **e.** cleaning teeth

_1_ **f.** drilling a tooth

Hospital pages 120 and 121, CD 2, Track 38

Look at page 120 in your dictionary. Who said . . . ? Check (✓) the answers.

1. ✓ **a.** obstetrician   ☐ **b.** oncologist
2. ☐ **a.** cardiologist   ☐ **b.** pediatrician
3. ☐ **a.** ophthalmologist   ☐ **b.** radiologist
4. ☐ **a.** psychiatrist   ☐ **b.** registered nurse
5. ☐ **a.** dietician   ☐ **b.** surgical nurse
6. ☐ **a.** internist   ☐ **b.** orderly
7. ☐ **a.** certified nursing assistant   ☐ **b.** administrator

A Health Fair pages 122 and 123, CD 2, Track 39

Look in your dictionary. Listen. Where are the people? Check (✓) the booths.

	Acupuncture	Eye Exam	Good Foods Market	Healthy Cooking	Medical Screening	Nutrition Lecture	Aerobic Exercise
1.					✓		
2.							
3.							
4.							
5.							
6.							
7.							

Downtown pages 124 and 125, CD 3, Track 2

Look in your dictionary. Listen. *True* or *False*? Check (✓) the answers.

	True	False
1.	✓	☐
2.	☐	☐
3.	☐	☐
4.	☐	☐
5.	☐	☐
6.	☐	☐

City Streets pages 126 and 127, CD 3, Track 3

Listen. Circle the words to complete the sentences.

1. She's going to church / (the gym).

2. He's going to the coffee shop / shopping mall.

3. She's going to the car dealership / home improvement store.

4. He's looking for the mosque / motel.

5. They're going to go to the movie theater / stadium.

6. He's going to the furniture / office supply store.

7. She's going to the bakery / supermarket.

An Intersection pages 128 and 129, CD 3, Track 4

Listen. What are they going to get? Write the number.

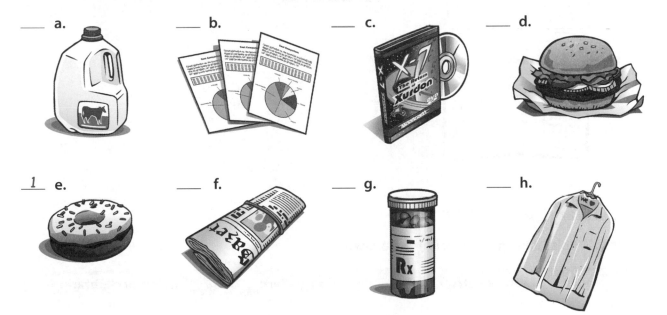

___ a.

___ b.

___ c.

___ d.

_1_ e.

___ f.

___ g.

___ h.

A Mall pages 130 and 131, CD 3, Track 5

Look in your dictionary. *True* or *False*? Check (✓) the answers.

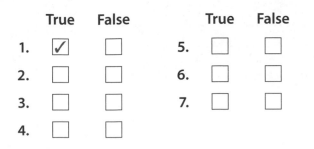

	True	False		True	False
1.	✓	☐	5.	☐	☐
2.	☐	☐	6.	☐	☐
3.	☐	☐	7.	☐	☐
4.	☐	☐			

The Bank page 132, CD 3, Track 6

Listen. Write the number of the conversation.

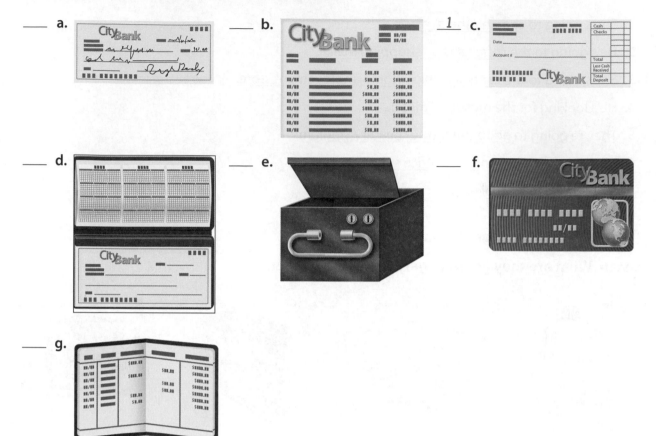

____ a.

____ b.

__1__ c.

____ d.

____ e.

____ f.

____ g.

The Library page 133, CD 3, Track 7

Listen. Who's talking? Check (✓) the answers.

	Library Patron	Library Clerk	Reference Librarian
1.	✓		
2.			
3.			
4.			
5.			
6.			
7.			

The Post Office pages 134 and 135, CD 3, Track 8

Listen. Check (✓) the columns.

	Priority Mail®	Express Mail®	Media Mail®	Certified Mail™	Airmail	Ground Post
1.					✓	
2.						
3.						
4.						
5.						
6.						

Department of Motor Vehicles (DMV) pages 136 and 137, CD 3, Track 9

Listen. Circle the words to complete the sentences.

1. He's taking a (vision exam) / written test.

2. She's showing her identification / proof of insurance.

3. He's getting a learner's permit / studying the handbook.

4. She got a registration sticker / passed a driving test.

5. He's getting his license / paying the application fee.

6. She's talking about her driver's license / license plate.

7. She's taking his fingerprint / photo.

Government and Military Service pages 138 and 139, CD 3, Track 10

Listen. Write the number of the conversation.

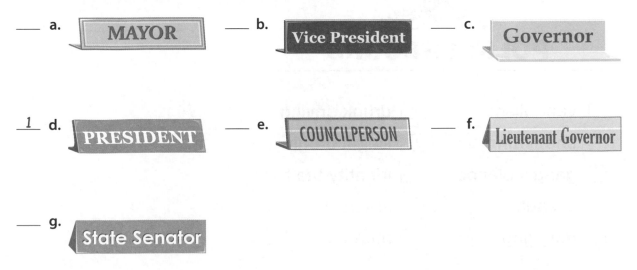

____ a. MAYOR

____ b. Vice President

____ c. Governor

_1_ d. PRESIDENT

____ e. COUNCILPERSON

____ f. Lieutenant Governor

____ g. State Senator

Civic Rights and Responsibilities page 140, CD 3, Track 11

Listen. Circle the words to complete the sentences.

1. He's <u>serving on a jury</u> / <u>voting.</u>

2. This is an example of <u>peaceful assembly</u> / <u>a fair trial.</u>

3. This is an example of freedom of <u>the press</u> / <u>religion.</u>

4. He's <u>registering with Selective Services</u> / <u>paying taxes.</u>

5. She is <u>informed</u> / <u>taking a citizenship test.</u>

6. He's <u>18</u> / <u>20</u> or older.

The Legal System page 141, CD 3, Track 12

Listen. Who said . . . ? Check (✓) the answers.

1. ☑ **a.** the defense attorney ☐ **b.** the prosecuting attorney
2. ☐ **a.** the convict ☐ **b.** the witness
3. ☐ **a.** the bailiff ☐ **b.** the judge
4. ☐ **a.** the defendant ☐ **b.** the guard
5. ☐ **a.** the judge ☐ **b.** the police officer
6. ☐ **a.** the police officer ☐ **b.** the prisoner
7. ☐ **a.** the court reporter ☐ **b.** the jury

Crime page 142, CD 3, Track 13

Listen. Complete the form. Check (✓) the crimes.

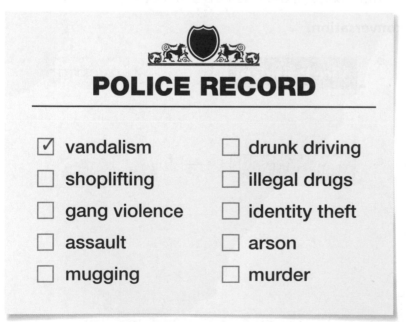

POLICE RECORD

☑ vandalism ☐ drunk driving

☐ shoplifting ☐ illegal drugs

☐ gang violence ☐ identity theft

☐ assault ☐ arson

☐ mugging ☐ murder

Public Safety page 143, CD 3, Track 14

Listen. *True* or *False*? Check (✓) the answers.

	True	False
1. She's walking with a friend.	✓	☐
2. She's shopping on a secure site.	☐	☐
3. She's opening the door to a stranger.	☐	☐
4. They're going to stay on well-lit streets.	☐	☐
5. He's reporting a crime to the police.	☐	☐
6. She's drinking and driving.	☐	☐
7. They're aware of their surroundings.	☐	☐

Emergencies and Natural Disasters pages 144 and 145, CD 3, Track 15

Listen. Write the number of the news story.

___ a. MIAMI NEWS **Hurricane Hits Miami Beach**

___ b. Media *WATCH* **Blizzard Closes Schools**

___ c. *STAR Plus* **Firefighters Put Out Downtown Fire**

___ d. Brown Town Metro **Five-Car Accident at Busy Intersection**

_1_ e. Aviation News **Airplane Crash— Everyone OK!**

___ f. MOUNTAIN POST **Earthquake Shakes City**

Emergency Procedures pages 146 and 147, CD 3, Track 16

Listen. What are they doing? Check (✓) the answers.

1. ☐ **a.** cleaning up debris ✓ **b.** inspecting utilities
2. ☐ **a.** calling out-of-state contacts ☐ **b.** helping people with disabilities
3. ☐ **a.** seeking shelter ☐ **b.** taking cover
4. ☐ **a.** following directions ☐ **b.** staying calm
5. ☐ **a.** evacuating the area ☐ **b.** staying away from windows
6. ☐ **a.** paying attention to warnings ☐ **b.** watching the weather

Community Cleanup pages 148 and 149, CD 3, Track 17

Look in your dictionary. Listen. Who said . . . ? Check (✓) the columns.

	Marta Lopez	Florist	Hardware Store Owner	City Council
1.			✓	
2.				
3.				
4.				
5.				
6.				

Basic Transportation pages 150 and 151, CD 3, Track 18

Listen. Where are the passengers? Check (✓) the answers.

1. ☐ **a.** subway   ✓ **b.** taxi
2. ☐ **a.** helicopter   ☐ **b.** plane
3. ☐ **a.** bus   ☐ **b.** car
4. ☐ **a.** motorcycle   ☐ **b.** truck
5. ☐ **a.** bus   ☐ **b.** taxi
6. ☐ **a.** bus   ☐ **b.** train

Public Transportation page 152, CD 3, Track 19

Listen. Write the number of the conversation.

___ **a.**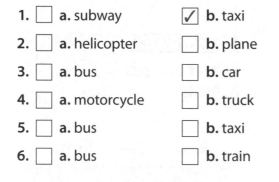

___ **b.** New York City Transit — MTA Transfer — ◄ Going your way

___ **c.** Riders 1 — RUSSO/VINCENT — From RALEIGH, NC To NEWTON, NC — Carrier 2V Train 276 Date 17 OCT 10 — Price $10 Form of Payment V XXXX228871 — Space/Car COACH CL

___ **d.**
BUS 10 Northbound
Main	Elm	Oak
6:00	6:10	6:13
6:30	6:40	6:43
7:00	7:10	7:13
7:30	7:40	7:43

___ **e.** Riders 1 — NOVAK/ANNA — From RALEIGH, NC To NEWTON, NC — Carrier 2V Train 276 Date 17 OCT 10 — From NEWTON, NC To RALEIGH, NC — Carrier 2V Train 276 Date 22 OCT 10 — Price $18 Form of Payment M XXXX939979 — Space/Car COACH CL

_1_ **f.** MTA RED LINE — OPENING DAY JUNE 24, 2000 — 1 FARE — NORTH HOLLYWOOD

Prepositions of Motion   page 153, CD 3, Track 20

Listen. Circle the words you hear.

1. Go <u>over</u> / ⟨under⟩ the bridge.
2. Go <u>across</u> / <u>around</u> that small park.
3. Get <u>on</u> / <u>off</u> the highway at Exit 21.
4. Walk <u>up</u> / <u>down</u> those steps.
5. He's getting <u>into</u> / <u>out of</u> a taxi.
6. Drive <u>around</u> / <u>through</u> that tunnel.

Traffic Signs   page 154, CD 3, Track 21

Listen. Write the number of the conversation.

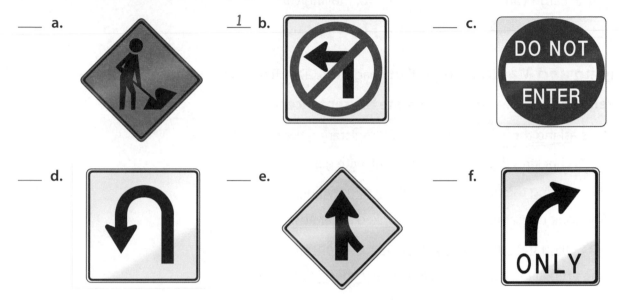

____ a.

_1_ b.

____ c.

____ d.

____ e.

____ f.

Directions and Maps   page 155, CD 3, Track 22

Listen. Use your pen or pencil to follow the directions.

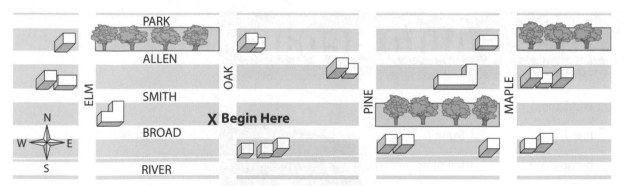

Cars and Trucks page 156, CD 3, Track 23

Listen. What do they drive? Check (✓) the answers.

1. ☑ **a.** sports car ☐ **b.** sedan
2. ☐ **a.** 2-door car ☐ **b.** 4-door car
3. ☐ **a.** RV ☐ **b.** SUV
4. ☐ **a.** minivan ☐ **b.** sedan
5. ☐ **a.** tank truck ☐ **b.** tow truck
6. ☐ **a.** cargo van ☐ **b.** moving van
7. ☐ **a.** pickup truck ☐ **b.** dump truck

Buying and Maintaining a Car page 157, CD 3, Track 24

Listen. Circle the words to complete the sentences.

1. He's asking the seller about the car / registering the car.
2. She's checking the oil / filling the tank with gas.
3. He's getting the title from the seller / negotiating a price.
4. She took the car to a mechanic / looked at car ads.
5. He's filling the tank with gas / filling a tire with air.
6. She's replacing the windshield wipers / checking the oil.

Parts of a Car pages 158 and 159, CD 3, Track 25

Listen. Check (✓) the car parts that have problems.

Rick's Auto Repair

☑ windshield ☐ hubcaps

☐ hood ☐ trunk

☐ bumper ☐ tail pipe

☐ sideview mirror ☐ headlights

☐ rearview mirror ☐ tail lights

☐ tires ☐ brake lights

Professional Auto Repair, Personalized Service

An Airport   pages 160 and 161, CD 3, Track 26

Listen. Circle the words to complete the sentences.

1. The passenger should go to the (gate) / screening area now.

2. The plane just took off / landed.

3. The pilot / flight attendant is talking.

4. Passengers must fasten their seat belts / turn off their cell phones now.

5. Passengers must claim their baggage / stow their carry-on bags now.

6. Flight 28 is delayed / on time.

7. This information is about checking / claiming your baggage.

Taking a Trip   pages 162 and 163, CD 3, Track 27

Look in your dictionary. Listen. Who's talking? Check (✓) the columns.

	Rob / Joe	Gas Station Attendant	Police Officer	Tow Truck Driver
1.	✓			
2.				
3.				
4.				
5.				
6.				

The Workplace   pages 164 and 165 , CD 3, Track 28

Look in your dictionary. Listen. Who are they looking for? Check (✓) the answers.

1. ☐ **a.** employer   ✓ **b.** receptionist
2. ☐ **a.** payroll clerk   ☐ **b.** supervisor
3. ☐ **a.** customer   ☐ **b.** supervisor
4. ☐ **a.** receptionist   ☐ **b.** supervisor
5. ☐ **a.** boss   ☐ **b.** employee

Jobs and Occupations A–C page 166, CD 3, Track 29

Listen. What are their jobs? Circle the words to complete the sentences.

1. He's an <u>assembler</u> / <u>auto mechanic.</u>

2. They are <u>actors</u> / <u>artists.</u>

3. She's a <u>baker</u> / <u>butcher.</u>

4. He's <u>an accountant</u> / <u>a cashier.</u>

5. She's a <u>businessperson</u> / <u>babysitter.</u>

6. He's an <u>appliance repair person</u> / <u>architect.</u>

Jobs and Occupations C–H page 167, CD 3, Track 30

Listen. Who should they call? Write the number of the conversation.

—— a. Ethier's Yardworks — Professional Gardeners — 555-3234

—— b. THE COMPUTER DOC — Computer Technician 555-5424

—— c. flo's flower Pot FLORIST — 555-5456 ffp@eol.us

—— d. HELPING HAND — CERTIFIED HOME HEALTH CARE AIDES — 555-4776

1 e. ELECTRONICS REPAIR PERSON — T.V. JONES — 555-7676

—— f. The Beauty Spot — MARIE DeVito — HAIR STYLIST 555-9997

Jobs and Occupations H–P page 168, CD 3, Track 31

Look in your dictionary. Listen. What are their jobs? Circle the words to complete the sentences.

1. They're machine operators / (movers.)
2. She's a homemaker / housekeeper.
3. She's a model / an occupational therapist.
4. He's a lawyer / messenger.
5. He's a musician / translator.
6. She's a housepainter / manicurist.

Jobs and Occupations P–W page 169, CD 3, Track 32

Listen. Check (✓) the jobs you hear.

1. ☐ printer   ✓ receptionist   ✓ retail clerk
   ☐ server   ✓ security guard   ☐ stock clerk

2. ☐ servers   ☐ retail clerks   ☐ stock clerks
   ☐ telemarketers   ☐ truck drivers   ☐ welders

3. ☐ truck driver   ☐ telemarketer   ☐ writer
   ☐ soldier   ☐ stock clerk   ☐ retail clerk

4. ☐ printer   ☐ writer   ☐ reporter
   ☐ welder   ☐ server   ☐ social worker

Job Skills page 170, CD 3, Track 33

Listen. Check (✓) Andrea's job skills.

RRR Ron's Roadside Restaurant

JOB SKILLS

- ✓ cook
- ☐ wait on customers
- ☐ use a cash register
- ☐ speak another language
- ☐ supervise people
- ☐ repair appliances

Office Skills page 171, CD 3, Track 34

Listen. *True* or *False*? Check (✓) the answers.

	True	False
1. He's typing.	✓	☐
2. She's leaving a message.	☐	☐
3. He's faxing a document.	☐	☐
4. She's putting the caller on hold.	☐	☐
5. He's checking messages.	☐	☐
6. He's transcribing.	☐	☐

Career Planning page 172, CD 3, Track 35

Listen. Circle the words to complete the sentences.

1. Luisa got a new job /(promotion.)

2. He's going to talk to a recruiter / career counselor.

3. He's going to complete an interest / a skill inventory.

4. Erika is getting on-the-job / vocational training.

5. He's going to go to the resource center / job fair.

Job Search page 173, CD 3, Track 36

Listen. Check (✓) the things Amy does to find a job.

EZ EMPLOYMENT AGENCY

- ✓ go to an employment agency
- ☐ talk to friends and family / network
- ☐ look for help wanted signs
- ☐ look in the classifieds
- ☐ check Internet job sites
- ☐ write a resume

Interview Skills page 174, CD 3, Track 37

Listen. *True* or *False*? Check (✓) the answers.

		True	False
1.	Roger dressed appropriately for his interview.	✓	☐
2.	He greeted the interviewer.	☐	☐
3.	He brought his resume.	☐	☐
4.	He turned off his cell phone before the interview.	☐	☐
5.	He asked questions.	☐	☐
6.	He thanked the interviewer.	☐	☐

A Factory page 175 , CD 3, Track 38

Look in your dictionary. Listen. Who's talking? Check (✓) the answers.

1. ✓ **a.** factory worker ☐ **b.** shipping clerk
2. ☐ **a.** line supervisor ☐ **b.** shipping clerk
3. ☐ **a.** designer ☐ **b.** packer
4. ☐ **a.** factory owner ☐ **b.** factory worker
5. ☐ **a.** line supervisor ☐ **b.** packer
6. ☐ **a.** shipping clerk ☐ **b.** order puller

Landscaping and Gardening page 176, CD 3, Track 39

Listen. Check (✓) the jobs the gardening crew is doing today.

LAWNCARE
Landscaping and Gardening

✓ trim hedges	☐ rake leaves
☐ plant trees	☐ water plants
☐ mow lawn	☐ weed flower beds
☐ fertilize plants	☐ install sprinkler system

Farming and Ranching   page 177, CD 3, Track 40

Listen. Where are they? Check (✓) the columns.

	Vegetable Garden	Field	Barn	Orchard	Vineyard	Corral
1.	✓					
2.						
3.						
4.						
5.						
6.						

Construction   page 178, CD 3, Track 41

Listen. Check (✓) the supplies they are going to order.

R&J CONSTRUCTION SUPPLIES

- ☐ concrete
- ✓ tile
- ☐ bricks
- ☐ insulation

- ☐ stucco
- ☐ plywood
- ☐ lumber
- ☐ shingles

Job Safety   page 179 , CD 3, Track 42

Listen. What are the workers using or wearing? Check (✓) the answers.

1. ✓ **a.** ear plugs   ☐ **b.** knee pads
2. ☐ **a.** ear muffs   ☐ **b.** two-way radio
3. ☐ **a.** respirator   ☐ **b.** work gloves
4. ☐ **a.** safety boots   ☐ **b.** safety goggles
5. ☐ **a.** hard hat   ☐ **b.** fire extinguisher

Tools and Building Supplies pages 180 and 181, CD 3, Track 43

Look in your dictionary. Listen. _True_ or _False_? Check (✓) the answers.

	True	False
1.	✓	☐
2.	☐	☐
3.	☐	☐
4.	☐	☐
5.	☐	☐
6.	☐	☐

An Office pages 182 and 183, CD 3, Track 44

Listen. Check (✓) the items that are in the supply closet.

OFFICE SUPPLIES INVENTORY

☐ clear tape   ☐ mailing labels

☐ correction fluid   ☐ paper clips

☐ correction tape   ☐ rubber cement

☐ envelopes   ✓ staples

☐ glue   ☐ sticky notes

A Hotel page 184, CD 3, Track 45

Look in your dictionary. Who said . . . ? Circle the answers.

1. **a.** bell hop   **(b.)** parking attendant
2. **a.** desk clerk   **b.** doorman
3. **a.** bell captain   **b.** concierge
4. **a.** pool service   **b.** maintenance
5. **a.** guest   **b.** housekeeper
6. **a.** concierge   **b.** maintenance

Food Service page 185, CD 3, Track 46

Look in your dictionary. Listen. *True* or *False*? Check (✓) the answers.

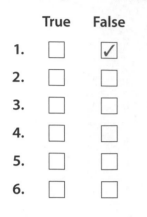

	True	False
1.	☐	✓
2.	☐	☐
3.	☐	☐
4.	☐	☐
5.	☐	☐
6.	☐	☐

A Bad Day at Work pages 186 and 187, CD 3, Track 47

Look in your dictionary. Who said . . . ? Check (✓) the columns.

	Contractor	Owner	Worker
1.	✓		
2.			
3.			
4.			
5.			
6.			
7.			

Schools and Subjects pages 188 and 189, CD 4, Track 2

Look at page 189 in your dictionary. Listen. Where can you hear . . . ? Check (✓) the answers.

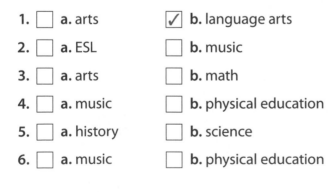

1. ☐ **a.** arts   ✓ **b.** language arts
2. ☐ **a.** ESL   ☐ **b.** music
3. ☐ **a.** arts   ☐ **b.** math
4. ☐ **a.** music   ☐ **b.** physical education
5. ☐ **a.** history   ☐ **b.** science
6. ☐ **a.** music   ☐ **b.** physical education

English Composition   pages 190 and 191, CD 4, Track 3

Listen. What is Marc doing? Circle the words to complete the sentences.

1. Marc is <u>brainstorming ideas</u> / (<u>getting feedback</u>.)

2. He's <u>revising / turning in</u> his paper.

3. He's <u>organizing his ideas / thinking about the assignment</u>.

4. He's <u>editing / writing</u> a first draft.

5. He's <u>organizing his ideas / revising</u>.

Mathematics   pages 192 and 193, CD 4, Track 4

Listen. *True* or *False*? Check (✓) the answers.

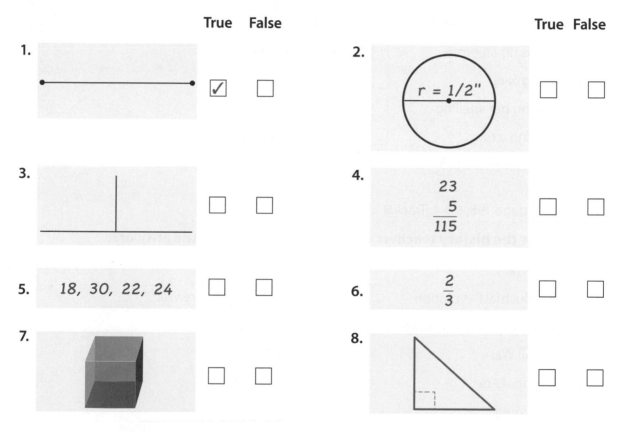

Science   pages 194 and 195, CD 4, Track 5

Listen. What are they talking about? Check (✓) the answers.

1. ☑ **a.** balance   ☐ **b.** prism

2. ☐ **a.** formula   ☐ **b.** periodic table

3. ☐ **a.** funnel   ☐ **b.** graduated cylinder

4. ☐ **a.** Bunsen burner   ☐ **b.** magnet

5. ☐ **a.** electron   ☐ **b.** nucleus

6. ☐ **a.** microscope   ☐ **b.** photosynthesis

Computers page 196, CD 4, Track 6

Listen. Circle the words to complete the sentences.

1. Her <u>flash drive</u> / (<u>hard drive</u>) isn't working.

2. He is having problems with his <u>mouse / motherboard</u>.

3. She has a <u>desktop computer / laptop</u>.

4. The cable goes into the <u>printer / USB port</u>.

5. She probably needs a new <u>microprocessor / monitor</u>.

The Internet page 197, CD 4, Track 7

Listen. What is Carla doing? Check (✓) the answers.

1. ☐ **a.** addressing an email   ✓ **b.** typing a message

2. ☐ **a.** addressing an email   ☐ **b.** typing her password

3. ☐ **a.** clicking *Send*   ☐ **b.** clicking *Sign In*

4. ☐ **a.** checking her spelling   ☐ **b.** typing the subject

5. ☐ **a.** attaching a file   ☐ **b.** attaching a picture

6. ☐ **a.** typing her password   ☐ **b.** typing the subject

U.S. History page 198, CD 4, Track 8

Listen. What are the history teachers talking about? Check (✓) the answers.

1. ✓ **a.** World War I   ☐ **b.** World War II

2. ☐ **a.** the Industrial Revolution   ☐ **b.** the Revolutionary War

3. ☐ **a.** the first Continental Congress   ☐ **b.** the first president

4. ☐ **a.** the Civil War   ☐ **b.** the Cold War

5. ☐ **a.** the Global Age   ☐ **b.** the Space Age

6. ☐ **a.** minutemen   ☐ **b.** redcoats

7. ☐ **a.** Native Americans   ☐ **b.** slaves

World History   page 199, CD 4, Track 9

Listen. *True* or *False*? Check (✓) the answers.

		True	False
1.	The woman is a monarch.	✓	☐
2.	These people are explorers.	☐	☐
3.	This is a news report about an invention.	☐	☐
4.	They're listening to a composition.	☐	☐
5.	This program is about a modern civilization.	☐	☐
6.	This program is about a political movement.	☐	☐

North America and Central America   pages 200 and 201, CD 4, Track 10

Look in your dictionary. Listen. Check (✓) the answers.

1. ☐ **a.** British Columbia   ✓ **b.** Saskatchewan
2. ☐ **a.** The Maritime Provinces   ☐ **b.** Ontario
3. ☐ **a.** Oregon   ☐ **b.** Nevada
4. ☐ **a.** Louisiana   ☐ **b.** Georgia
5. ☐ **a.** The Yucatan Peninsula   ☐ **b.** The Chiapas Highlands

World Map   pages 202 and 203, CD 4, Track 11

Listen. Circle the words to complete the sentences.

1. ⃝Austria / Australia won the World Cup in downhill skiing.
2. Iran / Oman is having very hot weather.
3. The President is going to Swaziland / Switzerland.
4. The singers come from Iceland / Ireland.
5. The movie takes place in Chile / China.
6. The paintings come from Niger / Nigeria.

Geography and Habitats   page 204, CD 4, Track 12

Listen. Where are they? Check (✓) the answers.

1. ☐ **a.** canyon   ✓ **b.** mountain peak
2. ☐ **a.** bay   ☐ **b.** rainforest
3. ☐ **a.** meadow   ☐ **b.** sand dune
4. ☐ **a.** beach   ☐ **b.** valley
5. ☐ **a.** desert   ☐ **b.** pond
6. ☐ **a.** canyon   ☐ **b.** hills

The Universe   page 205, CD 4, Track 13

Listen. Look at the pictures. Write the number of the conversation.

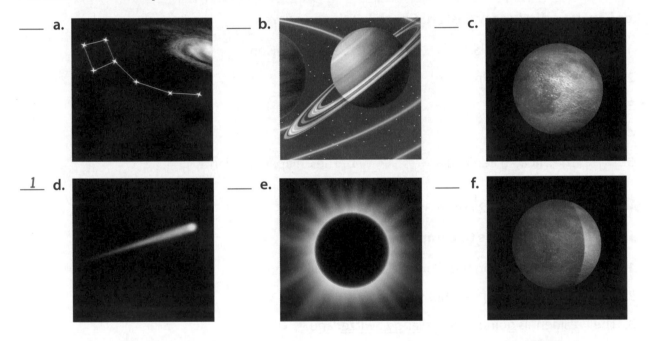

___ **a.**   ___ **b.**   ___ **c.**

_1_ **d.**   ___ **e.**   ___ **f.**

A Graduation   pages 206 and 207, CD 4, Track 14

Listen. *True* or *False*? Check (✓) the answers.

		True	False
1.	The photographer is taking a picture.	✓	☐
2.	The students are crying.	☐	☐
3.	The guest speaker is talking.	☐	☐
4.	The students are receiving their caps and gowns.	☐	☐
5.	The photographer wants to take a funny photo.	☐	☐

Nature Center pages 208 and 209, CD 4, Track 15

Look in your dictionary. Listen. *True* or *False*? Check (✓) the answers.

	True	False
1.	☐	✓
2.	☐	☐
3.	☐	☐
4.	☐	☐
5.	☐	☐
6.	☐	☐
7.	☐	☐

Trees and Plants page 210, CD 4, Track 16

Look in your dictionary. Which trees or plants are they talking about? Check (✓) the answers.

1. ☐ a. magnolia   ✓ b. redwood
2. ☐ a. holly   ☐ b. maple
3. ☐ a. dogwood   ☐ b. oak
4. ☐ a. oak   ☐ b. palm
5. ☐ a. birch   ☐ b. pine
6. ☐ a. pine   ☐ b. willow
7. ☐ a. cactus   ☐ b. poison ivy

Flowers page 211, CD 4, Track 17

Listen. Complete the orders. Check (✓) the flowers.

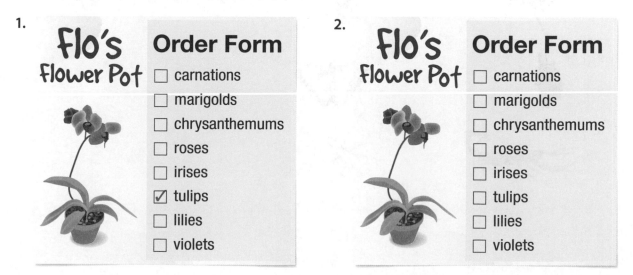

1. flo's flower Pot **Order Form**
☐ carnations
☐ marigolds
☐ chrysanthemums
☐ roses
☐ irises
✓ tulips
☐ lilies
☐ violets

2. flo's flower Pot **Order Form**
☐ carnations
☐ marigolds
☐ chrysanthemums
☐ roses
☐ irises
☐ tulips
☐ lilies
☐ violets

Marine Life, Amphibians, and Reptiles pages 212 and 213, CD 4, Track 18

Listen. What are they looking at? Check (✓) the answers.

1. ☐ **a.** jellyfish   ✓ **b.** octopus
2. ☐ **a.** starfish   ☐ **b.** swordfish
3. ☐ **a.** sea anemone   ☐ **b.** sea urchin
4. ☐ **a.** frog   ☐ **b.** toad
5. ☐ **a.** dolphin   ☐ **b.** sea lion
6. ☐ **a.** crocodile   ☐ **b.** cobra

Birds, Insects, and Arachnids page 214, CD 4, Track 19

Listen. Check (✓) the pictures.

1. a. ✓   b. ☐
2. a. ☐   b. ☐
3. a. ☐   b. ☐
4. a. ☐   b. ☐
5. a. ☐   b. ☐
6. a. ☐   b. ☐
7. a. ☐   b. ☐

Domestic Animals and Rodents page 215, CD 4, Track 20

Listen. Circle the words to complete the sentences.

1. It's a <u>rabbit /</u>(rooster.)
2. It's a <u>parakeet / squirrel</u>.
3. It's a <u>cow / puppy</u>.
4. It's a <u>cat / rat</u>.
5. It's a <u>dog / kitten</u>.
6. It's a <u>goat / horse</u>.

Mammals pages 216 and 217, CD 4, Track 21

Look in your dictionary. *True* or *False*? Check (✓) the answers.

	True	False		True	False
1.	✓	☐	5.	☐	☐
2.	☐	☐	6.	☐	☐
3.	☐	☐	7.	☐	☐
4.	☐	☐	8.	☐	☐

Energy and Conservation pages 218 and 219, CD 4, Track 22

Listen. Number the energy sources in order. (1 = the most production)

____ **a.** biomass

_1_ **b.** coal

____ **c.** geothermal energy

____ **d.** hydroelectric power

____ **e.** natural gas

____ **f.** nuclear energy

____ **g.** oil

____ **h.** solar energy

U.S. National Parks pages 220 and 221, CD 4, Track 23

Listen to the park rangers. What are they talking about? Check (✓) the answers.

1. ☑ **a.** the ferry   ☐ **b.** wildlife
2. ☐ **a.** a cave   ☐ **b.** a park ranger
3. ☐ **a.** a landmark   ☐ **b.** coral
4. ☐ **a.** a tour   ☐ **b.** the ferry
5. ☐ **a.** wildlife   ☐ **b.** coral
6. ☐ **a.** landmarks   ☐ **b.** caves

Places to Go pages 222 and 223, CD 4, Track 24

Look in your dictionary. Listen. Where are they? Check (✓) the answers.

1. ☐ **a.** aquarium   ☑ **b.** zoo
2. ☐ **a.** classical concert   ☐ **b.** rock concert
3. ☐ **a.** night club   ☐ **b.** bowling alley
4. ☐ **a.** art museum   ☐ **b.** county fair
5. ☐ **a.** amusement park   ☐ **b.** play
6. ☐ **a.** opera   ☐ **b.** movies
7. ☐ **a.** botanical garden   ☐ **b.** swap meet

The Park and Playground page 224, CD 4, Track 25

Look in your dictionary. Listen. _True_ or _False_? Check (✓) the answers.

	True	False
1.	☐	☑
2.	☐	☐
3.	☐	☐
4.	☐	☐
5.	☐	☐
6.	☐	☐
7.	☐	☐
8.	☐	☐

The Beach   page 225, CD 4, Track 26

Listen. What does the beach have? Check (✓) the answers.

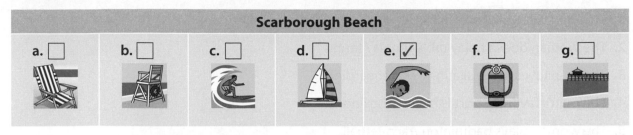

Scarborough Beach						
a. ☐	b. ☐	c. ☐	d. ☐	e. ✓	f. ☐	g. ☐

Outdoor Recreation   page 226, CD 4, Track 27

Listen. What are the people doing? Circle the words to complete the sentences.

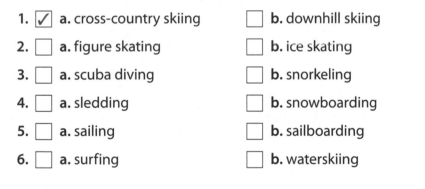

1. They're going (fishing) / mountain biking.

2. They're canoeing / camping.

3. They're going hiking / canoeing.

4. They're backpacking / boating.

5. They're horseback riding / rafting.

Winter and Water Sports   page 227, CD 4, Track 28

Listen. Which sports do people like more? Check (✓) the answers.

1. ✓ **a.** cross-country skiing   ☐ **b.** downhill skiing

2. ☐ **a.** figure skating   ☐ **b.** ice skating

3. ☐ **a.** scuba diving   ☐ **b.** snorkeling

4. ☐ **a.** sledding   ☐ **b.** snowboarding

5. ☐ **a.** sailing   ☐ **b.** sailboarding

6. ☐ **a.** surfing   ☐ **b.** waterskiing

Individual Sports page 228, CD 4, Track 29

Listen. Circle the words to complete the sentences.

1. The man likes (bowling)/ billiards.

2. The woman doesn't play table tennis / tennis.

3. The man loves inline skating / skateboarding.

4. The man's favorite sport is biking / boxing.

5. The woman plays badminton /racquetball.

6. The woman doesn't like weightlifting / wrestling.

Team Sports page 229, CD 4, Track 30

Listen. Check (✓) the columns.

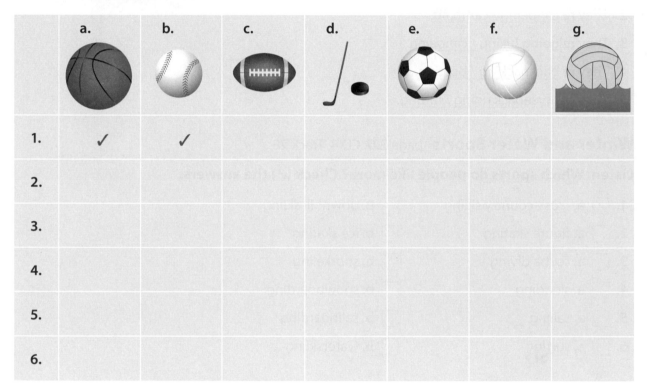

	a.	b.	c.	d.	e.	f.	g.
1.	✓	✓					
2.							
3.							
4.							
5.							
6.							

Sports Verbs page 230, CD 4, Track 31

Listen. Write the numbers.

___ a.

___ b.

___ c.

_1_ d.

___ e.

___ f.

___ g.

___ h.

Sports Equipment page 231, CD 4, Track 32

Look in your dictionary. What are they talking about? Check (✓) the answers.

1. ☐ **a.** bow and arrow   ✓ **b.** flying discs

2. ☐ **a.** shin guards   ☐ **b.** weights

3. ☐ **a.** inline skate   ☐ **b.** ski pole

4. ☐ **a.** glove   ☐ **b.** target

5. ☐ **a.** baseball bat   ☐ **b.** snowboard

6. ☐ **a.** basketball   ☐ **b.** bowling ball

Hobbies and Games pages 232 and 233, CD 4, Track 33

Listen. *True* or *False*? Check (✓) the answers.

	True	False
1. They're playing cards.	✓	☐
2. She's quilting.	☐	☐
3. She's painting.	☐	☐
4. They are pretending.	☐	☐
5. They're knitting.	☐	☐
6. He's doing crafts.	☐	☐
7. They're playing a game.	☐	☐

Electronics and Photography pages 234 and 235, CD 4, Track 34

Listen. What are they using? Check (✓) the answers.

1. ☐ **a.** speakers   ✓ **b.** universal remote
2. ☐ **a.** portable DVD Player   ☐ **b.** tripod
3. ☐ **a.** adapter   ☐ **b.** MP3 player
4. ☐ **a.** digital camera   ☐ **b.** photo album
5. ☐ **a.** battery pack   ☐ **b.** film
6. ☐ **a.** camera case   ☐ **b.** zoom lens

Entertainment pages 236 and 237, CD 4, Track 35

Listen. Write the number of the channel.

Music page 238, CD 4, Track 36

Listen. Check (✓) the instruments you hear.

1. ✓ **a.** guitar   ☐ **b.** trumpet
2. ☐ **a.** flute   ☐ **b.** piano
3. ☐ **a.** accordion   ☐ **b.** drums
4. ☐ **a.** saxophone   ☐ **b.** organ
5. ☐ **a.** tambourine   ☐ **b.** violin
6. ☐ **a.** cello   ☐ **b.** trombone

Holidays page 239, CD 4, Track 37

Listen. Write the number of the conversation.

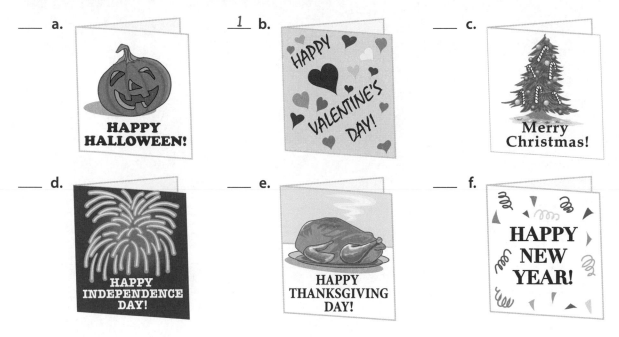

___ **a.** HAPPY HALLOWEEN!

_1_ **b.** HAPPY VALENTINE'S DAY!

___ **c.** Merry Christmas!

___ **d.** HAPPY INDEPENDENCE DAY!

___ **e.** HAPPY THANKSGIVING DAY!

___ **f.** HAPPY NEW YEAR!

A Birthday Party pages 240 and 241, CD 4, Track 38

Listen. What are the people doing? Check (✓) the answers.

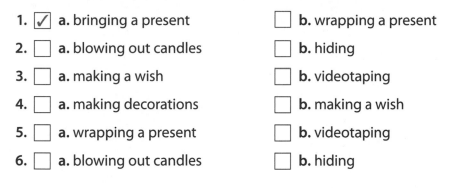

1. ☑ **a.** bringing a present   ☐ **b.** wrapping a present
2. ☐ **a.** blowing out candles   ☐ **b.** hiding
3. ☐ **a.** making a wish   ☐ **b.** videotaping
4. ☐ **a.** making decorations   ☐ **b.** making a wish
5. ☐ **a.** wrapping a present   ☐ **b.** videotaping
6. ☐ **a.** blowing out candles   ☐ **b.** hiding